What Readers Are Saying About *Metaprogramming Ruby*

Reading this book was like diving into a new world of thinking. I tried a mix of Java and JRuby metaprogramming on a recent project. Using Java alone would now feel like entering a sword fight carrying only a banana, when my opponent is wielding a one-meter-long Samurai blade.

> ► **Sebastian Hennebrüder**
> Java Consultant and Trainer, *laliluna.de*

This Ruby book fills a gap between language reference manuals and programming cookbooks. Not only does it explain various meta-programming facilities, but it also shows a pragmatic way of making software smaller and better. There's a caveat, though; when the new knowledge sinks in, programming in more mainstream languages will start feeling like a chore.

> ► **Jurek Husakowski**
> Software Designer, Philips Applied Technologies

Before this book, I'd never found a clear organization and explanation of concepts like the Ruby object model, closures, DSLs definition, and eigenclasses all spiced with real-life examples taken from the gems we usually use every day. This book is definitely worth reading.

> ► **Carlo Pecchia**
> Software Engineer

I've had a lot of trouble finding a good way to pick up these meta-programming techniques, and this book is bar none the best way to do it. Paolo Perrotta makes it painless to learn Ruby's most complex secrets and use them in practical applications.

> ► **Chris Bunch**
> Software Engineer

Metaprogramming Ruby

Program Like the Ruby Pros

Metaprogramming Ruby
Program Like the Ruby Pros

Paolo Perrotta

The Pragmatic Bookshelf
Raleigh, North Carolina   Dallas, Texas

Many of the designations used by manufacturers and sellers to distinguish their products are claimed as trademarks. Where those designations appear in this book, and The Pragmatic Programmers, LLC was aware of a trademark claim, the designations have been printed in initial capital letters or in all capitals. The Pragmatic Starter Kit, The Pragmatic Programmer, Pragmatic Programming, Pragmatic Bookshelf and the linking *g* device are trademarks of The Pragmatic Programmers, LLC.

Every precaution was taken in the preparation of this book. However, the publisher assumes no responsibility for errors or omissions, or for damages that may result from the use of information (including program listings) contained herein.

Our Pragmatic courses, workshops, and other products can help you and your team create better software and have more fun. For more information, as well as the latest Pragmatic titles, please visit us at

http://www.pragprog.com

ISBN-10: 1-934356-47-6

ISBN-13: 978-1-934356-47-0

Printed on acid-free paper.

P1.0 printing, January 2010

Version: 2010-1-15

To Carlo.

Contents

Foreword

Ruby inherits characteristics from various languages—Lisp, Smalltalk, C, and Perl, to name a few. Metaprogramming comes from Lisp (and Smalltalk). It's a bit like magic, which makes something astonishing possible. There are two kinds of magic: white magic, which does good things, and black magic, which can do nasty things. Likewise, there are two aspects to metaprogramming. If you discipline yourself, you can do good things, such as enhancing the language without tweaking its syntax by macros or enabling internal domain-specific languages. But you can fall into the dark side of metaprogramming. Metaprogramming can confuse easily.

Ruby trusts you. Ruby treats you as a grown-up programmer. It gives you great power such as metaprogramming. But you need to remember that with great power comes great responsibility.

Enjoy programming in Ruby.

matz
October 2009

Acknowledgments

Before I begin, I need to thank a few people. I'm talking to you, gentlemen: Joe Armstrong, Satoshi Asakawa, Paul Barry, Emmanuel Bernard, Roberto Bettazzoni, Ola Bini, Piergiuliano Bossi, Simone Busoli, Andrea Cisternino, Davide D'Alto, Mauro Di Nuzzo, Marco Di Timoteo, Mauricio Fernandez, Jay Fields, Michele Finelli, Neal Ford, Florian Frank, Sanne Grinovero, Federico Gobbo, Florian Groß, Sebastian Hennebrüder, Doug Hudson, Jurek Husakowski, Lyle Johnson, Luca Marchetti, MenTaLguY, Carlo Pecchia, Andrea Provaglio, Mike Roberts, Martin Rodgers, Jeremy Sydik, Andrea Tomasini, Marco Trincardi, Ivan Vaghi, Giancarlo Valente, Davide Varvello, Jim Weirich, and the dozens of readers who reported problems and errata while this book was in beta. Whether you provided reviews, quotes, fixes, opinions, or moral support, there's at least one line in this book that changed for the better because of you. Did I say one line? For some of you, make that "a few chapters." In particular, Ola, Satoshi, and Jurek deserve a special place on this page and my enduring gratitude.

Thanks to the staff at the Pragmatic Bookshelf: Janet Furlow, Seth Maislin, Steve Peter, Susannah Davidson Pfalzer, and Kim Wimpsett. Dave and Andy, thank you for believing in this project when times got rough. Jill, thank you for making my awkward prose look so effortless. Our crunch week in Venice was a lot of hard work, but it was definitely worth it. And speaking of Venice: thank you, Lucio, for being such a dear old friend.

Mom and Dad, thank you for your support, for your love, and for never asking why I was taking so long to finish this book.

Most authors' closing thanks go to their partners, and now I know why. When you're about to finish a book, you turn back to the day when you started writing, and it feels so far away. I remember writing over lunch breaks, nights, and weekends, locked for days or weeks inside my study, a hotel room in some foreign city, or a seashore house that would have suited a hermit. It's such a lonesome endeavor—and yet, I never felt alone. Thank you, Mirella.

Will write code that writes code that writes code for food.
► Martin Rodgers

Introduction

Metaprogramming... it sounds cool! It sounds like a design technique for high-level enterprise architects or a fashionable buzzword that has found its way into press releases.

In fact, far from being an abstract concept or a bit of marketing-speak, metaprogramming is a collection of down-to-earth, pragmatic coding techniques. It doesn't just sound cool; it *is* cool. Here are some of the things you can do with metaprogramming in the Ruby language:

- Say you want to write a Ruby program that connects to an external system—maybe a web service or a Java program. With metaprogramming, you can write a wrapper that takes *any* method call and routes it to the external system. If somebody adds methods to the external system later, you don't have to change your Ruby wrapper; the wrapper will support the new methods right away. That's magic!

- Maybe you have a problem that would be best solved with a programming language that's specific to that problem. You could go to the trouble of writing your own language, custom parser and all. Or you could just use Ruby, bending its syntax until it looks like a specific language for your problem. You can even write your own little interpreter that reads code written in your Ruby-based language from a file.

- You can remove duplication from your Ruby program at a level that Java programmers can only dream of. Let's say you have twenty methods in a class, and they all look the same. How about defining all those methods at once, with just a few lines of code? Or maybe you want to call a sequence of similarly named methods. How would you like a single short line of code that calls all the methods whose names match a pattern—like, say, all methods that begin with *test*?

- You can stretch and twist Ruby to meet your needs, rather than adapt to the language as it is. For example, you can enhance any class (even a core class like Array) with that method you miss so dearly, you can wrap logging functionality around a method that you want to monitor, you can execute custom code whenever a client inherits from your favorite class. . . the list goes on. You are limited only by your own, undoubtedly fertile, imagination.

Metaprogramming gives you the power to do all these things. Let's see what it looks like.

The "M" Word

You're probably expecting a definition of metaprogramming right from the start. Here's one for you:

Metaprogramming is writing code that writes code.

We'll get to a more precise definition in a short while, but this one will do for now. What do I mean by "code that writes code," and how is that useful in your daily work? Before I answer those questions, let's take a step back and look at programming languages themselves.

Ghost Towns and Marketplaces

Think of your source code as a world teeming with vibrant citizens: variables, classes, methods, and so on. If you want to get technical, you can call these citizens *language constructs*.

In many programming languages, language constructs behave more like ghosts than fleshed-out citizens: you can see them in your source code, but they disappear before the program runs. Take C++, for example. Once the compiler has finished its job, things like *variable* and *method* have lost their concreteness; they are just locations in memory. You can't ask a class for its instance methods, because by the time you ask the question, the class has faded away. In languages like C++, runtime is an eerily quiet place—a ghost town.

In other languages, such as Ruby, runtime looks more like a busy marketplace. Most language constructs are still there, buzzing all around. You can even walk up to a construct and ask it questions about itself. This is called *introspection*. Let's watch introspection in action.

Code Generators and Compilers

In metaprogramming, you write code that writes code. But isn't that what code generators and compilers do? For example, you can write annotated Java code and then use a code generator to output XML configuration files. In a broad sense, this XML generation is an example of metaprogramming. In fact, many people think about code generation when the "m" word comes up.

This particular brand of metaprogramming implies that you use a program to generate or otherwise manipulate a second, distinct program—and then you run the second program. After you run the code generator, you can actually read the generated code and (if you want to test your tolerance for pain) even modify it by hand before you finally run it. This is also what happens under the hood with C++ templates: the compiler turns your templates into a regular C++ program before compiling them, and then you run the compiled program.

In this book, I'll stick to a different meaning of *metaprogramming*, focusing on code that manipulates itself at runtime. Only a few languages can do that effectively, and Ruby is one of them. You can think of this as *dynamic* metaprogramming to distinguish it from the *static* metaprogramming of code generators and compilers.

Introspection

Take a look at this code:

Introduction/Introspection.rb

```
class Greeting
  def initialize(text)
    @text = text
  end

  def welcome
    @text
  end
end

my_object = Greeting.new("Hello")
```

I defined a Greeting class and created a Greeting object. I can now turn to the language constructs and ask them questions.

```
my_object.class                          # => Greeting
my_object.class.instance_methods(false)  # => [:welcome]
my_object.instance_variables             # => [:@text]
```

I asked my_object about its class, and it replied in no uncertain terms: "I'm a Greeting." Then I asked the class for a list of its instance methods. (The false argument means, "List only instance methods you defined yourself, not those ones you inherited.") The class answered with an array containing a single method name: welcome(). I also peeked into the object itself, asking for its instance variables. Again, the object's reply was loud and clear. Since objects and classes are first-class citizens in Ruby, you can get a lot of information out of running code.

However, this is only half the picture. Sure, you can read language constructs at runtime, but what about *writing* them? What if you want to add new instance methods to Greeting, alongside welcome(), while the program is running? You might be wondering why on Earth anyone would want to do that. Allow me to explain by telling a story.

The Story of Bob, Metaprogrammer

Bob, a Java coder who's just starting to learn Ruby, has a grand plan: he'll write the biggest Internet social network ever for movie buffs. To do that, he needs a database of movies and movie reviews. Bob makes it a practice to write reusable code, so he decides to build a simple library to persist objects in the database.

Bob's First Attempt

Bob's library maps each class to a database table and each object to a record. When Bob creates an object or accesses its attributes, the object generates a string of SQL and sends it to the database. All this functionality is wrapped in a base class:

introduction/orm.rb

```ruby
class Entity
  attr_reader :table, :ident

  def initialize(table, ident)
    @table = table
    @ident = ident
    Database.sql "INSERT INTO #{@table} (id) VALUES (#{@ident})"
  end

  def set(col, val)
    Database.sql "UPDATE #{@table} SET #{col}='#{val}' WHERE id=#{@ident}"
  end
```

```
  def get(col)
    Database.sql("SELECT #{col} FROM #{@table} WHERE id=#{@ident}")[0][0]
  end
end
```

In Bob's database, each table has an id column. Each Entity stores the content of this column and the name of the table to which it refers. When Bob creates an Entity, the Entity saves itself to the database. Entity#set() generates SQL that updates the value of a column, and Entity#get() generates SQL that returns the value of a column. (In case you care, Bob's Database class returns record sets as arrays of arrays.)

Bob can now subclass Entity to map to a specific table. For example, class Movie maps to a database table named movies:

```
class Movie < Entity
  def initialize(ident)
    super("movies", ident)
  end

  def title
    get("title")
  end

  def title=(value)
    set("title", value)
  end

  def director
    get("director")
  end

  def director=(value)
    set("director", value)
  end
end
```

A Movie has two methods for each field: a reader such as Movie#title() and a writer such as Movie#title=(). Bob can now load a new movie into the database by firing up the Ruby command-line interpreter and typing the following:

```
movie = Movie.new(1)
movie.title = "Doctor Strangelove"
movie.director = "Stanley Kubrick"
```

This code creates a new record in movies, which has values 1, Doctor Strangelove, and Stanley Kubrick for the fields id, title, and director, respectively.[1]

Proud of himself, Bob shows the code to his older, more experienced colleague Bill. Bill stares at the screen for a few seconds and proceeds to shatter Bob's pride into tiny little pieces. "There's a lot of duplicated code here," Bill says. "You have a movies table with a title column in the database, and you have a Movie class with a @title field in the code. You also have a title() method, a title=() method, and two "title" string constants. You can solve this problem with way less code if you sprinkle some metaprogramming magic over it."

Enter Metaprogramming

At the suggestion of his expert-coder friend, Bob looks for a metaprogramming-based solution. He finds that very thing in the ActiveRecord library, a popular Ruby library that maps objects to database tables.[2] After a short tutorial, Bob is able to write the ActiveRecord version of the Movie class:

```
class Movie < ActiveRecord::Base
end
```

Yes, it's as simple as that. Bob just subclassed the ActiveRecord::Base class. He didn't have to specify a table to map Movies to. Even better, he didn't have to write boring, almost identical methods such as title() and director(). Everything just works:

```
movie = Movie.create
movie.title = "Doctor Strangelove"
movie.title                        # => "Doctor Strangelove"
```

The previous code creates a Movie object that wraps a record in the movies table, then accesses the record's title field by calling Movie#title() and Movie#title=(). But these methods are nowhere to be found in the source code. How can title() and title=() exist, if they're not defined anywhere? You can find out by looking at how ActiveRecord works.

The table name part is straightforward: ActiveRecord looks at the name of the class through introspection and then applies some simple con-

---

1. You probably know this already, but it doesn't hurt to refresh your memory: in Ruby, movie.title = "Doctor Strangelove" is actually a disguised call to the title=() method—the same as movie.title=("Doctor Strangelove").

2. ActiveRecord is part of Rails, the quintessential Ruby framework. You'll read more about Rails and ActiveRecord in Chapter 7, *The Design of ActiveRecord*, on page 171.

ventions. Since the class is named Movie, ActiveRecord maps it to a table named movies. (This library knows how to find plurals for English words.)

What about methods like title=() and title(), which access object attributes (*accessor methods* for short)? This is where metaprogramming comes in: Bob doesn't have to write those methods. ActiveRecord defines them automatically, after inferring their names from the database schema. ActiveRecord::Base reads the schema at runtime, discovers that the movies table has two columns named title and director, and defines accessor methods for two attributes of the same name. This means that ActiveRecord defines methods such as Movie#title() and Movie#director=() out of thin air while the program runs![3]

This is the "yang" to the introspection "yin": rather than just reading from the language constructs, you're writing into them. If you think this is an extremely powerful feature, well, you would be right.

The "M" Word Again

Now you have a more formal definition of metaprogramming:

Metaprogramming is writing code that manipulates language constructs at runtime.

How did the authors of ActiveRecord apply this concept? Instead of writing accessor methods for each class's attributes, they wrote code that defines those methods at runtime for *any* class that inherits from ActiveRecord::Base. This is what I meant when I talked about "writing code that writes code."

You might think that this is exotic, seldom-used stuff, but if you look at Ruby, as we're about to do, you'll see that it's used all around the place.

Metaprogramming and Ruby

Remember our earlier talk about ghost towns and marketplaces? If you want to "manipulate language constructs," those constructs must exist at runtime. In this respect, some languages are definitely better than others. Take a quick glance at a few languages and how much control they give you at runtime.

---

3. The real implementation of accessors in ActiveRecord is a bit more subtle than I describe here, as you'll see in Chapter 8, *Inside ActiveRecord*, on page 187.

A program written in C spans two different worlds: compile time, where you have language constructs such as variables and functions, and runtime, where you just have a bunch of machine code. Since most information from compile time is lost at runtime, C doesn't support metaprogramming or introspection. In C++, some language constructs do survive compilation, and that's why you can ask a C++ object for its class. In Java, the distinction between compile time and runtime is even fuzzier. You have enough introspection available to list the methods of a class or climb up a chain of superclasses.

Ruby is arguably the most metaprogramming-friendly of the current fashionable languages. It has no compile time at all, and most constructs in a Ruby program are available at runtime. You don't come up against a brick wall dividing the code that you're writing from the code that your computer executes when you run the program. There is just one world.

In this one world, metaprogramming is everywhere. In fact, metaprogramming is so deeply entrenched in the Ruby language that it's not even sharply separated from "regular" programming. You can't look at a Ruby program and say, "This part here is metaprogramming, while this other part is not." In a sense, metaprogramming is a routine part of every Ruby programmer's job.

To be clear, metaprogramming isn't an obscure art reserved for Ruby gurus, and it's also not a bolt-on power feature that's useful only for building something as sophisticated as ActiveRecord. If you want to take the path to advanced Ruby coding, you'll find metaprogramming at every step. Even if you're happy with the amount of Ruby you already know and use, you're still likely to stumble on metaprogramming in your coding travels: in the source of popular frameworks, in your favorite library, and even in small examples from random blogs. Until you master metaprogramming, you won't be able to tap into the full power of the Ruby language.

There is also another, less obvious reason why you might want to learn metaprogramming. As simple as Ruby looks at first, you can quickly become overwhelmed by its subtleties. Sooner or later, you'll be asking yourself questions such as "Can an object call a **private** method on another object of the same class?" or "How can you define class methods by importing a module?" Ultimately, all of Ruby's seemingly complicated behaviors derive from a few simple rules. Through metaprogramming, you can get an intimate look at the language, learn those rules, and get answers to your nagging questions.

Now that you know what metaprogramming is about, you're ready to dive in this book.

About This Book

Part I, *Metaprogramming Ruby*, is the core of the book. It tells the story of your week in the office, paired with Bill, an experienced Ruby coder:

- Ruby's object model is the land in which metaprogramming lives. Chapter 1, *Monday: The Object Model*, on page 3 provides a map to this land. This chapter introduces you to the most basic metaprogramming techniques. It also reveals the secrets behind Ruby classes and *method lookup*, the process by which Ruby finds and executes methods.

- Once you understand method lookup, you can do some fancy things with methods: you can create methods at runtime, intercept method calls, route calls to another object, or even accept calls to methods that don't exist. All these techniques are explained in Chapter 2, *Tuesday: Methods*, on page 37.

- Methods are just one member of a larger family also including entities such as blocks and lambdas. Chapter 3, *Wednesday: Blocks*, on page 69, is your field manual for everything related to these entities. It also presents an example of writing a *domain-specific language*, a powerful conceptual tool that's gaining popularity in today's development community. And, of course, this chapter comes with its own share of tricks, explaining how you can package code and execute it later or how you can carry variables across scopes.

- Speaking of scopes, Ruby has a special scope that deserves a close look: the scope of class definitions. Chapter 4, *Thursday: Class Definitions*, on page 101, talks about this scope and introduces you to some of the most powerful weapons in a metaprogrammer's arsenal. It also introduces *eigenclasses* (also known as *singleton classes*), the last concept you need to make sense of Ruby's most perplexing features.

- Finally, Chapter 5, *Friday: Code That Writes Code*, on page 139 puts it all together through an extended example that uses techniques from all the previous chapters. The chapter also rounds out your metaprogramming training with two new topics: the somewhat controversial eval() method and the callback methods that you can use to intercept object model events.

Part II of the book, *Metaprogramming in Rails*, is a case study in metaprogramming. It contains three short chapters that focus on different areas of Rails, the flagship Ruby framework. By looking at Rails' source code, you'll see how master Ruby coders use metaprogramming in the real world to develop great software.

Before you get down to reading this book, you should know about the three appendixes. Appendix A, on page 223, describes some common techniques that you'll probably find useful even if they're not, strictly speaking, metaprogramming. Appendix B, on page 235, is a look at domain-specific languages. Appendix C, on page 239, is a quick reference to all the spells in the book, complete with code examples.

"Wait a minute," I can hear you saying. "What the heck are *spells*?" Oh, right, sorry. Let me explain.

Spells

This book contains a number of metaprogramming techniques that you can use in your own code. Some people might call these *patterns* or maybe *idioms*. Neither of these terms is very popular among Rubyists, so I'll call them *spells* instead. Even if there's nothing magical about them, they *do* look like magic spells to Ruby newcomers!

You'll find references to spells everywhere in the book. I reference a spell by using the convention *Blank Slate (61)* or *String of Code (142)*, for example. The number in parentheses is the page where the spell receives a name. If you need a quick reference to a spell, in Appendix C, on page 239, you'll find a complete spell book.

Quizzes

Every now and then, this book also throws a quiz at you. You can skip these quizzes and just read the solution, but you'll probably want to solve them just because they're fun.

Some quizzes are traditional coding exercises; others require you to get off your keyboard and think. All quizzes include a solution, but most quizzes have more than one possible answer. Go wild and experiment!

Notation Conventions

Throughout this book, I use a typewriter-like font for code examples. To show you that a line of code results in a value, I print that value as a comment on the same line:

```
-1.abs          # => 1
```

If a code example is supposed to print a result rather than return it, I show that result after the code:

```
puts 'Testing... testing...'
```

⇒ Testing... testing...

In most cases, the text uses the same code syntax that Ruby uses: MyClass.my_method is a class method, MyClass::MY_CONSTANT is a constant defined within a class, and so on. There are a couple of exceptions to this rule. First, I identify instance methods with the *hash* notation, like the Ruby documentation does (MyClass#my_method). This is useful when trying to differentiate class methods and instance methods. Second, I use a hash prefix to identify eigenclasses (#MyEigenclass).

Some of the code in this book comes straight from existing open source libraries. To avoid clutter (or to make the code easier to understand in isolation), I'll sometimes take the liberty of editing the original code slightly. However, I'll do my best to keep the spirit of the original source intact.

Unit Tests

This book follows two developers as they go about their day-to-day work. As the story unfolds, you may notice that the developers rarely write unit tests. Does this book condone untested code?

Please rest assured that it doesn't. In fact, the original draft of this book included unit tests for all code examples. In the end, I found that those tests distracted from the metaprogramming techniques that are the meat of the book—so the tests fell on the cutting-room floor.

This doesn't mean you shouldn't write tests for your own metaprogramming endeavors! In fact, you'll find specific advice on testing metaprogramming code in Chapter 9, *Metaprogramming Safely*, on page 205.

Ruby Versions

One of the joys of Ruby is that it's continuously changing and improving. However, this very fluidity can be problematic when you try a piece of code on the latest version of the language only to find that it doesn't work anymore. This is not overly common, but it can happen with metaprogramming, which pushes Ruby to its limits.

As I write this text, the latest stable release of Ruby is 1.9.1 and is labeled a "developer" version. Developer versions are meant as test beds for new language features, but Ruby 1.9 is generally considered stable enough for real production work—so I used it to write this book. You can stick with Ruby 1.8 if you prefer. Throughout the text, I'll tell you which features behave differently on the two versions of Ruby.

The next production version of Ruby is going to be Ruby 2.0, which will likely introduce some big changes. At the time of writing this book, this version is still too far away to either worry or rejoice about. Once 2.0 comes out, I'll update the text.

When I talk about Ruby versions, I'm talking about the "official" interpreter (sometimes called MRI for *Matz's Ruby Interpreter*[4]). To add to all the excitement (and the confusion) around Ruby, some people are also developing alternate versions of the language, like JRuby, which runs on the Java Virtual Machine,[5] or IronRuby, which runs on the Microsoft .NET platform.[6] As I sit here writing, most of these alternate Ruby implementations are progressing nicely, but be aware that some of the examples in this book might not work on some of these alternate implementations.

About You

Most people consider metaprogramming an advanced topic. To play with the constructs of a Ruby program, you have to know how these constructs work in the first place. How do you know whether you're enough of an "advanced" Rubyist to deal with metaprogramming? Well, if you understood the code in the previous sections without much trouble, you are well equipped to move forward.

If you're not confident about your skills, you can take a simple self-test. Which kind of code would you write to iterate over an array? If you thought about the each() method, then you know enough Ruby to follow the ensuing text. If you thought about the **for** keyword, then

---

4. http://www.ruby-lang.org
5. http://jruby.codehaus.org
6. http://www.ironruby.net

you're probably new to Ruby. In the second case, you can still embark on this metaprogramming adventure—just take an introductory Ruby text along with you![7]

Are you on board, then? Great! Let's dive in.

---

7. I suggest the seminal *Pickaxe* [TFH08] book. You can also find an excellent interactive introduction in the *Try Ruby!* tutorial on http://tryruby.sophrinix.com.

Part I

Metaprogramming Ruby

## Chapter 1

Monday: The Object Model

Just glance at any Ruby program, and you'll see objects everywhere. Do a double take, and you'll see that objects are just citizens of a larger world that also includes language constructs such as classes, modules, and instance variables. Metaprogramming manipulates these language constructs, so you need to know a few things about them right off the bat.

You are about to dig into the first concept: all these constructs live together in a system called the *object model*. The object model is where you'll find answers to questions such as "Which class does this method come from?" and "What happens when I include this module?"

Delving into the object model, at the very heart of Ruby, you'll learn some powerful techniques, and you'll also learn how to steer clear of a few pitfalls. Monday promises to be a full day, so set your IM status to Away, hold all your calls, grab an extra donut, and get ready to start!

1.1 Monday with Bill

Where you meet Bill, your new mentor and programming buddy.

Welcome to your new job as a Ruby programmer. After you've settled yourself at your new desk with a shiny, latest-generation monitor and a cup of coffee, you can meet Bill, your mentor, experienced in all things Ruby. Yes, you have your first assignment at your new company, a new language to work with, and a new pair-programming buddy. What a Monday!

Your assignment is with the Enterprise Integration Department (which is corporate-speak for "the folks hammering the legacy systems back into shape"). Given that Ruby is a new language for you, you've been practicing for a few weeks already. Bill, who has some months of Ruby under his belt, looks like a nice chap, so you know you're going to have a good time—at least until your first petty fight over coding conventions.

The boss wants you and Bill to get to know each other, so she's asked the two of you to review the source of a small application called Book-worm. The company developed Bookworm to manage its large internal library of books. The program has slowly grown out of control as many different developers added their pet features to the mix, from text previews to magazine management and the tracking of borrowed books. As a result, the Bookworm source code is in dire need of refactoring. You and your new pal Bill have been selected to whip the Bookworm source back into shape.

You and Bill are ready to get to work. With Bill sitting next to you at your desk, you fire up your text editor.

1.2 Open Classes

Where Bill gives you your first taste of Ruby classes.

You and Bill have been browsing through the Bookworm source code for a few minutes when you spot your first refactoring opportunity. To print book titles on limited supports like tape labels, Bookworm has a function that strips all punctuation and special characters out of a string, leaving only alphanumeric characters and spaces:

`object_model/alphanumeric.rb`
```
def to_alphanumeric(s)
  s.gsub /[^\w\s]/, ''
end
```

This method also comes with its own unit test:

```
require 'test/unit'

class ToAlphanumericTest < Test::Unit::TestCase
  def test_strips_non_alphanumeric_characters
    assert_equal '3 the Magic Number', to_alphanumeric('#3, the *Magic, Number*?')
  end
end
```

"This to_alphanumeric() method is not very object oriented, is it?" Bill muses. "It'd be better if we could just ask the string to convert itself, rather than pass it through an external method."

Even though you're the new guy on the block, you can't help but interrupt. "But this is just a regular String. To add methods to it, we'd have to write a whole new AlphanumericString class. I'm not sure it would be worth it."

"I think I have a simpler solution to this problem," Bill replies. He *opens* the String class and plants the to_alphanumeric() method there:

```
class String
  def to_alphanumeric
    gsub /[^\w\s]/, ''
  end
end
```

Bill also changes the callers to use String#to_alphanumeric(). For example, the test becomes as follows:

```
require 'test/unit'

class StringExtensionsTest < Test::Unit::TestCase
  def test_strips_non_alphanumeric_characters
    assert_equal '3 the Magic Number', '#3, the *Magic, Number*?'.to_alphanumeric
  end
end
```

To understand Bill's trick, you need to know a thing or two about Ruby classes. Bill is only too happy to teach you. . . .

Inside Class Definitions

In Ruby there is no real distinction between code that defines a class and code of any other kind. You can put any code you want in a class definition, as Bill demonstrates with a quick example:

```
3.times do
  class C
    puts "Hello"
  end
end
```
⇒
```
Hello
Hello
Hello
```

Ruby executed the code within the class just as it would execute any other code. Does that mean you defined three classes with the same name? The answer is no, as Bill demonstrates with a second example:

```
class D
  def x; 'x'; end
end
```

> ### Where Should You Put Your Methods?
>
> In Section 1.2, *Open Classes*, on page 4, Bill demonstrates how you can move the to_alphanumeric( ) method to the String class. But even if you *can* do this, you might wonder whether you *should* do it. Is it right to have every string in the system expose a to_alphanumeric( ) method? Wouldn't it be better to leave the String class alone?
>
> This time around, you're dealing with a pretty generic functionality that makes sense for all strings—so you can argue it makes sense to follow Bill's suggestion and put alphanumeric conversion in the String class. In general, however, you should think hard before you pollute Ruby's standard libraries with a lot of domain-specific methods. After all, a class such as String already comes with loads of methods that you have to remember.
>
> You do have alternatives to using an *Open Class (7)*. You could define a new AlphanumericString class or even add specific methods like to_alphanumeric( ) only to a few, selected strings (you'll learn how to do that in the discussion of *Singleton Methods (112)*). You'll learn more Open Class alternatives and variations in the rest of this book.

```ruby
class D
  def y; 'y'; end
end

obj = D.new
obj.x       # => "x"
obj.y       # => "y"
```

When the previous code mentions class D for the first time, no class by that name exists yet. So, Ruby steps in and defines the class—and the x() method. At the second mention, class D already exists, so Ruby doesn't need to define it. Instead, it just *reopens* the existing class and defines a method named y() there.

In a sense, the **class** keyword in Ruby is more like a scope operator than a class declaration. Yes, it does create classes that don't yet exist, but you might argue that it does this as a side effect. For **class**, the core job is to move you in the context of the class, where you can define methods.

You might think that Bill is just nitpicking here, but this distinction about the **class** keyword is not an academic detail. It has an important practical consequence: you can always reopen existing classes, even standard library classes such as String or Array, and modify them on the fly. You can simply call this technique *Open Class*.

Spell: Open Class

To demonstrate how people use Open Classes in practice, Bill runs through a quick example from a real-life library.

The Money Example

As an example of Open Classes, Bill opens your eyes to the Money gem, a set of utility classes for managing money and currencies.[1] Here's how you create a Money object:

```
cents = 9999
# 99.99 US Dollars:
bargain_price = Money.new(cents)
```

As a shortcut, you can also convert any number to a Money object by calling Numeric#to money():

```
# 100.00 US Dollars:
standard_price = 100.to_money()
```

Since Numeric is a standard Ruby class, you might wonder where the Numeric#to_money method comes from. Look through the source of the Money gem, and you'll find code that reopens Numeric and defines that method:

`gems/money-2.1.3/lib/money/core_extensions.rb`

```
class Numeric
  def to_money
    Money.new(self * 100)
  end
end
```

It's quite common for libraries to use Open Classes this way.

The Problem with Open Classes

You and Bill don't have to look much further before you stumble upon another opportunity to use Open Classes. The Bookworm source contains a method that replaces elements in an array.

---

1. Money was written by Tobias Luetke. Install it with gem install money.

`object_model/replace.rb`

```ruby
def replace(array, from, to)
  array.each_with_index do |e, i|
    array[i] = to if e == from
  end
end
```

Instead of focusing on the internal workings of replace(), you can look at Bookworm's unit tests to see how that method is supposed to be used:

```ruby
def test_replace
  book_topics = ['html', 'java', 'css']
  replace(book_topics, 'java', 'ruby')
  expected = ['html', 'ruby', 'css']
  assert_equal expected, book_topics
end
```

This time, you know what to do. You grab the keyboard (taking advantage of Bill's slower reflexes) and move the method to the Array class:

```ruby
class Array
  def replace(from, to)
    each_with_index do |e, i|
      self[i] = to if e == from
    end
  end
end
```

Then you change all calls to replace() into calls to Array#replace(). For example, the test becomes as follows:

```ruby
def test_replace
  book_topics = ['html', 'java', 'css']
  book_topics.replace('java', 'ruby')
  expected = ['html', 'ruby', 'css']
  assert_equal expected, book_topics
end
```

Everything looks like it's in order until you run Bookworm's unit tests. Not only do they break, but the failing tests seem to have nothing to do with the code you just edited. Bummer! What gives?

Monkey See, Monkey Patch

Your pal Bill comes to the rescue. "I think I know what just happened," he mumbles. He fires up an irb session and gets a list of all methods in Ruby's standard Array that begin with *re*:[2]

```
[].methods.grep /^re/  # => [:replace, :reject, :reject!, :respond_to?, ...
```

Yipes! In looking at the irb output, you spot the problem. Class Array already has a method named replace(). When you defined your own replace() method, you inadvertently overwrote the original replace(), a method that some other part of Bookworm was relying on.

This is the dark side to Open Classes: if you casually add bits and pieces of functionality to classes, you can end up with bugs like the one you just encountered. Some people would frown upon this kind of reckless patching of classes, and they would refer to the previous code with a derogatory name: they'd call it a *Monkeypatch*.

Spell: Monkeypatch

You and Bill then rename your own version of Array#replace() to Array# substitute() and fix both the tests and the calling code. You just learned a lesson the hard way, but that didn't spoil your attitude. If anything, this incident piqued your curiosity about Ruby classes. As it turns out, Bill is only too happy to tell you more about this topic.

1.3 The Truth About Classes

Where Bill reveals surprising facts about objects, classes, and constants.

"At this stage," Bill observes, "it's probably a good idea to take a break from coding and give a long, hard look at the theory behind Ruby classes." He warns you that this will be a lot of theory in a single shot and adds that there is no escaping this if you want to understand the mechanics behind Ruby classes and objects.

"I'll be asking for your full attention, so let's go find a quiet place to talk." He grabs your arm and hustles you to the conference room.

---

2. You probably already know about irb, the interactive Ruby interpreter. You might want to keep an irb session open at all times to run quick experiments as you read through this book—or any other Ruby book, for that matter.

Is Monkeypatching Evil?

In Section 1.2, *Monkey See, Monkey Patch*, on the previous page, Bill told you that *Monkeypatch* is a derogatory term. However, the same term is sometimes used in a positive sense, to refer to *Open Classes (7)* in general. You might argue that there are two types of *Monkeypatches (9)*. Some happen by mistake, like the one that you and Bill experienced, and they're invariably evil. Others are applied on purpose, and they're quite useful—especially when you want to bend an existing library to your needs.

Even when you think you're in control, you should still Monkeypatch with care. Like any other global modification, Monkeypatches can be difficult to track in a large code base. (Some languages solve this problem with *selector namespaces*, which are like Monkeypatches confined to a limited scope. This feature might eventually find its way into Ruby 2.0—but don't hold your breath.)

So, Monkeypatches are useful but also dangerous. How do you minimize their dangers while still reaping their benefits? Carefully check the existing methods in a class before you define your own methods. Be aware that some changes are riskier than others. For example, adding a new method is usually safer than modifying an existing one. Also, test your code thoroughly.

You'll see more defensive techniques to manage Monkeypatches in Section 9.2, *Defusing Monkeypatches*, on page 213.

What's in an Object

"Let's start with the basics: objects and classes," Bill announces as you take your place in the conference room. He opens his laptop, launches irb, and types some code:

```ruby
class MyClass
  def my_method
    @v = 1
  end
end

obj = MyClass.new
obj.class          # => MyClass
```

Bill homes in on the obj object. If you could open the Ruby interpreter and look into obj, what would you see?

Instance Variables

Most importantly, objects contain instance variables. You're not really supposed to peek at them, but you can do that anyway by calling Object#instance_variables(). Bill's example object has just a single instance variable:

```
obj.my_method
obj.instance_variables  # => [:@v]
```

Unlike in Java or other static languages, in Ruby there is no connection between an object's class and its instance variables. Instance variables just spring into existence when you assign them a value, so you can have objects of the same class that carry different sets of instance variables. For example, if Bill hadn't called obj.my_method(), then obj would have no instance variable at all. You can think of the names and values of instance variables as keys and values in a hash. Both the keys and the values can be different for each object.

Bill stretches his arms in an attempt at dramatic gesturing. "That's all there is to know about instance variables really. Now, let's move on to methods."

Methods

Besides having instance variables, objects also have methods. You can get a list of an object's methods by calling Object#methods(). Most objects (including obj in Bill's example code) inherit a number of methods from Object, so this list of methods is usually quite long. Bill uses Array#grep() to show you that my_method() is in obj's list:[3]

```
obj.methods.grep(/my/)  # => [:my_method]
```

If you could pry open the Ruby interpreter and look into obj, you'd notice that this object doesn't really carry a list of methods. On the inside, an object simply contains its instance variables and a reference to its class.[4] So, where are the methods?

---

3. In earlier versions of Ruby, Object#methods() returned a list of strings. Starting with Ruby 1.9, it now returns a list of symbols.

4. To be precise, it also contains a unique identifier (the one returned by Object#object_id()) and a set of flags that mark special states such as "tainted" or "frozen."

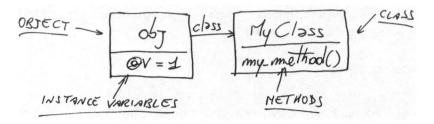

Figure 1.1: INSTANCE VARIABLES LIVE IN OBJECTS, AND METHODS LIVE IN CLASSES.

Bill walks over to the conference-room whiteboard and starts scribbling all over it. "Think about it for a minute," he says, drawing Figure 1.1. "Objects that share the same class also share the same methods, so the methods must be stored in the class, not the object."

While you're looking at the picture, Bill also takes the chance to highlight an important distinction in the terminology. You can rightly say that "obj has a method called my_method()," meaning that you're able to call obj.my_method(). By contrast, you shouldn't say that "MyClass has a method named my_method()." That would be confusing, because it would imply that you're able to call MyClass.my_method() as if it were a class method.

To remove the ambiguity, you should say that my_method() is an *instance method* (not just "a method") of MyClass, meaning that it's defined in MyClass, and you actually need an instance of MyClass to call it. It's the same method, but when you talk about the class, you call it an *instance method*, and when you talk about the object, you simply call it a *method*. Remember this distinction, and you won't get confused when writing introspective code like this:

```
String.instance_methods == "abc".methods    # => true
String.methods == "abc".methods             # => false
```

Bill wraps it all up: an object's instance variables live in the object itself, and an object's methods live in the object's class. That's why objects of the same class share methods but don't share instance variables.

That's all you really have to know about objects, instance variables, and methods. But since he's brought classes into the picture, Bill suggests you take a closer look.

Classes Revisited

"Now, my friend, this might be the most important thing you'll ever learn about the Ruby object model," Bill exclaims, pausing for dramatic effect. "*Classes themselves are nothing but objects.*"

Since a class is an object, everything that applies to objects also applies to classes. Classes, like any object, have their own class, as instances of a class called Class:

```
"hello".class   # => String
String.class    # => Class
```

Like any object, classes also have methods. Remember what Bill covered in Section 1.3, *What's in an Object*, on page 10? The methods of an object are also the instance methods of its class. This means that the methods of a class are the instance methods of Class:

```
inherited = false
Class.instance_methods(inherited)   # => [:superclass, :allocate, :new]
```

You already know about new(), because you use it all the time to create objects. The allocate() method plays a support role to new(), and superclass() does exactly what its name suggests, returning the class's superclass:

```
String.superclass       # => Object
Object.superclass       # => BasicObject
BasicObject.superclass  # => nil
```

All classes ultimately inherit from Object, which in turn inherits from BasicObject, the root of the Ruby class hierarchy.[5] Bill also shows you the superclass of Class:

```
Class.superclass        # => Module
Module.superclass       # => Object
```

So, a class is just a souped-up module with three additional methods— new(), allocate(), and superclass()—that allow you to create objects or arrange classes into hierarchies. Apart from these (admittedly important) differences, classes and modules are pretty much the same. Most of what you will learn about classes also applies to modules, and vice versa.

---

5. Before Ruby 1.9, the root of the Ruby object hierarchy was Object. Ruby 1.9 introduced BasicObject as a superclass of Object. You'll have to wait until the sidebar on page 66 to understand the reason why BasicObject even exists.

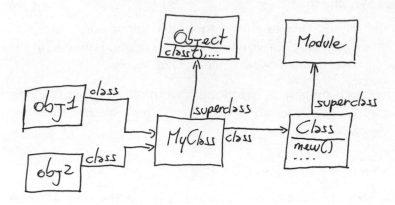

Figure 1.2: CLASSES ARE JUST OBJECTS.

Bill concludes his lecture on classes with a piece of code and a white-board diagram:

```
class MyClass; end
obj1 = MyClass.new
obj2 = MyClass.new
```

"See?" Bill asks, pointing at the diagram (Figure 1.2). "Classes and regular objects live together happily."

According to your programming pal, there's one last wrinkle in the "Classes are objects" theme: just like you do with regular objects, you hold onto classes with *references*. If you look at the previous code, you'll see that obj1 and MyClass are both references—the only difference being that obj1 is a variable, while MyClass is a constant. To put this differently, just as classes are nothing but objects, class names are nothing but constants. Bill takes the opportunity to dive into a sermon about constants.[6]

Constants

Any reference that begins with an uppercase letter, including the names of classes and modules, is a *constant*. The scope of constants follows

---

6. This information is important but not strictly necessary on your first pass through this chapter. If you want, you can safely snooze through Bill's talk on constants, jumping straight to Section 1.3, *Objects and Classes Wrap-Up*, on page 19, and come back to the discussion of constants later.

But Aren't Java Classes Objects, Too?

It's true that classes in both Java and C# are themselves instances of a class named Class. C# even allows you to add methods to existing classes, pretty much like Ruby's *Open Classes (7)* do.

However, classes in Java and C# are quite different from, and more limited than, regular objects. For example, you can't create a class at runtime, change a class's methods, or pull most other tricks from this book. In a sense, Class objects are more like class descriptors than "real" classes, in the same way that Java's File class is a file descriptor rather than the actual file.

This flexibility is typical of Ruby's metaprogramming: while other languages allow you to read class-related information, Ruby allows you to *write* that information at runtime. For example, as you will see in Chapter 4, *Thursday: Class Definitions*, on page 101, you can actually call Class.new to create new classes at runtime.

What Are Modules Good For?

In Section 1.3, *Classes Revisited*, on page 13, you learned that a module is basically a bunch of instance methods and that a class is just a module with a couple of additional features (a superclass and a new( ) method). Actually, classes and modules are so closely related that you might wonder why this distinction exists at all. Couldn't Ruby get away with a single "thing" that plays both roles?

The main reason for having both modules and classes is clarity: by carefully picking either a class or a module, you can make your code more explicit. Usually, you pick a module when you mean it to be included somewhere (or maybe to be used as a *Namespace (17)*), and you pick a class when you mean it to be instantiated or inherited. So, although you can use classes and modules interchangeably in many situations, you'll probably want to make your intentions clear by using them for different purposes.

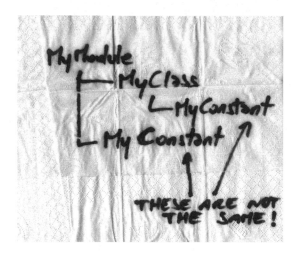

Figure 1.3: Bill's napkin drawing of a constants tree

its own special rules, different from the scope of variables.[7] Your pair-programming partner Bill shows you a quick example:

```ruby
module MyModule
  MyConstant = 'Outer constant'

  class MyClass
    MyConstant = 'Inner constant'
  end
end
```

Ignoring the whiteboard behind him, Bill picks up a napkin from his shirt pocket and sketches out the constants in this code (Figure 1.3). As he points out, all the constants in a program are arranged in a tree similar to a file system, where modules (and classes) are *directories* and regular constants are *files*. Just like in a file system, you can have multiple files with the same name, as long as they live in different directories. You can even refer to a constant by its *path*, just as you'd do with a file. For example, you can write MyModule::MyClass::MyConstant.[8]

---

7. Apart from this difference, a Ruby constant is very similar to a variable—to the extent that you can change the value of a constant, although you will get a warning from the interpreter. If you're in a destructive mood, you can even break Ruby beyond repair by changing the value of the String class name.

8. You can read more about the paths of constants in the sidebar on page 18.

The similarities between Ruby constants and files go even further: you can use modules to organize your constants, the same way that you use directories to organize your files. As usual, Bill has an example handy.

The Rake Example

The first versions of Rake, the popular Ruby build system, defined classes with obvious names such as Task and FileTask.[9] These names had a good chance of clashing with other class names from different libraries. To prevent clashes, recent versions of Rake define the classes inside a Rake module:

`gems/rake-0.8.7/lib/rake.rb`

```
module Rake
  class Task
    # ...
```

Now the full name of the Task class is Rake::Task, which is unlikely to clash with someone else's name. A module such as Rake, which only exists to be a container of constants, is called a *Namespace*.

Spell: Namespace

What if you have an old Rake build file lying around, one that still references the earlier, non-namespaced class names? To maintain compatibility with older build files, Rake provides a command-line option named classic-namespace. This option loads an additional source file that assigns the new, safer constant names to the old, unsafe ones:

`gems/rake-0.8.7/lib/rake/classic_namespace.rb`

```
Task = Rake::Task
FileTask = Rake::FileTask
FileCreationTask = Rake::FileCreationTask
# ...
```

Now both Task and Rake::Task reference the same Class instance, so you can use either constant. (Of course, now that you have the old names around, you have to worry about clashes again—so it would probably be a good idea to update your build file instead.)

Enough of this digression on constants. It's time to go back to the focus of Bill's improvised lecture—objects and classes—and wrap up what you've just learned.

---

9. Rake was written by Jim Weirich. Install it with gem install rake.

The Paths of Constants

In Section 1.3, *Constants*, on page 14, you learned that constants are nested like directories and files. Also like directories and files, constants are uniquely identified by their paths. Constants' paths use a double colon as a separator (this is akin to the scope operator in C++):

```ruby
module M
  class C
    X = 'a constant'
  end

  C::X # => "a constant"
end

M::C::X # => "a constant"
```

If you're sitting deep inside the tree of constants, you can provide the absolute path to an outer constant by using a leading double colon as root:

```ruby
module M
  Y = 'another constant'

  class C
    ::M::Y    # => "another constant"
  end
end
```

The Module class also provides an instance method and a class method that, confusingly, are both called constants(). Module#constants() returns all constants in the current scope, like your file system's ls command (or dir command, if you're running Windows). Module.constants() returns all the top-level constants in the current program, including class names:

```ruby
M.constants              # => [:C, :Y]
Module.constants[0..1]   # => [:Object, :Module]
```

Finally, if you need the current path, check out Module.nesting():

```ruby
module M
  class C
    module M2
      Module.nesting     # => [M::C::M2, M::C, M]
    end
  end
end
```

Pruning Your Tree of Constants

Imagine finding a motd.rb file on the Net that displays a "message of the day" on the console. You want to incorporate this code into your latest program, so you load the file to execute it and display the message:

```
load('motd.rb')
```

Using load(), however, has a side effect. The motd.rb file probably defines variables and classes. Although variables fall out of scope when the file has finished loading, constants don't. As a result, motd.rb can pollute your program with the names of its own constants—in particular, class names.

You can force motd.rb to keep its constants to itself by passing a second, optional argument to load():

```
load('motd.rb', true)
```

If you load a file this way, Ruby creates an anonymous module, uses that module as a *Namespace (17)* to contain all the constants from motd.rb, and then destroys the module.

The require() method is quite similar to load(), but it's meant for a different purpose. You use load() to execute code, and you use require() to import libraries. That's why require() has no second argument: those leftover class names are probably the reason why you imported the file in the first place.

Objects and Classes Wrap-Up

What's an object? It's just a bunch of instance variables, plus a link to a class. The object's methods don't live in the object—they live in the object's class, where they're called the *instance methods* of the class.

What's a class? It's just an object (an instance of Class), plus a list of instance methods and a link to a superclass. Class is a subclass of Module, so a class is also a module.

Like any object, a class has its own methods, such as new(). These are instance methods of the Class class. Also like any object, classes must be accessed through references. You already have a constant reference to each class: the class's name.

"That's pretty much all there is to know about objects and classes," Bill asserts. "If you can understand this, you're well on your way to understanding metaprogramming. Now, let's turn back to the code."

Another Learning Opportunity

It takes only a short while for you and Bill to get a chance to apply your newfound knowledge about classes. After ten minutes sifting through the Bookworm source code, you stumble upon a class that represents a snippet of text out of a book:

```
class TEXT
  # ...
```

Since the names of Ruby classes are conventionally camel cased,[10] you and Bill rename this class Text:

```
class Text
  # ...
```

You change the name of the class everywhere it's used, you run the unit tests, and—surprise!—the tests fail with a cryptic error message:

⇒   `TypeError: Text is not a class`

"D'oh! Of course it *is*," you exclaim. Bill is as puzzled as you are, so it takes the two of you some time to find the cause of the problem. As it turns out, the Bookworm application requires a popular library named ActionMailer. ActionMailer, in turn, uses a text-formatting library that defines a module named—you guessed it—Text:

```
module Text
  # ...
```

That's where the problem lies: since Text is already the name of a module, Ruby complains that it can't also be the name of a class at the same time. In a sense, you were lucky that this name clash was readily apparent. If ActionMailer's Text had been a class, you might have never noticed that this name already existed. Instead, you'd have inadvertently *Monkeypatched (9)* the existing Text class, with unpredictable results. (On the other hand, as Bill puts it, "That's what unit tests are for.")

---

10. In camel case, words are chained together, and the first letter of each word is capitalized, as in ThisTextIsCamelCased.

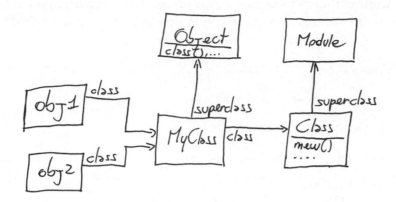

Figure 1.4: BILL'S OBJECT MODEL DIAGRAM AGAIN

Fixing the clash between your Text class and ActionMailer's Text module is as easy as wrapping your class in a *Namespace (17)*:

```
module Bookworm
  class Text
    # ...
```

You and Bill also change all references to Text into references to Bookworm::Text. It's unlikely that an external library defines a class named Bookworm::Text, so you should be safe from clashes now.

That was a lot of learning in a single sitting! You deserve a break and a cup of coffee—and a little quiz.

1.4 Quiz: Missing Lines

Where you prove to Bill that you can find your way around the Ruby object model.

Back in Section 1.3, *Classes Revisited*, on page 13, Bill showed you how objects and classes are related. As an example, he used a snippet of code (reprinted here) and a whiteboard diagram (shown in Figure 1.4):

```
class MyClass; end
obj1 = MyClass.new
obj2 = MyClass.new
```

Bill had drawn arrows to show you some of the connections between the program entities. Now he's asking you to add more lines and boxes to the diagram and answer these questions:

- What's the class of Object?

- What's the superclass of Module?

- What's the class of Class?

- Imagine that you execute this code:

  ```
  obj3 = MyClass.new
  obj3.instance_variable_set("@x", 10)
  ```

  Can you add obj3 to the diagram?

You can use irb and the Ruby documentation to find out the answers.

Quiz Solution

Your enhanced version of Bill's diagram is in Figure 1.5, on the next page. As you can easily check in irb, the superclass of Module is Object. You don't even need irb to know what the class of Object is: since Object is a class, its class must be Class. This is true of all classes, meaning that the class of Class must be Class itself. Don't you just love self-referential logic?

Finally, calling instance_variable_set() blesses obj3 with its own instance variable @x. If you find this concept surprising, remember that in a dynamic language such as Ruby every object has its own list of instance variables, independent of other objects—even other objects of the same class.

1.5 What Happens When You Call a Method?

Where you learn that a humble method call requires a lot of work on Ruby's part and you shed light on a twisted piece of code.

After some hours working on Bookworm, you and Bill already feel confident enough to fix some minor bugs here and there—but now, as your working day is drawing to a close, you find yourself stuck. Attempting to fix a long-standing bug, you've stumbled upon a tangle of classes, modules, and methods that you can't make head or tail of.

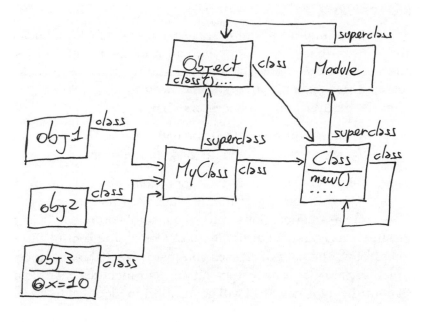

Figure 1.5: BILL'S DIAGRAM, ENHANCED BY YOU

"Stop!" Bill shouts, startling you. "This code is too complicated! To understand it, you have to learn in detail what happens when you call a method." And before you can react, he dives into yet another lecture.

When you call a method, Bill explains, Ruby does two things:

1. It finds the method. This is a process called *method lookup*.

2. It executes the method. To do that, Ruby needs something called **self**.

This process—find a method and then execute it—happens in every object-oriented language. In a very dynamic language like Ruby, however, it's particularly important that you understand the process in depth. Have you ever found yourself wondering where a particular method was defined? If you have, then you should definitely know more about method lookup and **self**.

Bill is going to explain method lookup first, and he'll come around to **self** later.

Method Lookup

You already know about the simplest case of method lookup. Look back at Figure 1.1, on page 12. When you call a method, Ruby looks into the object's class and finds the method there. Before you look at a more complicated example, though, you need to know about two new concepts: the receiver and the ancestors chain.

The *receiver* is simply the object that you call a method on. For example, if you write my_string.reverse(), then my_string is the receiver.

To understand the concept of an *ancestors chain*, just look at any Ruby class. Then imagine moving from the class into its superclass, then into the superclass's superclass, and so on, until you reach Object (the default superclass) and then, finally, BasicObject (the root of the Ruby class hierarchy). The path of classes you just traversed is the ancestors chain of the class. (The ancestors chain also includes modules, but forget about them for now. Bill will get around to modules in a bit.)

Now that you know what a receiver is and what an ancestors chain is, you can sum up the process of method lookup in a single sentence: to find a method, Ruby goes in the receiver's class, and from there it climbs the ancestors chain until it finds the method. Bill grabs the keyboard and writes an example:

`object_model/lookup.rb`
```ruby
class MyClass
  def my_method; 'my_method()'; end
end

class MySubclass < MyClass
end

obj = MySubclass.new
obj.my_method()        # => "my_method()"
```

As he draws Figure 1.6, on the next page, Bill wraps up the process of method lookup.[11] When you call my_method(), Ruby goes *right* from obj, the receiver, into MySubclass. Since it can't find my_method() there, Ruby continues its search by going *up* into MyClass, where it finally finds the

---

11. If you're used to UML diagrams, this picture might look confusing to you. Why is obj, a humble object, hanging around in the same diagram with a class hierarchy? Don't get confused—this is not a class diagram. Every box in the diagram is an object. It's just that some of these objects happen to be classes, and classes are linked together through the superclass() method.

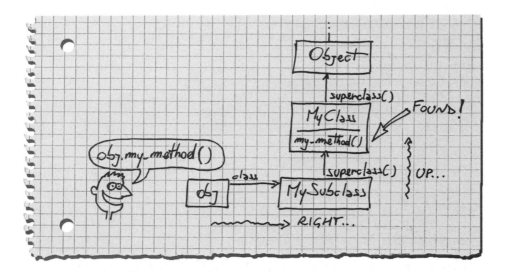

Figure 1.6: METHOD LOOKUP GOES "ONE STEP TO THE RIGHT, THEN UP."

method. If it hadn't found the method there, Ruby would have climbed higher up the chain into Object and then BasicObject. Because of the way most people draw diagrams, this behavior is also called the "one step to the right, then up" rule: go *one step to the right* into the receiver's class, and then go *up* the ancestors chain until you find the method.

"You don't even have to draw the ancestors chain like I did," Bill adds. Instead, he shows you how to ask a class for its ancestors chain with the ancestors() method:

```
MySubclass.ancestors # => [MySubclass, MyClass, Object, Kernel, BasicObject]
```

"Hey, what's Kernel doing there in the ancestors chain?" you ask. "You told me about a chain of superclasses, but I'm pretty sure that Kernel is a module, not a class."

"Whoops, you're right!" Bill exclaims, slapping his forehead. "I forgot to tell you about modules. They're easy...."

Modules and Lookup

You learned that the ancestors chain goes from class to superclass. Actually, the ancestors chain also includes modules.

Bill shows you an example:

```
object_model/lookup_modules.rb
```

```ruby
module M
  def my_method
    'M#my_method()'
  end
end

class C
  include M
end

class D < C; end

D.new.my_method() # => "M#my_method()"
```

When you include a module in a class (or even in another module), Ruby plays a little trick. It creates an anonymous class that wraps the module and inserts the anonymous class in the chain, just above the including class itself:[12]

```ruby
D.ancestors # => [D, C, M, Object, Kernel, BasicObject]
```

As he draws Figure 1.7, on the facing page, Bill also explains that these "wrapper" classes are called *include classes* (or sometimes *proxy classes*). Include classes are a well-kept secret of Ruby. The superclass() method pretends that they don't even exist, and in general you cannot access them from regular Ruby code. Still, you should know about them, if nothing else because they can help you make sense of complex hierarchies with lots of modules.

"While we're here," Bill continues, "I'd also like to tell you about that Kernel module that keeps popping up everywhere."

The Kernel

Ruby includes some methods, such as print(), that you can call from anywhere in your code. It looks like each and every object has the print() method. As Bill is quick to show you, methods such as print() are actually private instance methods of module Kernel:

```ruby
Kernel.private_instance_methods.grep(/^pr/) # => [:printf, :print, :proc]
```

The trick here is that class Object includes Kernel, so Kernel gets into every object's ancestors chain. And since you're always sitting inside

---

12. If you're using Ruby 1.8 or a previous version, don't get confused by BasicObject. This class didn't exist before Ruby 1.9.

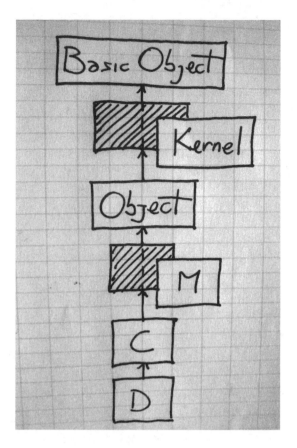

Figure 1.7: METHOD LOOKUP WITH MODULES

an object, you can call the Kernel methods from anywhere. This gives you the illusion that print is a language keyword, when it's actually a method. "Neat, isn't it?" Bill says.[13]

You can take advantage of this mechanism yourself: if you add a method to Kernel, this *Kernel Method* will be available to all objects. To prove this is actually useful, Bill shows you an example from one of Ruby's most popular libraries.

Spell: Kernel Method

---

13. If you're not convinced that you're always inside an object, wait for the sidebar on page 30.

The RubyGems Example

RubyGems, the Ruby package manager, includes a gem() method that activates a specific version of a gem:[14]

```ruby
require 'rubygems'
gem 'rails', '= 2.3.2'
```

You can call gem() from anywhere because it's a *Kernel Method (27)*, which you can verify by peeking into the RubyGems source code:

```
gems/rubygems-update-1.3.3/lib/rubygems.rb
```
```ruby
module Kernel
  def gem(gem_name, *version_requirements)
    # ...
```

"After this foray into Ruby modules and the Kernel," Bill says, "we can go back to our original track."

Method Execution

Bill sums up what you've learned so far. When you call a method, Ruby does two things: first, it finds the method, and second, it executes the method. Up to now, you focused on the finding part. Now you can finally look at the execution part.

Imagine being the Ruby interpreter. Somebody called a method named, say, my_method(). You found the method by going "one step to the right, then up," and it looks like this:

```ruby
def my_method
  temp = @x + 1
  my_other_method(temp)
end
```

To execute this method, you need to answer two questions. First, what object does the instance variable @x belong to? And second, what object should you call my_other_method() on?

Being a smart human being (as opposed to a dumb computer program), you can probably answer both questions intuitively: both @x and my_other_method() belong to the *receiver*—the object that my_method() was originally called upon. However, Ruby doesn't have the luxury of intuition. When you call a method, it needs to tuck away a reference to the receiver. Thanks to this reference, it can remember who the receiver is as it executes the method.

---

14. RubyGems was written by Chad Fowler, Rich Kilmer, Jim Weirich, and others.

That reference to the receiver can be useful for you, as well—so Bill gives you the lowdown on it.

Discovering self

Every line of Ruby code is executed inside an object—the so–called *current object*. The current object is also known as **self**, because you can access it with the **self** keyword.

Only one object can take the role of **self** at a given time, but no object holds that role for a long time. In particular, when you call a method, the receiver becomes **self**. From that moment on, all instance variables are instance variables of **self**, and all methods called without an explicit receiver are called on **self**. As soon as your code explicitly calls a method on some other object, that other object becomes **self**.

Bill writes an artfully complicated example to show you **self** in action:

`object_model/self.rb`
```
class MyClass
  def testing_self
    @var = 10      # An instance variable of self
    my_method()    # Same as self.my_method()
    self
  end

  def my_method
    @var = @var + 1
  end
end

obj = MyClass.new
obj.testing_self  # => #<MyClass:0x510b44 @var=11>
```

As soon as you call testing_self(), the receiver obj becomes **self**. Because of that, the instance variable @var is an instance variable of obj, and the method my_method() is called on obj(). As my_method() is executed, obj is still **self**, so @var is still an instance variable of obj. Finally, testing_self() returns a reference to **self** (you can also check the output to verify that @var is now worth 11).

"If you want to become a master of Ruby," Bill warns you, "you should always know which object has the role **self** at any given moment." In most cases, that's easy. You just have to track which object was the last method receiver. However, there are some corner cases that you should be aware of, and Bill wants to show you one of them right away.

The Top Level

In Section 1.5, *Discovering self*, on the preceding page, you learned that every time you call a method on an object, that object becomes **self**. But then, who's **self** if you haven't called any method yet? You can run irb and ask Ruby itself for an answer:

```
self        # => main
self.class  # => Object
```

As soon as you start a Ruby program, you're sitting within an object named main that the Ruby interpreter created for you.* This object is sometimes called the *top-level context*, because it's the object you're in when you're at the top level of the call stack: either you haven't called any method yet or all the methods that you called have returned.

---

*. In case you're wondering, Ruby's main has nothing to do with the main() functions in C and Java.

Class Definitions and self

Usually the role of **self** is taken by the last object who received a method call. However, in a class or module definition (and outside of any method), the role of **self** is taken by the class or module:

```
class MyClass
  self        # => MyClass
end
```

This detail is not going to be useful right now, but it will become a central concept in Chapter 4, *Thursday: Class Definitions*, on page 101. For now, you can set it aside.

Everything that you learned about method execution can be summed up in a few short sentences. When you call a method, Ruby looks up the method by following the "one step to the right, then up" rule and then executes the method with the receiver as **self**. There are some special cases in this procedure (for example, when you include a module), but there are no exceptions.

While you're lost in thought, pondering the elegant simplicity of the Ruby object model, Bill has beaten you to the keyboard, and he's ready to throw a quiz at you.

What private Really Means

Now that you know about **self**, you can cast a new light over Ruby's **private** keyword. Private methods are governed by a single simple rule: you cannot call a private method with an explicit receiver. In other words, every time you call a private method, it must be on the implicit receiver—**self**. Let's see a corner case:

```
class C
  def public_method
    self.private_method
  end

  private

  def private_method; end
end

C.new.public_method
```

⇒ `NoMethodError: private method 'private_method' called [...]`

You can make this code work by removing the **self** keyword.

This contrived example shows that private methods come from two rules working together: first, you need an explicit receiver to call a method on an object that is not yourself, and second, **private** methods can be called only with an implicit receiver. Put these two rules together, and you'll see that you can only call a **private** method on yourself. You can call this the "**private** rule."

You could find Ruby's private methods perplexing—especially if you come from Java or C#, where **private** behaves very differently. When you're in doubt, just go back to the **private** rule, and everything will make sense. Can object x call a private method on object y if the two objects share the same class? The answer is no, because no matter which class you belong to, you still need an explicit receiver to call another object's method. Can you call a **private** method that you inherited from a superclass? The answer is yes, because you don't need an explicit receiver to call inherited methods on yourself.

1.6 Quiz: Tangle of Modules

You can finally go back to the problem that prompted Bill to launch into his discussion on method lookup and **self**. You've had trouble making sense of a complicated arrangement of classes and modules. Here's the confusing part:

`object_model/tangle.rb`
```ruby
module Printable
  def print
    # ...
  end

  def prepare_cover
    # ...
  end
end

module Document
  def print_to_screen
    prepare_cover
    format_for_screen
    print
  end

  def format_for_screen
    # ...
  end

  def print
    # ...
  end
end

class Book
  include Document
  include Printable

  # ...
end
```

Another source file creates a Book and calls print_to_screen():

```ruby
b = Book.new
b.print_to_screen
```

According to the company's bug management application, there is a problem with this code: print_to_screen() is not calling the right print() method. The bug report doesn't provide any more details.

Can you guess which version of print() gets called—the one in Printable or the one in Document? Try drawing the chain of ancestors on paper. How can you quickly fix the code so that print_to_screen() calls the other version of print() instead?

Quiz Solution

You can ask Ruby itself for the ancestors chain of Book:

```
Book.ancestors  # => [Book, Printable, Document, Object, Kernel, BasicObject]
```

If you draw this ancestors chain on your whiteboard, it will look like Figure 1.8, on the following page. Let's see how Ruby builds the chain. Since Book doesn't have an explicit superclass, it implicitly inherits from Object, which, in turn, includes Kernel and inherits from BasicObject. When Book includes Document, Ruby creates an include class for Document and adds it to Book's ancestors chain right above Book itself. Immediately after that, Book includes Printable. Again, Ruby creates an include class for Printable and slips it in the chain right above Book, pushing up the rest of the chain—from Document upward.

When you call b.print_to_screen, the object referenced by b becomes **self**, and method lookup begins. Ruby finds the print_to_screen() method in Document, and that method then calls other methods—including print(). All methods called without an explicit receiver are called on **self**, so method lookup starts once again from Book (**self**'s class) and goes up until it finds a method named print(). The lowest print() in the chain is Printable#print(), so that's the one that gets called.

The bug report hints that the original author of the code intended to call Document#print() instead. In real production code, you'd probably want to get rid of this confusion and rename one of the clashing print() methods. However, if you just want to solve this quiz, the cheapest way to do it is to swap the order of inclusion of the modules in Book so that Document gets lower than Printable in the ancestors chain:

`object_model/tangle_untwisted.rb`
```
module Printable
  # ...
end

module Document
  # ...
end
```

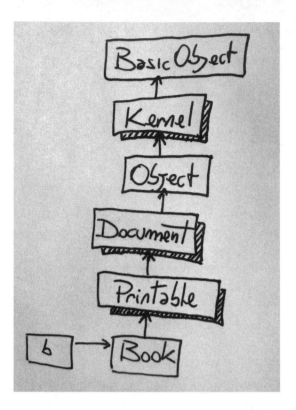

Figure 1.8: The ancestors chain of the Book class

```
class Book
►   include Printable
►   include Document

    ancestors  # => [Book, Document, Printable, Object, Kernel, BasicObject]
end
```

Bill points out that the previous code implicitly calls ancestors() on Book, because in a class definition the role of **self** is taken by the class. He also hints at another interesting detail: the ancestors chain of Book also contains a third method named print()—but Bill is not telling you where it is. If you're curious, you'll have to find it yourself, maybe with some help from your friend irb.

It's almost time to go home after an exhausting, but very satisfying, day of work. But before you call it a day, Bill does a complete wrap-up of what you learned.

1.7 Object Model Wrap-Up

Here's a checklist of what you learned today:

- An object is composed of a bunch of instance variables and a link to a class.

- The methods of an object live in the object's class (from the point of view of the class, they're called *instance methods*).

- The class itself is just an object of class Class. The name of the class is just a constant.

- Class is a subclass of Module. A module is basically a package of methods. In addition to that, a class can also be instantiated (with new()) or arranged in a hierarchy (through its superclass()).

- Constants are arranged in a tree similar to a file system, where the names of modules and classes play the part of directories and regular constants play the part of files.

- Each class has an ancestors chain, beginning with the class itself and going up to BasicObject.

- When you call a method, Ruby goes *right* into the class of the receiver and then *up* the ancestors chain, until it either finds the method or reaches the end of the chain.

- Every time a class includes a module, the module is inserted in the ancestors chain right above the class itself.

- When you call a method, the receiver takes the role of **self**.

- When you're defining a module (or a class), the module takes the role of **self**.

- Instance variables are always assumed to be instance variables of **self**.

- Any method called without an explicit receiver is assumed to be a method of **self**.

Checked... checked... done! Now it's time to go home before your brain explodes with all the information you crammed into it today.

Chapter 2

Tuesday: Methods

Yesterday you learned about the Ruby object model and how to make Ruby classes sing and dance for you. Today you're holding all calls to focus on *methods*.

As you know, the objects in your code talk to each other all the time. Some languages—Java, for one—feature a compiler that presides over this chatting. For every method call, the compiler checks to see that the receiving object has a matching method. This is called *static type checking*, and the languages that adopt it are called *static languages*. So, for example, if you call talk_simple() on a Lawyer object that has no such method, the compiler protests loudly.

Dynamic languages—such as Python and Ruby—don't have a compiler policing method calls. As a consequence, you can start a program that calls talk_simple() on a Lawyer, and everything works just fine—that is, until that specific line of code is executed. Only then does the Lawyer complain that it doesn't understand that call.

Admittedly, that's one advantage of static type checking: the compiler can spot some of your mistakes before the code runs. Before you ask the obvious question, realize that this protectiveness comes at a high price. Static languages force you to write lots of tedious, repetitive methods— these are the so-called boilerplate methods—just to make the compiler happy. (If you're a Java programmer, just think of all the "get" and "set" methods you've written in your life or the innumerable methods that do nothing but delegate to some other object.)

In Ruby, boilerplate methods aren't a problem, because you can easily avoid them with techniques that would be impractical or just plain impossible in a static language. In this chapter, we home in on those techniques.

2.1 A Duplication Problem

Where you and Bill have a problem with duplicated code.

Your boss is happy with the job that you and Bill did yesterday. Today, she gives the two of you a more serious integration assignment.

To give you a bit of history, some folks in the purchasing department are concerned that developers are spending oodles of company money on computing gear. To make sure things don't get out of hand, they're requesting a system that automatically flags expenses more than $99. (You read that right: *ninety-nine.* The purchasing department isn't fooling around.)

Before you and Bill, some developers took a stab at the project, coding a report that lists all the components of each computer in the company and how much each component costs. To date they haven't plugged in any real data. Here's where you and Bill come in.

The Legacy System

Right from the start, the two of you have a challenge on your hands: the data you need to load into the already established program is stored in a legacy system stuck behind an awkwardly coded class named DS (for "data source"):

`methods/computer/data_source.rb`

```
class DS
  def initialize # connect to data source...
  def get_mouse_info(workstation_id) # ...
  def get_mouse_price(workstation_id) # ...
  def get_keyboard_info(workstation_id) # ...
  def get_keyboard_price(workstation_id) # ...
  def get_cpu_info(workstation_id) # ...
  def get_cpu_price(workstation_id) # ...
  def get_display_info(workstation_id) # ...
  def get_display_price(workstation_id) # ...
  # ...and so on
```

DS#initialize() connects to the data system when you create a new DS() object. The other methods—and there are dozens of them—take a workstation identifier and return descriptions and prices for the computer's components. The output is in the form of strings, with prices expressed as integer numbers rounded to the nearest dollar. With Bill standing by to offer moral support, you quickly try the class in irb:

```
ds = DS.new
ds.get_cpu_info(42)      # => 2.16 Ghz
ds.get_cpu_price(42)     # => 150
ds.get_mouse_info(42)    # => Dual Optical
ds.get_mouse_price(42)   # => 40
```

It looks like workstation number 42 has a 2.16GHz CPU and a luxurious $40 dual optical mouse. This is enough data to get you started.

Double, Treble... Trouble

You and Bill have to wrap DS into an object that fits the reporting application. This means each Computer must be an object. This object has a single method for each component, returning a string describing both the component and its price. Remember that price limit the purchasing department set? Keeping this requirement in mind, you know that if the component costs $100 or more, the string must begin with an asterisk to draw people's attention.

You kick off development by writing the first three methods in the Computer class:

`methods/computer/boring.rb`

```
class Computer
  def initialize(computer_id, data_source)
    @id = computer_id
    @data_source = data_source
  end

  def mouse
    info = @data_source.get_mouse_info(@id)
    price = @data_source.get_mouse_price(@id)
    result = "Mouse: #{info} ($#{price})"
    return "* #{result}" if price >= 100
    result
  end

  def cpu
    info = @data_source.get_cpu_info(@id)
    price = @data_source.get_cpu_price(@id)
    result = "Cpu: #{info} ($#{price})"
    return "* #{result}" if price >= 100
    result
  end
end
```

```ruby
  def keyboard
    info = @data_source.get_keyboard_info(@id)
    price = @data_source.get_keyboard_price(@id)
    result = "Keyboard: #{info} ($#{price})"
    return "* #{result}" if price >= 100
    result
  end

  # ...
end
```

At this point in the development of Computer, you find yourself bogged down in a swampland of repetitive copy and paste. You have a long list of methods left to deal with, and you should also write tests for each and every method, because it's easy to make mistakes in duplicated code. This is getting boring fast—not to mention painful.

Bill is right there with you, verbalizing precisely what's going through your head: "This is just the same method again and again, with some minor changes." You turn to each other and ask simultaneously, as if on cue, "How can we refactor it?"

Bill's Plan

"I can think of not one but *two* different ways to remove this duplication," Bill brags. He suggests using either Dynamic Methods or a special method called method_missing(). By trying both solutions, you and Bill can decide which one you like better. You agree to start with Dynamic Methods and get to method_missing() after that.

2.2 Dynamic Methods

Where you learn how to call and define methods dynamically and remove the duplicated code.

"As I mentioned, we can remove the duplication in our code with either Dynamic Methods or method_missing()," Bill recalls. "Forget about method_missing() for now—we'll get to that this afternoon. To introduce Dynamic Methods, allow me to tell you a story from my youth," he says.

"When I was a young developer learning C++," Bill muses, "my mentors told me that when you call a method, you're actually sending a message to an object. It took me a while to get used to that concept. Of course, if I'd been using Ruby back then, that notion of sending messages would have come more naturally to me." Bill launches into a mini-presentation.

Calling Methods Dynamically

When you call a method, you usually do so using the standard dot notation:

```
methods/dynamic_call.rb
```

```ruby
class MyClass
  def my_method(my_arg)
    my_arg * 2
  end
end

obj = MyClass.new
obj.my_method(3)   # => 6
```

Bill demonstrates how you can also call MyClass#my_method() using Object#send() in place of the dot notation:

```ruby
obj.send(:my_method, 3)    # => 6
```

The previous code still calls my_method(), but it does so through send(). The first argument to send() is the message that you're sending to the object—that is, the name of a method. You can use a string or a symbol, but symbols are considered more kosher (see the sidebar on the next page). Any remaining arguments (and the block, if one exists) are simply passed on to the method.

"Wait a minute," you interject. "Why on Earth would I use send() instead of the plain old dot notation?" Bill is glad you asked, pointing out that this is one of the cool things about Ruby. With send(), the name of the method that you want to call becomes just a regular argument. You can wait literally until the very last moment to decide which method to call, *while* the code is running. This technique is called *Dynamic Dispatch*, and you'll find it wildly useful. To help reveal its magic, Bill shows you a couple of real-life examples.

Spell: Dynamic Dispatch

The Camping Example

One example of Dynamic Dispatch comes from Camping, a minimalist Ruby web framework. A Camping application stores its configuration parameters as key-value pairs in a file created with YAML, a simple and very popular serialization format.[1]

---

1. Camping, a framework written by "_why the lucky stiff," can be installed with gem install camping. YAML stands for "Yaml Ain't Markup Language," and you can learn more about it at http://www.yaml.org.

Symbols

If you prefix any sequence of characters with a colon (actually, any sequence that would make a legal variable name), it becomes a *symbol*:

```
x = :this_is_a_symbol
```

Symbols and strings are not related, and they belong to entirely different classes. Nevertheless, symbols are similar enough to strings that most Ruby beginners are confused by them. "What's the point of having symbols at all? Why can't I just use regular strings everywhere?" they ask.

Different people will provide different answers to these questions. Some might point out that symbols are different from strings because symbols are *immutable*: you can change the characters inside a string, but you can't do that for symbols. Also, some operations (such as comparisons) are faster on symbols than they are on strings. But, choosing between symbols and strings basically comes down to conventions. In most cases, symbols are used as names of things—in particular, names of metaprogramming-related things such as methods.

For example, when you call Object#send(), you need to pass it the name of a method as a first argument. Although send() accepts this name as either a symbol or a string, symbols are usually considered more appropriate:

```
# rather than: 1.send("+", 2)
1.send(:+, 2)    # => 3
```

Regardless, you can easily convert a string to a symbol (by calling either String#to_sym() or String#intern()) or back (by calling either Symbol#to_s() or Symbol#id2name()).

The configuration file for a blog application might look like this:

```
admin : Bill
title : Rubyland
topic : Ruby and more
```

Camping copies keys and values from the file into its own configuration object. (This object is an OpenStruct. You can read more about this class in Section 2.3, *The OpenStruct Example*, on page 52.) Assume that you store your application's configuration in a conf object. In an ideal world, the configuration code for the blog application would look like this:

```
conf.admin = 'Bill'
conf.title = 'Rubyland'
conf.topic = 'Ruby and more'
```

The sad fact is, in real life, Camping's source can't contain this kind of code. That's because it can't know in advance which keys you need in your specific application—so it can't know which methods it's supposed to call. It can discover the keys you need only at runtime, by parsing the YAML file. For this reason, Camping resorts to Dynamic Dispatch. For each key-value pair, it composes the name of an assignment method, such as admin=(), and sends the method to conf:

`gems/camping-1.5/bin/camping`

```
# Load configuration if any
if conf.rc and File.exists?( conf.rc )
  YAML.load_file(conf.rc).each do |k,v|
    conf.send("#{k}=", v)
  end
end
```

Neat, huh?

The Test::Unit Example

Another example of *Dynamic Dispatch (41)* comes from the Test::Unit standard library. Test::Unit uses a naming convention to decide which methods are tests. A TestCase looks inside its own public methods and selects the methods that have names starting with *test*:

```
method_names = public_instance_methods(true)
tests = method_names.delete_if {|method_name| method_name !~ /^test./}
```

Now TestCase has an array of all test methods. Later, it uses send() to call each method in the array.[2] This particular flavor of Dynamic Dispatch

---

2. To nitpick, TestCase uses a synonym of send() named __send__(). You'll find out why in the sidebar on page 64.

Privacy Matters

Remember what Spiderman's uncle used to say? "With great power comes great responsibility." The Object#send() method is very powerful—perhaps *too* powerful. In particular, you can call any method with send(), including private methods. Short of using a *Context Probe (83)*, this is the easiest way to peek into an object's private matters.

Some Rubyists think that send() makes it too easy to unwillingly break encapsulation. Ruby 1.9 experimented with changing send()'s behavior, but the changes were ultimately reverted. As of Ruby 1.9.1, send() can still call private methods—and many libraries use it just for that purpose. On the other hand, you have a new public_send() method that respects the receiver's privacy.

Spell: Pattern Dispatch is sometimes called *Pattern Dispatch*, because it filters methods based on a pattern in their names.

Bill leans back in his chair. "Now you know about send() and Dynamic Dispatch, but there is more to Dynamic Methods than that. You're not limited to calling methods dynamically. You can also *define* methods dynamically. I'll show you how."

Defining Methods Dynamically

You can define a method on the spot with Module#define_method(). You just need to provide a method name and a block, which becomes the method body:

methods/dynamic_definition.rb

```
class MyClass
  define_method :my_method do |my_arg|
    my_arg * 3
  end
end

obj = MyClass.new
obj.my_method(2)  # => 6
```

define_method( ) is executed within MyClass, so my_method( ) is defined as an instance method of MyClass.[3] This technique of defining a method at runtime is called a *Dynamic Method*.

Spell: Dynamic Method

You learned how to use Module#define_method( ) in place of the **def** keyword to define a method and how to use send( ) in place of the dot notation to call a method. Now you can go back to your and Bill's original problem and put this knowledge to work.

Refactoring the Computer Class

Recall the code that pulled you and Bill into this dynamic discussion:

methods/computer/boring.rb

```ruby
class Computer
  def initialize(computer_id, data_source)
    @id = computer_id
    @data_source = data_source
  end

  def mouse
    info = @data_source.get_mouse_info(@id)
    price = @data_source.get_mouse_price(@id)
    result = "Mouse: #{info} ($#{price})"
    return "* #{result}" if price >= 100
    result
  end

  def cpu
    info = @data_source.get_cpu_info(@id)
    price = @data_source.get_cpu_price(@id)
    result = "Cpu: #{info} ($#{price})"
    return "* #{result}" if price >= 100
    result
  end

  def keyboard
    info = @data_source.get_keyboard_info(@id)
    price = @data_source.get_keyboard_price(@id)
    result = "Keyboard: #{info} ($#{price})"
    return "* #{result}" if price >= 100
    result
  end

  # ...
end
```

---

3. There is also an Object#define_method( ) that defines a *Singleton Method (112)*.

Now that you know about send() and define_method(), you and Bill can get to work and remove the duplication in Computer. Time to refactor!

Step 1: Adding Dynamic Dispatches

You and Bill start, extracting the duplicated code into its own message-sending method:

methods/computer/send.rb

```ruby
class Computer
  def initialize(computer_id, data_source)
    @id = computer_id
    @data_source = data_source
  end

  def mouse
    component :mouse
  end

  def cpu
    component :cpu
  end

  def keyboard
    component :keyboard
  end

  def component(name)
    info = @data_source.send "get_#{name}_info", @id
    price = @data_source.send "get_#{name}_price", @id
    result = "#{name.to_s.capitalize}: #{info} ($#{price})"
    return "* #{result}" if price >= 100
    result
  end
end
```

A call to mouse() is delegated to component(), which in turn calls DS# get_mouse_info() and DS#get_mouse_price(). The call also writes the capitalized name of the component in the resulting string. (Since component() expects the name as a symbol, it converts the symbol to a string with Symbol#to_s().) You open an irb session and smoke-test the new Computer:

```ruby
my_computer = Computer.new(42, DS.new)
my_computer.cpu   # => * Cpu: 2.16 Ghz ($220)
```

This new version of Computer is a step forward, because it contains far fewer duplicated lines, but you still have to write dozens of similar methods. To avoid writing all those methods, use define_method().

Step 2: Generating Methods Dynamically

You and Bill refactor Computer to use define_method():

methods/computer/dynamic.rb

```
class Computer
  def initialize(computer_id, data_source)
    @id = computer_id
    @data_source = data_source
  end

▶   def self.define_component(name)
▶     define_method(name) {
▶       info = @data_source.send "get_#{name}_info", @id
▶       price = @data_source.send "get_#{name}_price", @id
▶       result = "#{name.to_s.capitalize}: #{info} ($#{price})"
▶       return "* #{result}" if price >= 100
▶       result
▶     }
▶   end
▶
▶   define_component :mouse
▶   define_component :cpu
▶   define_component :keyboard
end
```

Note that define_method() is executed inside the definition of Computer, where Computer is the implicit **self**.[4] This means you're calling define_component() on Computer, so it must be a class method.

You quickly test the slimmed-down Computer class in irb and discover that it still works. This is great news!

Step 3: Sprinkling the Code with Introspection

The latest Computer contains minimal duplication, but you can push it even further and remove the duplication altogether. How? By getting rid of all the define_component() methods. You can do that by introspecting the data_source argument and extracting the names of all components:

methods/computer/more_dynamic.rb

```
class Computer
  def initialize(computer_id, data_source)
    @id = computer_id
    @data_source = data_source
▶     data_source.methods.grep(/^get_(.*)_info$/) { Computer.define_component $1 }
  end
```

---

4. See Section 1.5, *Discovering self*, on page 29.

```
    def self.define_component(name)
      define_method(name) {
        info = @data_source.send "get_#{name}_info", @id
        price = @data_source.send "get_#{name}_price", @id
▶       result = "#{name.capitalize}: #{info} ($#{price})"
        return "* #{result}" if price >= 100
        result
      }
  end
end
```

The new line in initialize() is where the magic happens. To understand it, you need to know a couple of things. First, if you pass a block to String#grep(), the block is evaluated for each element that matches the regular expression. Second, the string matching the parenthesized part of the regular expression is stored in the global variable $1. So, if data_source has methods named get_cpu_info() and get_mouse_info(), this code ultimately calls Computer.define_component() twice, with the strings "cpu" and "mouse". Note that you're calling define_component() with a string rather than a symbol, so you don't need to convert the argument to string.

The duplicated code is finally gone for good. As a bonus, you don't even have to write or maintain the list of components. If someone adds a new component to DS, the Computer class will support it automatically. Wonderful!

Let's Try That Again!

Your refactoring was a resounding success, but Bill is not willing to stop here. "We said that we were going to try *two* different solutions to this problem, remember? We've only found one, involving *Dynamic Dispatch (41)* and *Dynamic Methods (45).*" Although it has served the two of you well, to be fair, you need to give the other solution a chance.

"For this second solution," Bill continues, "we need to talk about some strange methods that are not really methods and a very special method named method_missing()."

2.3 method_missing()

Where you listen to spooky stories about Ghost Methods and dynamic proxies and you try a second way to remove duplicated code.

"With Ruby, there's no compiler to enforce method calls," Bill pronounces. "This means you can call a method that doesn't exist." For example:

```
methods/method_missing.rb
```

```ruby
class Lawyer; end

nick = Lawyer.new
nick.talk_simple
```

⇒ `NoMethodError: undefined method 'talk_simple' for #<Lawyer:0x3c848> [...]`

Do you remember how method lookup works? When you call talk_simple, Ruby goes into nick's class and browses its instance methods. If it can't find talk_simple() there, it searches up the ancestors chain into Object and eventually into Kernel.

Since Ruby can't find talk_simple() anywhere, it admits defeat by calling a method named method_missing() on nick, the original receiver. Ruby knows that method_missing() is there, because it's an instance method of Kernel that every object inherits.

You and Bill decide to experiment by calling method_missing() yourselves. It's a private method, but you can get to it through send():[5]

```ruby
nick.send :method_missing, :my_method
```

⇒ `NoMethodError: undefined method 'my_method' for #<Lawyer:0x3c7f8>`

You've just done exactly what Ruby does. You told the object, "I tried to call a method named my_method() on you, and you didn't understand." Kernel#method_missing() responded by raising a NoMethodError. This is what method_missing() does for a living. It's like an object's dead-letter office, the place where unknown messages eventually end up (and also, the place where NoMethodErrors come from).

Overriding method_missing()

Most likely, you will never need to call method_missing() yourself. Instead, you can override it to intercept unknown messages. Each message landing on method_missing()'s desk includes the name of the method that was called, plus any arguments and blocks associated with the call.

---

5. See the sidebar on page 44.

```
methods/more_method_missing.rb
class Lawyer
  def method_missing(method, *args)
    puts "You called: #{method}(#{args.join(', ')})"
    puts "(You also passed it a block)" if block_given?
  end
end

bob = Lawyer.new
bob.talk_simple('a', 'b') do
  # a block
end
```

⇒ You called: talk_simple(a, b)
  (You also passed it a block)

Overriding method_missing() allows you to call methods that don't really exist. Let's take a closer look at these Ghost Methods.

Ghost Methods

When you need to define many similar methods, you can spare yourself the definitions and just respond to calls through method_missing(). This is like saying to the object, "If they ask you something and you don't understand, do this."

Spell: Ghost Method

A message that's processed by method_missing() looks like a regular call from the caller's side but has no corresponding method on the receiver's side. This is named a *Ghost Method*. The following are some Ghost Method examples.

The Ruport Example

Ruport is a Ruby reporting library.[6] You can use the Ruport::Data::Table class to create tabular data and convert it to different formats—text, for example:

```
methods/ruport_example.rb
require 'ruport'

table = Ruport::Data::Table.new :column_names => ["country", "wine"],
                                :data => [["France", "Bordeaux"],
                                          ["Italy", "Chianti"],
                                          ["France", "Chablis"]]

puts table.to_text
```

---

6. You can install Ruport, by Gregory T. Brown, with gem install ruport.

```
⇒    +-------------------+
     | country |   wine   |
     +-------------------+
     | France  | Bordeaux |
     | Italy   | Chianti  |
     | France  | Chablis  |
     +-------------------+
```

Let's say you select only the French wines and convert them to comma-separated values:

```
found = table.rows_with_country("France")
found.each do |row|
  puts row.to_csv
end
```

```
⇒    France, Bordeaux
     France, Chablis
```

What you just did is call a method named rows_with_country() on Ruport::Data::Table. But how could the author of this class know you were going to have a column named country? The fact is, the author *didn't* know that. If you look inside Ruport, you see that both rows_with_country() and to_csv() are Ghost Methods:

gems/ruport-1.6.1/lib/ruport/data/table.rb

```
class Table
  def method_missing(id,*args,&block)
    return as($1.to_sym,*args,&block) if id.to_s =~ /^to_(.*)/
    return rows_with($1.to_sym => args[0]) if id.to_s =~ /^rows_with_(.*)/
    super
  end

  # ...
```

A call to rows_with_country() becomes a call to a more traditional-looking method, rows_with(:country), which takes the column name as an argument. Also, a call to to_csv() becomes a call to as(:csv). If the method name doesn't start with either of these two prefixes, Ruport falls back to Kernel#method_missing(), which throws a NoMethodError. (That's what the **super** keyword is for.)

Ghost Methods like rows_with_country() are just syntactic sugar; they can't do anything that a regular method couldn't. Still, you have to admit, they look sexier than regular methods. If you use Ruport to define new output formats (say, xsl) or new columns (say, price), you'll get methods such as to_xsl() and rows_with_price() automatically.

This example focused on very specific libraries, but Ghost Methods are also widely used in Ruby's built-in, standard libraries. Consider this next example.

The OpenStruct Example

The OpenStruct class is a little bit of magic from the Ruby standard libraries. The attributes of an OpenStruct object work like Ruby variables. If you want a new attribute, just assign it a value, and it will spring into existence:

```ruby
require 'ostruct'

icecream = OpenStruct.new
icecream.flavor = "strawberry"
icecream.flavor                    # => "strawberry"
```

This works because the attributes of an OpenStruct object are actually Ghost Methods. OpenStruct#method_missing() catches the call to flavor=() and chops off the "=" at the end to get the attribute name. Then it stores the attribute name and its value into a hash. When you call a method that doesn't end with an "=", method_missing() looks up the method name in the hash and returns the result. The code from OpenStruct is a tad complex, because it covers special cases such as error conditions. However, it's easy to write your own, simplified version of an open structure:

```ruby
methods/my_ostruct.rb
class MyOpenStruct
  def initialize
    @attributes = {}
  end

  def method_missing(name, *args)
    attribute = name.to_s
    if attribute =~ /=$/
      @attributes[attribute.chop] = args[0]
    else
      @attributes[attribute]
    end
  end
end

icecream = MyOpenStruct.new
icecream.flavor = "vanilla"
icecream.flavor                 # => "vanilla"
```

Dynamic Proxies

Ghost Methods (50) are usually icing on the cake, but some objects actually rely almost exclusively on them. These objects are often wrappers for something else—maybe another object, a web service, or code written in a different language. They collect method calls through method_ missing() and forward them to the wrapped object. Bill decides to demonstrate this technique. "I'll give you a real-life example, but it's going to be a tad complex," he warns you. "So, I'll have to ask for your full attention for a few minutes. Have you ever used Flickr?"

The Flickr Example

Flickr[7] is an online service that people use to upload and "tag" (that is, label) photographs. It also exposes a public HTTP API, which provides methods such as flickr.people.findByUsername(). You pass a username to this method, and it returns the identifier of that user. You can call methods such as findByUsername() with a regular HTTP GET, for example by writing the following URL in a browser.[8] You must also provide an API key, which you can get for free from http://www.flickr.com/services/api/keys/:

http://api.flickr.com/services/rest/?method=flickr.people.findByUsername& username=duncandavidson&api_key=*your API key here*

You'll get back a snippet of XML containing the identifier for user duncandavidson:

```
⇒ <rsp stat="ok">
    <user id="59532755@N00" nsid="59532755@N00">
      <username>duncandavidson</username>
    </user>
  </rsp>
```

Now that you have a user identifier, you can access the user's data. For example, you can get duncandavidson's photo tags by calling flickr.tags. getListUser(). But instead of using HTTP, you can do that through the flickr gem, a Ruby wrapper for Flickr.[9] Just replace the dots in the Flickr

---

7. http://www.flickr.com

8. The Flickr API may have changed by the time you read this. As you'll see, this tendency of online services to evolve is the point of the whole example—but it may prove inconvenient if you want to try the code on your computer. Here, you just need to trust that this example is running fine on the author's computer. (You're probably thinking, "Hmm, where have I heard that before?")

9. The flickr gem was written by Scott Raymond. Install it with gem install flickr.

method name with underscores so that it becomes a valid Ruby method name:

```
require 'flickr'
flickr = Flickr.new([your API key here])
xml = flickr.tags_getListUser('user_id'=>'59532755@N00')
tags = xml['who']['tags']['tag']
tags.grep /rails/  # => ["railsconf07", "railsconf08", "railsconf09", ...
```

The Flickr class converts the XML returned from Flickr to a tree-like object. The previous code peers into this object and finds out that this duncandavidson guy is a regular at Rails conferences.

What if the Flickr API gets extended? You might assume that you'd have to wait for an updated version of the flickr library. Actually, the library supports changes in the API without flinching. In fact, the version of the Flickr API used to write this example was written before the flickr.tags.getListUser() method became available.

This library manages to support new methods in the Flickr API even *before* they're written, thanks to a little bit of metaprogramming magic: if you look into the source of the flickr library, you see that Flickr#tags_getListUser() and the other Flickr API methods are actually Ghost Methods:

gems/flickr-1.0.2/flickr.rb

```
class Flickr
  # Takes a Flickr API method name and set of parameters;
  # returns an XmlSimple object with the response
  def request(method, *params)
    response =
      XmlSimple.xml_in(http_get(request_url(method, params)),
                       { 'ForceArray' => false })
    raise response['err']['msg'] if response['stat'] != 'ok'
    response
  end

  def method_missing(method_id, *params)
    request(method_id.id2name.gsub(/_/, '.'), params[0])
  end

  # ...
```

Flickr#method_missing() replaces all underscores in the method name with dots. Then it takes the first argument of the method, which it assumes to be an array of arguments, and forwards the name and arguments to Flickr#request(). In turn, this method forwards the call to Flickr via HTTP, checks the resulting XML for errors, and finally returns it.

Delegates

You can get a quick, ready-to-use *Dynamic Proxy (55)* by using Ruby's delegate library:

methods/delegator.rb

```ruby
require 'delegate'

class Assistant
  def initialize(name)
    @name = name
  end

  def read_email
    "(#{@name}) It's mostly spam."
  end

  def check_schedule
    "(#{@name}) You have a meeting today."
  end
end

class Manager < DelegateClass(Assistant)
  def initialize(assistant)
    super(assistant)
  end

  def attend_meeting
    "Please hold my calls."
  end
end
```

DelegateClass() is a *Mimic Method (224)* that creates and returns a new Class. This class defines a method_missing() that forwards calls to a wrapped object, such as an Assistant. Manager inherits this method_missing(), so it becomes a proxy of the wrapped object. As a result, the Manager forwards to her Assistant all the messages she doesn't understand:

```ruby
frank = Assistant.new("Frank")
anne = Manager.new(frank)
anne.attend_meeting     # => "Please hold my calls."
anne.read_email         # => "(Frank) It's mostly spam."
anne.check_schedule     # => "(Frank) You have a meeting today."
```

The flickr library also provides object-oriented wrappers for the Flickr API, but ultimately all these wrappers call Flickr#method_missing(). An object that catches Ghost Methods and forwards them to another object, maybe wrapping some logic around the call, is called a *Dynamic Proxy.*

Spell: Dynamic Proxy

Refactoring the Computer Class (Again)

"OK, you now know about method_missing()," Bill observes. "Let's go back to the Computer class and remove the duplication."

Once again, here's the original Computer class:

methods/computer/boring.rb

```ruby
class Computer
  def initialize(computer_id, data_source)
    @id = computer_id
    @data_source = data_source
  end

  def mouse
    info = @data_source.get_mouse_info(@id)
    price = @data_source.get_mouse_price(@id)
    result = "Mouse: #{info} ($#{price})"
    return "* #{result}" if price >= 100
    result
  end

  def cpu
    info = @data_source.get_cpu_info(@id)
    price = @data_source.get_cpu_price(@id)
    result = "Cpu: #{info} ($#{price})"
    return "* #{result}" if price >= 100
    result
  end

  def keyboard
    info = @data_source.get_keyboard_info(@id)
    price = @data_source.get_keyboard_price(@id)
    result = "Keyboard: #{info} ($#{price})"
    return "* #{result}" if price >= 100
    result
  end

  # ...
end
```

Computer is just a wrapper that collects calls, tweaks them a bit, and routes them to a data source. To remove all those duplicated methods, you and Bill can turn Computer into a Dynamic Proxy.

Refactor It!

It only takes a method_missing() to remove all the duplication from the Computer class.

methods/computer/proxy.rb

```ruby
class Computer
  def initialize(computer_id, data_source)
    @id = computer_id
    @data_source = data_source
  end

  def method_missing(name, *args)
    super if !@data_source.respond_to?("get_#{name}_info")
    info = @data_source.send("get_#{name}_info", args[0])
    price = @data_source.send("get_#{name}_price", args[0])
    result = "#{name.to_s.capitalize}: #{info} ($#{price})"
    return "* #{result}" if price >= 100
    result
  end
end
```

What happens when you call a method such as Computer#mouse()? The call gets routed to method_missing(), which checks whether the wrapped data source has a get_mouse_info() method. If it doesn't have one, the call falls back to Kernel#method_missing(), which throws a NoMethodError. If the data source knows about the component, the original call is converted into two calls to DS#get_mouse_info() and DS#get_mouse_price(). The values returned from these calls are used to build the final result. You try the new class in irb:

```ruby
my_computer = Computer.new(42, DS.new)
my_computer.cpu    # => * Cpu: 2.16 Ghz ($220)
```

Hey! It worked.

Overriding respond_to?()

Bill is concerned about one last detail. As he points out, you called mouse() and its ilk Ghost Methods—but they're not *really* methods. For example, they don't appear in the generated documentation, and they're not listed by Object#methods(). Also, if you specifically ask a Computer whether it responds to a Ghost Method, it will flat-out lie:

```ruby
cmp = Computer.new(0, DS.new)
cmp.respond_to?(:mouse)        # => false
```

You can avoid this kind of lie in your code if you override respond_to?() when you override method_missing():

```ruby
class Computer
  def respond_to?(method)
    @data_source.respond_to?("get_#{method}_info") || super
  end

  # ...
```

---

const_missing()

If you like Object#method_missing(), you should also check out Module#const_missing(). When you reference a constant that doesn't exist, Ruby passes the name of the constant to const_missing() as a symbol.

You can define const_missing() on a specific *Namespace (17)* (either a module or a class). If you define it on the Object class, then all objects inherit it, including the top-level main object:

```
def Object.const_missing(name)
  name.to_s.downcase.gsub(/_/, ' ')
end

MY_CONSTANT   # => "my constant"
```

Now Computer#respond_to?() knows about Ghost Methods:

```
cmp.respond_to?(:mouse)   # => true
```

The call to **super** in respond_to?() guarantees that the default respond_to?() is called for all other methods.

You might think that it would also be a good idea to override Object# methods() so that it takes Ghost Methods into account. Bill concedes that this overriding would be sensible in some cases, but not in every case. For example, you probably don't want to override methods() on an object that responds to thousands, or maybe infinite, Ghost Method calls. After a brief debate, you and Bill decide that you can live with the default Object#methods() in this particular case and move on to wrap up your work.

Refactoring Wrap-Up

You solved the same problem in two different ways. The first version of Computer introspects DS to get a list of methods to wrap and uses *Dynamic Methods (45)* and *Dynamic Dispatches (41)*, which delegate to the legacy system. The second version of Computer does the same with *Ghost Methods (50)*. Bill likes the second version better (he's a method_missing() kind of guy), so you send that to the folks in purchasing. You and your pal Bill pat each other on the back and head out for a well-deserved lunch break and an unexpected quiz.

2.4 Quiz: Bug Hunt

Where you and Bill discover that bugs in a method_missing() can be diffi-cult to squash.

Over lunch, Bill has a quiz for you. "My previous team followed a cruel office ritual," he says. "Every morning, each team member picked a random number. Whoever got the smallest number had to take a trip to the nearby Starbucks and buy coffee for the whole team."

Bill explains that the team even wrote a class that was supposed to provide a random number (and some Wheel of Fortune–style suspense) when you called the name of a team member. Here's the class:

`methods/bug_hunt.rb`
```ruby
class Roulette
  def method_missing(name, *args)
    person = name.to_s.capitalize
    3.times do
      number = rand(10) + 1
      puts "#{number}..."
    end
    "#{person} got a #{number}"
  end
end
```

You can use the Roulette like this:

```ruby
number_of = Roulette.new
puts number_of.bob
puts number_of.frank
```

And here's what the result is supposed to look like:

```
⇒    5...
     6...
     10...
     Frank got a 10
     7...
     4...
     3...
     Bob got a 3
```

"Unfortunately," Bill continues, "this code didn't work as expected. Can you spot the problem? If you can't, try running it on your computer. Now, can you explain the result?"

Quiz Solution

The Roulette contains a bug that causes an infinite loop. It prints a long list of numbers and finally crashes.

```
⇒    2...
     7...
     1...
     5...
     (...more numbers here...)
     bug_hunt.rb:7:in 'method_missing': stack level too deep (SystemStackError)
```

This bug is nasty and difficult to spot. The variable number is defined within a block (the block that gets passed to times()) and falls out of scope by the last line of method_missing(). When Ruby executes that line, it can't know that the number there is supposed to be a variable. As a default, it assumes that number must be a parentheses-less method call on **self**.

In normal circumstances, you would get an explicit NoMethodError that makes the problem obvious. But in this case you have a method_missing(), and that's where the call to number() ends. The same chain of events happens again—and again and again—until the call stack overflows.

This is a common problem with Ghost Methods: since unknown calls become calls to method_missing(), your object might accept a call that's just plain wrong. Finding a bug like this one in a large program can be pretty painful.

To avoid this kind of trouble, don't introduce more Ghost Methods than necessary. For example, Roulette might be better off if it simply accepts the names of people on Frank's team. Also, remember to fall back on Kernel#method_missing() when you get a call that you don't know how to deal with. Here's a better Roulette:

methods/bug_hunt_solution.rb

```
class Roulette
  def method_missing(name, *args)
    person = name.to_s.capitalize
    super unless %w[Bob Frank Bill].include? person
    number = 0
    3.times do
      number = rand(10) + 1
      puts "#{number}..."
    end
    "#{person} got a #{number}"
  end
end
```

You can also develop this code in bite-sized steps. Start by writing regular methods; then, when you're confident that your code is working, refactor the methods to a method_missing(). This way, you won't inadvertently hide a bug behind a Ghost Method.

2.5 More method_missing()

Where you and Bill learn to avoid another common method_missing() trap.

As you've just seen, method_missing() has its own share of problems. Now you're going to experience some more yourself, but don't panic. This will be a great opportunity to learn a new spell.

When Methods Clash

Once you get back from lunch, you find an unexpected problem waiting for you at the office. The developer who wrote the reporting application stumbled upon what he thinks is "the strangest bug ever": the Computer class can't retrieve information about the workstations' displays. All the other methods work fine, but Computer#display() doesn't.

You try the display() method in irb, and sure enough, it fails:

```
my_computer = Computer.new(42, DS.new)
my_computer.display    # => nil
```

Why does Computer#display() return nil? You triple-check the code and the back-end data source, but everything seems to be fine. Bill has a sudden insight, and he lists the instance methods of Object that begin with a *d*:

```
Object.instance_methods.grep /^d/   # => [:dup, :display, :define_singleton_method]
```

It seems that Object defines a method named display() (a seldom-used method that prints an object on a port and always returns nil). Computer inherits from Object, so it gets the display() method. The call to Computer#display() finds a real method by that name, so it never lands on method_missing(). You're calling a real, live method instead of a *Ghost Method (50)*.

This problem tends to crop up with *Dynamic Proxies (55)*. Whenever the name of a Ghost Method clashes with the name of a real, inherited method, the latter wins. If you don't need the inherited method, you can fix the problem by removing it. To stay on the safe side, you might want to remove most inherited methods from your proxies right away. The result is called a *Blank Slate*, a class that has fewer methods than the Object class itself.

Spell: Blank Slate

You can remove a method in two easy ways. The drastic Module#undef_method() removes all methods, including the inherited ones. The kinder Module#remove_method() removes the method from the receiver, but it leaves inherited methods alone. For your current job, undef_method() is the way to go. Before you and Bill start hacking away, though, let's look at a concrete example.

The Builder Example

The Builder library is an XML generator with a twist.[10] You can generate XML tags by calling methods on Builder::XmlMarkup:

```
methods/builder_example.rb
require 'builder'
xml = Builder::XmlMarkup.new(:target=>STDOUT, :indent=>2)

xml.coder {
  xml.name 'Matsumoto', :nickname => 'Matz'
  xml.language 'Ruby'
}
```

⇒ `<coder> <name nickname="Matz">Matsumoto</name> <language>Ruby</language> </coder>`

Builder cleverly bends the syntax of Ruby to support nested tags, attributes, and other niceties. The core idea of Builder is simple: calls like name() and language() are processed by XmlMarkup#method_missing(), which generates an XML tag for every call.

Now pretend you have to generate a piece of XML describing a university course. It might look like this:

⇒ `<semester> <class>Egyptology</class> <class>Ornithology</class> </semester>`

So, you'd have to write code like this:

```
methods/builder_example.rb
xml.semester {
  xml.class 'Egyptology'
  xml.class 'Ornithology'
}
```

You may be wondering whether the calls to class() clash with the inherited method class() in Object. They don't, because the XmlMarkup class in Builder inherits from a *Blank Slate (61)*, which removes class() and most other methods from Object.

---

10. Builder was written by Jim Weirich. Install it with gem install builder.

Performance Anxiety

In these pages, we mention some downsides of *Ghost Methods (50)*, such as name clashes and mysterious bugs. Some people would add another item to this list of weaknesses: in general, Ghost Methods are slower than regular methods, because method lookup tends to take a longer route when you call a Ghost Method. Here's a simple benchmark that compares a concrete method and its ghostly counterpart:

methods/methods_benchmark.rb

```ruby
class String
  def method_missing(method, *args)
    method == :ghost_reverse ? reverse : super
  end
end

require 'benchmark'

Benchmark.bm do |b|
  b.report 'Normal method' do
    1000000.times { "abc".reverse }
  end
  b.report 'Ghost method ' do
    1000000.times { "abc".ghost_reverse }
  end
end
```

On my computer, the benchmark shows that ghost_reverse() is about twice as slow as reverse():

```
                user      system      total         real
Normal method  0.930000  0.010000  0.940000  (  0.976292)
Ghost method   1.800000  0.020000  1.820000  (  1.871905)
```

This performance issue is something that you should be aware of, but usually it's not really a problem. Avoid guesswork, and measure your code's performance with a profiler before you start worrying too much about optimizations. If the performance of Ghost Methods ever turns out to be a problem, you can sometimes find a middle ground. For example, you might be able to arrange things so that the first call to a Ghost Method defines a *Dynamic Method (45)* for the next calls. You'll see an example of this technique and a discussion of its trade-offs in Chapter 8, *Inside ActiveRecord*, on page 187.

> ### Reserved Methods
>
> Some of the methods in Object are used internally by Ruby. If you redefine or remove them, the language might break in subtle ways. To make this less likely to happen, Ruby identifies these methods with a leading double underscore and issues a warning if you mess with them.
>
> At the time of writing, Ruby has two such reserved methods, __send__() and __id__(), which are synonyms for send() and id(). Some libraries, such as Test::Unit, protect themselves from maverick client code by calling the reserved methods rather than their "regular" counterparts. In general, you don't have to worry that much: just call the regular methods, unless you know for certain that they've been redefined.

gems/builder-2.1.2/lib/blankslate.rb

```
class BlankSlate
  # Hide the method named +name+ in the BlankSlate class.  Don't
  # hide +instance_eval+ or any method beginning with "__".
  def self.hide(name)
    if instance_methods.include?(name.to_s) and
      name !~ /^(__|instance_eval)/
      @hidden_methods ||= {}
      @hidden_methods[name.to_sym] = instance_method(name)
      undef_method name
    end
  end

  instance_methods.each { |m| hide(m) }

  # ...
```

The code in BlankSlate assumes that instance_methods() returns an array of strings. In Ruby 1.9, instance_methods() returns an array of symbols instead. Expect this code to change slightly when Builder is updated for Ruby 1.9.

Enough examples. Back to the real thing!

Fixing the Computer Class

You and Bill know what to do now: refactor Computer to transform it into a *Blank Slate (61)*. This refactoring doesn't take much:[11]

`methods/computer/blank.rb`

```
class Computer
▶    instance_methods.each do |m|
▶      undef_method m unless m.to_s =~ /method_missing|respond_to?/
▶    end

    # ...
```

This's not purely a blank slate, because you still want to access method_missing() and respond_to?() in both Computer and Object (through **super**).

You try the class in irb. The display() method now works, but Ruby issues a couple of warnings when you load the Computer class:

⇒ blank_slate_2.rb:3: warning: undefining '__id__' may cause serious problem
   blank_slate_2.rb:3: warning: undefining '__send__' may cause serious problem

Ruby is complaining that you also removed two reserved methods (see the sidebar on the preceding page). To stay on the safe side, you can leave double-underscored methods alone:

`methods/computer/more_blank.rb`

```
class Computer
    instance_methods.each do |m|
▶      undef_method m unless m.to_s =~ /^__|method_missing|respond_to?/
    end

    # ...
```

Now the class runs with no warnings. You're done, at long last!

Wrapping It Up

Let's review today's work. You and Bill started with a Computer class that contained lots of duplication (the original class is in Section 2.1, *Double, Treble...Trouble*, on page 39). You managed to remove the duplication in two different ways.

---

11. Depending on the Ruby version, instance_methods() can return either strings or symbols, so this code converts method names to strings to be compatible with all versions. The undef_method() method is not a problem, because it can take either a string or a symbol.

> ### BasicObject
>
> Starting with Ruby 1.9, *Blank Slates (61)* are an integral part of the language. In previous versions of Ruby, Object used to be the root of the class hierarchy. In Ruby 1.9, Object has a superclass named BasicObject that provides only a handful of essential methods:
>
> p BasicObject.instance_methods
>
> ⇒ [:==, :equal?, :!, :!=, :instance_eval, :instance_exec, :__send__]
>
> By default, classes still inherit from Object. Classes that inherit directly from BasicObject are automatically Blank Slates.

Your first attempt relied on *Dynamic Methods (45)* and *Dynamic Dispatch (41)*:

`methods/computer/more_dynamic.rb`

```ruby
class Computer
  def initialize(computer_id, data_source)
    @id = computer_id
    @data_source = data_source
    data_source.methods.grep(/^get_(.*)_info$/) { Computer.define_component $1 }
  end

  def self.define_component(name)
    define_method(name) {
      info = @data_source.send "get_#{name}_info", @id
      price = @data_source.send "get_#{name}_price", @id
      result = "#{name.capitalize}: #{info} ($#{price})"
      return "* #{result}" if price >= 100
      result
    }
  end
end
```

Your second attempt used a *Dynamic Proxy (55)* that is also a *Blank Slate (61)*:

`methods/computer/final.rb`

```ruby
class Computer
  instance_methods.each do |m|
    undef_method m unless m.to_s =~ /^__|method_missing|respond_to?/
  end
```

```ruby
  def initialize(computer_id, data_source)
    @id = computer_id
    @data_source = data_source
  end

  def method_missing(name, *args)
    super if !respond_to?(name)
    info = @data_source.send("get_#{name}_info", args[0])
    price = @data_source.send("get_#{name}_price", args[0])
    result = "#{name.to_s.capitalize}: #{info} ($#{price})"
    return "* #{result}" if price >= 100
    result
  end

  def respond_to?(method)
    @data_source.respond_to?("get_#{method}_info") || super
  end
end
```

Whichever of the two solutions you like best, neither would be practical without Ruby's dynamic capabilities. If you come from a static language, you're probably accustomed to spotting and removing duplication *inside* your methods. In Ruby, you might want to look for duplication *among* methods as well. Then you can remove that duplication with some of the spells from this chapter.

You and Bill can congratulate yourselves for a day chock-full of collaborative coding. It's time to say goodbye and head out of the office!

Chapter 3

Wednesday: Blocks

Yesterday you learned a lot about methods and method calls. Now it's Wednesday, aka "hump day." You're at the midpoint of your week. What's on your to-do list on this pivotal day?

Today you and Bill will deal with *blocks*. You're probably already familiar with blocks—you can't write much Ruby code without them. But what you might not know is that blocks are a powerful tool for controlling *scope*, meaning which variables and methods can be seen by which lines of code. In this chapter, you'll discover how this control of scope makes blocks a cornerstone of Ruby metaprogramming.

Blocks are just one member of a larger family of "callable objects," which include objects such as procs and lambdas. This chapter shows how you can use these and other callable objects to their greatest advantage—for example, to store a block and execute it later.

Just a short public service announcement before getting started: the previous chapters never strayed far from the usual object-oriented concepts such as classes, objects, and methods. Blocks have a different heritage that can be traced back to "functional programming languages."[1] If you think in objects and classes, expect to deal with some novel concepts in this chapter. You're likely to find these concepts strange and, at the same time, fascinating.

---

1.   If you like blocks, you'll probably want to learn more about functional programming. You have a few good languages and books to choose from, including *Lisp* [Gra96], *Haskell* [Tho99], and *Erlang* [Arm07]. The most popular new kids on the block are *Clojure* [Hal09] and *Scala* [OSV08].

With that sneak peek into what this chapter is all about, it's now time to step into the office!

3.1 How to Handle Hump Day

Where you and Bill agree to shun today's job, make a road map, and review the basics of blocks.

"Hey, what're you doing over there? It feels lonely here at my keyboard!"

"Oh, great," you think to yourself. You've barely had time to check your mail, and Bill is already making his way to your desk, eager to get to work.

"I talked with the boss about today's job," Bill says as he pulls up a chair. "I won't go into the details now," he continues, "but I can tell you that we're going to need *blocks* for today's project." He then points out that, before the two of you jump into the fray, you need to understand the nuances of blocks. You agree to spend the morning talking about blocks, putting off today's project until after lunch.

Today's Road Map

Bill picks up a sheet of paper on which he has enumerated all the things he wants to cover. Here's the list:

- A review of the basics of blocks

- An overview of *scopes* and how you can carry variables through scopes by using blocks as *closures*

- How you can further manipulate scopes by passing a block to instance_eval()

- How you can convert blocks into *callable objects* that you can set aside and call later, such as Procs and lambdas

Bill wastes no time getting started—with a review of the basics.[2]

Back to the Basics

"Do you remember how blocks work?" Bill queries. "I'll refresh your memory with a toy example, just to test you."

---

2. If you already know the basics of Ruby blocks, you can skip straight to Section 3.3, *Closures*, on page 74.

He scrawls this code on your whiteboard:

`blocks/basics.rb`

```ruby
def a_method(a, b)
  a + yield(a, b)
end

a_method(1, 2) {|x, y| (x + y) * 3 }   # => 10
```

You can define a block with either curly braces or the **do**...**end** keywords. Most programmers tend to use curly braces for single-line blocks and **do**...**end** for multiline blocks. However, this convention is not rigidly enforced. You're free to pick the idiom that you prefer for each block.

Bill explains that you can define a block only when you call a method. The block is passed straight into the method, and the method can then call back to the block with the **yield** keyword.

Optionally, a block can have arguments, like x and y in Bill's example. When you call back to the block, you can provide values for its arguments, just like you do when you call a method. Also, like a method, a block returns the result of the last line of code it evaluates.

The Current Block

Within a method, you can ask Ruby whether the current call includes a block. You can do that with the Kernel#block_given?() method:

```ruby
def a_method
  return yield if block_given?
  'no block'
end

a_method                          # => "no block"
a_method { "here's a block!" }    # => "here's a block!"
```

If you use **yield** when block_given?() is false, you'll get a runtime error.

"OK, we've made our way through a refresher of the basics," Bill says, "Now let's apply what we know about blocks to a real-life scenario."

3.2 Quiz: Ruby#

Where Bill challenges you to do something useful with blocks.

Bill shares a little secret: "You know, a few months ago I was making a living out of writing C# code. I don't miss C# much, but, I must admit, it does have a few nice features. I'll show you one of those."[3]

The using Keyword

Imagine that you're writing a C# program that connects to a remote server and you have an object that represents the connection:

```
RemoteConnection conn = new RemoteConnection("my_server");
String stuff = conn.readStuff();
conn.dispose();     // close the connection to avoid a leak
```

This code correctly disposes of the connection after using it. However, it doesn't deal with exceptions. If readStuff() throws an exception, then the last line is never executed, and conn is never disposed of. What the code *should* do is manage exceptions, disposing of the connection whether or not an exception is thrown. Luckily, C# provides a keyword named **using** that goes through the whole process for you:

```
RemoteConnection conn = new RemoteConnection("some_remote_server");
using (conn)
{
    conn.readSomeData();
    doSomeMoreStuff();
}
```

The **using** keyword expects that conn has a method named dispose(). This method is called automatically after the code in the curly braces, whether or not an exception is thrown.

The Challenge

"This **using** thing is cool, isn't it?" Bill exclaims. You nod your head in agreement. "I challenge you to write a Ruby version of **using**," he says, with what looks like a smirk. He gives you a test case:

blocks/using_test.rb

```
require 'using'
require 'test/unit'

class TestUsing < Test::Unit::TestCase
  class Resource
    def dispose
      @disposed = true
    end
```

---

3. Please be warned that after all this Ruby, the semicolons and brackets in the next section might hurt your eyes.

```
    def disposed?
      @disposed
    end
  end

  def test_disposes_of_resources
    r = Resource.new
    using(r) {}
    assert r.disposed?
  end

  def test_disposes_of_resources_in_case_of_exception
    r = Resource.new
    assert_raises(Exception) {
      using(r) {
        raise Exception
      }
    }
    assert r.disposed?
  end
end
```

Can you write a Ruby version of using and make this test pass? (Don't
peek at the solution. . . Bill is watching you!)

Quiz Solution

Take a look at this solution to the quiz:

blocks/using.rb

```
module Kernel
  def using(resource)
    begin
      yield
    ensure
      resource.dispose
    end
  end
end
```

You can't define a new keyword, but you can fake it with a *Kernel
Method (27)*. Kernel#using() takes the managed resource as an argument. It also takes a block, which it executes. Whether or not the block
completes normally, the **ensure** clause calls dispose() on the resource to
release it cleanly. In case of an exception, Kernel#using() also rethrows
the exception to the caller.

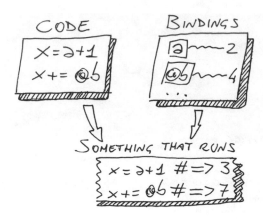

Figure 3.1: CODE THAT RUNS IS ACTUALLY MADE UP OF TWO THINGS: THE CODE ITSELF AND A SET OF BINDINGS.

"OK, we still remember the basic of blocks," Bill mumbles, checking the road map he jotted down in Section 3.1, *Today's Road Map*, on page 70. "Now we can get to the second point: closures."

3.3 Closures

Where you find there is more to blocks than meets the eye and you learn how to smuggle variables across scopes.

As Bill notes on a piece of scratch paper (Figure 3.1), a block is not just a floating piece of code. You can't run code in a vacuum. When code runs, it needs an *environment*: local variables, instance variables, **self**.... Since these entities are basically names bound to objects, you can call them the *bindings* for short. The main point about blocks is that they are all inclusive and come ready to run. They contain both the code *and* a set of bindings.

You're probably wondering where the block picks up its bindings. When you define the block, it simply grabs the bindings that are there at that moment, and then it carries those bindings along when you pass the block into a method:

blocks/closure.rb

```
def my_method
  x = "Goodbye"
```

```
  yield("cruel")
end

x = "Hello"
my_method {|y| "#{x}, #{y} world" } # => "Hello, cruel world"
```

Bill notes that when you create the block, you capture the local bindings, such as x. Then you pass the block to a method that has its own separate set of bindings. In the previous example, those bindings also include a variable named x. Still, the code in the block sees the x that was around when the block was defined, not the method's x, which is not visible at all in the block. Because of this property, a computer scientist would say that a block is a *closure*. For the rest of us, this means a block captures the local bindings and carries them along with it.

So, how do you use closures in practice? To understand that, you need to take a closer look at the place where all the bindings reside—the *scope*. Here you'll learn to identify the spots where a program changes scope, and you'll encounter a particular problem with changing scopes that can be solved with closures.

Scope

Imagine being a little debugger making your way through a Ruby program. You jump from statement to statement until you finally hit a breakpoint. Now, catch your breath and look around. See the scenery around you? That's your *scope*.

You can see bindings all over the scope. Look down at your feet, and you see a bunch of local variables. Raise your head, and you see that you're standing within an object, with its own methods and instance variables; that's the current object, also known as **self**. Further away, you see the tree of constants so clear that you could mark your current position on a map. Squint your eyes, and you can even see a bunch of global variables off in the distance.[4]

Now see what happens when you get tired of the scenery and decide to move on.

---

4. You already know about the tree of constants from Section 1.3, *Constants*, on page 14, as well as the current object from Section 1.5, *Discovering self*, on page 29. You'll learn about global variables in the sidebar on page 79.

Block-Local Variables

A block captures the bindings that are around when you first define the block. You can also define additional bindings inside the block, but they disappear after the block ends:

```ruby
def my_method
  yield
end

top_level_variable = 1
my_method do
  top_level_variable += 1
  local_to_block = 1
end
top_level_variable  # => 2
local_to_block      # => Error!
```

A word of warning: in Ruby 1.8 and earlier, block arguments contain a trap for the unwary. Contrary to what you might expect, blocks can overwrite local variables by the same name:

```ruby
def my_method
  yield(2)
end

x = 1
my_method do |x|
  # do nothing special
end
x   # => 2
```

When you name the block argument x, the block notices that there is already an x variable in the current context, and it uses that x as its argument. So, there is only a single x in the previous code, and it gets assigned the value that you pass to the block. This surprising behavior used to be a frequent cause of bugs, but the good news is that it has been fixed in Ruby 1.9.

Changing Scope

This example shows how scope changes as your program runs, tracking the names of bindings with the Kernel#local_variables() method:

`blocks/scopes.rb`
```ruby
v1 = 1

class MyClass
  v2 = 2
  local_variables    # => [:v2]

  def my_method
    v3 = 3
    local_variables
  end

  local_variables    # => [:v2]
end

obj = MyClass.new
obj.my_method    # => [:v3]
obj.my_method    # => [:v3]
local_variables    # => [:v1, :obj]
```

Bill tracks the program as it moves through scopes. It starts within the top-level scope, where it defines v1.[5] Then it enters the scope of MyClass's definition. What happens then?

Some languages, such as Java and C#, allow an "inner scope" to see variables from an "outer scope." That kind of nested visibility doesn't happen in Ruby, where scopes are sharply separated: as soon as you enter a new scope, the previous bindings are simply replaced by a new set of bindings. This means that when the program enters MyClass, v1 "falls out of scope" and is no longer visible.

In the scope of the definition of MyClass, the program defines v2 and a method. The code in the method isn't executed yet, so the program never opens a new scope until the end of the class definition. At that moment, the scope opened with the **class** keyword is closed forever, and the program gets back to the top-level scope.

Bill also explains what happens when the program creates a MyClass object and calls my_method() twice. The first time the program enters my_method(), it opens a new scope and defines a local variable, v3. Then the program exits the method, falling back to the top-level scope. At this

---

5. You became familiar with the top-level scope in the sidebar on page 30.

point, the method's scope is lost. When the program calls my_method( ) a second time, it opens yet another new scope, and it defines a new v3 variable (unrelated to the previous v3, which is now lost). Finally, the program returns to the top-level scope, where you can see v1 and obj again. Phew!

Bill stresses the example's important point: "Whenever the program changes scope, some bindings are replaced by a new set of bindings." Granted, this doesn't happen to all the bindings each and every time. For example, if a method calls another method on the same object, instance variables stay in scope through the call. In general, though, bindings tend to fall out of scope when the scope changes. In particular, local variables change at every new scope. (That's why they're "local"!)

As you can see, keeping track of scopes can be a boring task. You can spot scopes more quickly if you learn about *Scope Gates*.

Scope Gates

There are exactly three places where a program leaves the previous scope behind and opens a new one:

- Class definitions
- Module definitions
- Methods

Scope changes whenever the program enters (or exits) a class or module definition or a method. These three borders are marked by the keywords **class**, **module**, and **def**, respectively. Each of these keywords acts like a *Scope Gate*.

Spell: Scope Gate

For example, here is Bill's example program again, with Scope Gates clearly marked by comments:

```
v1 = 1

class MyClass        # SCOPE GATE: entering class
  v2 = 2
  local_variables    # => ["v2"]

  def my_method       # SCOPE GATE: entering def
    v3 = 3
    local_variables
  end                 # SCOPE GATE: leaving def

  local_variables    # => ["v2"]
end                   # SCOPE GATE: leaving class
```

Global Variables and Top-Level Instance Variables

Global variables can be accessed by any scope:

```
def a_scope
  $var = "some value"
end

def another_scope
  $var
end

a_scope
another_scope # => "some value"
```

The problem with global variables is that every part of the system can change them, so, in no time, you'll find it difficult to track who is changing what. For this reason, the general rule is this: when it comes to global variables, use them sparingly, if ever.

You can sometimes use a top-level instance variable in place of a global variable. These are the instance variables of the top-level main object, described in the sidebar on page 30:

```
@var = "The top-level @var"

def my_method
  @var
end

my_method # => "The top-level @var"
```

You can access a top-level instance variable whenever main takes the role of **self**, as in the previous example. When any other object is **self**, the top-level instance variable is out of scope.

```
class MyClass
  def my_method
    @var = "This is not the top-level @var!"
  end
end
```

Being less universally accessible, top-level instance variables are generally considered safer than global variables.

```
obj = MyClass.new
obj.my_method        # => [:v3]
obj.my_method        # => [:v3]
local_variables      # => [:v1, :obj]
```

Now it's easy to see that Bill's program opens four separate scopes: the top-level scope, one new scope when it enters MyClass, and one new scope each time it calls my_method().

There is a subtle difference between **class** and **module** on one side and **def** on the other. The code in a class or module definition is executed immediately. Conversely, the code in a method definition is executed later, when you eventually call the method. However, as you write your program, you usually don't care *when* it changes scope—you only care that it does.

Now you can pinpoint the places where your program changes scope— the spots marked by **class**, **module**, and **def**. But what if you want to pass a variable through one of these spots? This question takes you back to the topic of blocks.

Flattening the Scope

The more you become proficient in Ruby, the more you get into difficult situations where you want to pass bindings through a *Scope Gate (78)*:

blocks/flat_scope_1.rb

```
my_var = "Success"

class MyClass
  # We want to print my_var here...

  def my_method
    #  ..and here
  end
end
```

Scope gates are quite a formidable barrier. As soon as you walk through one of them, local variables fall out of scope. So, how can you carry my_var across not one but two Scope Gates?

Look at the **class** Scope Gate first. You can't pass my_var through it, but you can replace **class** with something else that is not a Scope Gate: a method. If you could use a method in place of **class**, you could capture my_var in a closure and pass that closure to the method. Can you think of a method that does the same thing that **class** does?

If you look at Ruby's documentation, you'll find the answer: Class.new()
is a perfect replacement for **class**. You can also define instance methods
in the class if you pass a block to Class.new():

`blocks/flat_scope_2.rb`

```
my_var = "Success"

MyClass = Class.new do
  # Now we can print my_var here...
  puts "#{my_var} in the class definition!"

  def my_method
    # ...but how can we print it here?
  end
end
```

Now, how can you pass my_var through the **def** Scope Gate? Once again,
you have to replace the keyword with a method. Instead of **def**, you can
use Module#define_method():[6]

`blocks/flat_scope_3.rb`

```
my_var = "Success"

MyClass = Class.new do
  puts "#{my_var} in the class definition!"

  define_method :my_method do
    puts "#{my_var} in the method!"
  end
end

MyClass.new.my_method
```

⇒
```
Success in the class definition!
Success in the method!
```

If you replace Scope Gates with methods, you allow one scope to see
variables from another scope. Technically, this trick should be called
nested lexical scopes, but many Ruby coders refer to it simply as "flat-
tening the scope," meaning that the two scopes share variables as if the
scopes were squeezed together. For short, you can call this spell a *Flat
Scope*.

Spell: Flat Scope

Bill also wants to show you a second spell that pushes the concept of
Flat Scopes even further.

---

6. You learned about Module#define_method() in the discussion about *dynamic methods*
(45).

Sharing the Scope

Once you know about *Flat Scopes (81)*, you can do pretty much whatever you want with scopes. For example, assume that you want to share a variable among a few methods, and you don't want anybody else to see that variable. You can do that by defining all the methods in the same Flat Scope as the variable:

```
blocks/shared_scope.rb
def define_methods
  shared = 0

  Kernel.send :define_method, :counter do
    shared
  end

  Kernel.send :define_method, :inc do |x|
    shared += x
  end
end

define_methods

counter          # => 0
inc(4)
counter          # => 4
```

This example defines two *Kernel Methods (27)*. (Bill had to use *Dynamic Dispatch (41)* to access the private method define_method() on Kernel.) Both Kernel#counter() and Kernel#inc() can see the shared variable. No other method can see shared, because it's protected by a *Scope Gate (78)*—that's what the define_methods() method is for. This smart way to control the sharing of variables is called a *Shared Scope*.

Spell: Shared Scope

With a combination of Scope Gates, Flat Scopes, and Shared Scopes, you can twist and bend your scopes to see exactly the variables you need, from the place you want. After gaining this kind of power, you can ease into Bill's wrap-up of Ruby scopes.

Scope Wrap-Up

Each Ruby scope contains a bunch of bindings, and the scopes are separated by *Scope Gates (78)*: **class**, **module**, and **def**. If you want to sneak a binding or two through a Scope Gate, you can replace the Scope Gate with a method call: you capture the current bindings in a closure and pass the closure to the method. You can replace **class** with Class.new(), **module** with Module.new, and **def** with Module#define_method(). This is a *Flat Scope (81)*, the basic closure-related spell. If you define multiple methods in the same Flat Scope, maybe protected by a Scope Gate, all those methods can share bindings. That's called a *Shared Scope (82)*.

Bill glances at the road map he created (see Section 3.1, *Today's Road Map*, on page 70). "Now that you've gotten a taste of Flat Scopes, we should move on to something more advanced: instance_eval()."

3.4 instance_eval()

Where you and Bill learn another way to mix code and bindings at will.

Bill shows you a short program to demonstrate Object#instance_eval(), which evaluates a block in the context of an object:

```
blocks/instance_eval.rb
class MyClass
  def initialize
    @v = 1
  end
end

obj = MyClass.new
obj.instance_eval do
  self        # => #<MyClass:0x3340dc @v=1>
  @v          # => 1
end
```

The block is evaluated with the receiver as **self**, so it can access the receiver's private methods and instance variables, such as @v. Even if instance_eval() changes **self**, it leaves all the other bindings alone, as Bill demonstrates with a few more lines of code:

```
v = 2
obj.instance_eval { @v = v }
obj.instance_eval { @v }       # => 2
```

The three lines in the previous example are evaluated in the same *Flat Scope (81)*, so they can all access the local variable v—but the blocks are evaluated with the object as **self**, so they can also access obj's instance variable @v. In all these cases, you can call the block that you pass to Instance_eval() a *Context Probe*, because it's like a snippet of code that you dip inside an object to do something in there.

Spell: Context Probe

---

instance_exec()

Ruby 1.9 introduced a method named instance_exec(). This is similar to instance_eval(), but it also allows you to pass arguments to the block:

```
class C
  def initialize
    @x, @y = 1, 2
  end
end

C.new.instance_exec(3) {|arg| (@x + @y) * arg }   # => 9
```

Breaking Encapsulation

At this point, you're wearing a look of horror on your face. With a *Context Probe (83)*, you can wreak havoc on encapsulation! No data is private data anymore. "Isn't that a Very Bad Thing?" you ask.

Bill answers you promptly. Pragmatically, there are some situations where encapsulation just gets in your way. For one, you might want to take a quick peek inside an object from an irb command line. In a case like this, breaking into the object with instance_eval() is often the shortest route.

The most socially acceptable reason to break encapsulation is arguably testing. Your pal provides an example.

The RSpec Example

The RSpec gem is a popular library for writing tests.[7] Among other things, it allows you to "stub" specific methods on an object that you want to test. For example, you can replace a method that accesses a database with a simple constant result:

`blocks/rspec.rb`

```
test_object.should_receive(:read_names).and_return(["Bill", "You"])
test_object.read_names  # => ["Bill", "You"]
```

To implement this feature, RSpec plays a few tricks behind the covers. Among other things, it adds an instance variable named @options to the object under test. But what if the object happens to already have an

---

7.   RSpec is a project by David Chelimsky and others. Install it with gem install rspec.

instance variable with that name? Will the stubbing feature still work? The RSpec authors like to eat their own dog food, so they wrote an RSpec test to check that the stubbing feature works in this edge case.

How would you write such a test? You need an object that has its own @options variable. The RSpec people get that object by enhancing a regular object with a *Context Probe (83)*. Here's their test:

`gems/rspec-1.2.6/spec/spec/mocks/partial_mock_spec.rb`

```
@object = Object.new
@object.instance_eval { @options = Object.new }
@object.should_receive(:blah)
@object.blah
```

As an alternative, you might create an entire class that defines @options in initialize() and then create an object of that class. However, in this case, a Context Probe lets you get away with just a single line of code.

Clean Rooms

Sometimes you create an object just to evaluate blocks inside it. An object like that can be called a *Clean Room*:

Spell: Clean Room

`blocks/clean_room.rb`

```
class CleanRoom
  def complex_calculation
    # ...
  end

  def do_something
    # ...
  end
end

clean_room = CleanRoom.new
clean_room.instance_eval do
  if complex_calculation > 10
    do_something
  end
end
```

A Clean Room is just an environment where you can evaluate your blocks, and it usually exposes a few useful methods that the block can call. You'll find a practical example of a Clean Room in Section 3.7, *Quiz: A Better DSL*, on page 96.

"That's all you have to know about instance_eval()," Bill promises. "Now we can get to the last topic in the road map: callable objects."

3.5 Callable Objects

Where Bill explains how blocks are just part of a larger family and demonstrates how you can set code aside and execute it later.

If you get to the bottom of it, using a block is a two-step process. First, you set some code aside, and second, you call the block (with **yield**) to execute the code. This "package code first, call it later" mechanism is not exclusive to blocks. There are at least three other places in Ruby where you can package code:

- In a *proc*, which is basically a block turned object

- In a *lambda*, which is a slight variation on a proc

- In a *method*

Procs and lambdas are the big ones to talk about here. Bill wants to start with them, and he'll bring methods back into the picture later.

Proc Objects

Bill starts by pointing out that although most things in Ruby are objects, blocks are not. But why would you care about that? Imagine that you want to store a block and execute it later. To do that, you need an object.

"To solve this problem," Bill clarifies, "Ruby provides the standard library class Proc." A Proc is a block that has been turned into an object. You can create a Proc by passing the block to Proc.new. Later, you can evaluate the block-turned-object with Proc#call():

```
inc = Proc.new {|x| x + 1 }
# more code...
inc.call(2) # => 3
```

Spell: Deferred Evaluation

This technique is called a *Deferred Evaluation*.

Ruby also provides two *Kernel Methods (27)* that convert a block to a Proc: lambda() and proc(). In a short while, you'll see that there are subtle differences between lambda(), proc(), and Proc.new(), but in most cases you can just use whichever one you like best:

```
dec = lambda {|x| x - 1 }
dec.class # => Proc
dec.call(2) # => 1
```

So far, Bill has shown not one, but three different ways to convert a block to a Proc. There is also a fourth way, which deserves its own section.

The & Operator

A block is like an additional, anonymous argument to a method. In most cases, you execute the block right there in the method, using **yield**. There are two cases where **yield** is not enough:

- You want to pass the block to another method.

- You want to convert the block to a Proc.

In both cases, you need to point at the block and say, "I want to use *this* block"—to do that, you need a name. To attach a binding to the block, you can add one special argument to the method. This argument must be the last in the list of arguments and prefixed by an & sign. Here's a method that passes the block to another method:

`blocks/ampersand.rb`

```
def math(a, b)
  yield(a, b)
end

def teach_math(a, b, &operation)
  puts "Let's do the math:"
  puts math(a, b, &operation)
end

teach_math(2, 3) {|x, y| x * y}
```

⇒
```
Let's do the math:
6
```

If you call teach_math() without a block, the &operation argument is bound to nil, and the **yield** operation in math() fails.

What if you want to convert the block to a Proc? As it turns out, if you referenced operation in the previous code, you'd already have a Proc object. The real meaning of the & is this: "This is a Proc that I want to use as a block." Just drop the &, and you'll be left with a Proc again:

```
def my_method(&the_proc)
  the_proc
end

p = my_method {|name| "Hello, #{name}!" }
puts p.class
puts p.call("Bill")
```

⇒
```
Proc
Hello, Bill!
```

You now know a bunch of different ways to convert a block to a Proc. But what if you want to convert it back? Again, you can use the & operator to convert the Proc to a block:

blocks/proc_to_block.rb
```ruby
def my_method(greeting)
  puts "#{greeting}, #{yield}!"
end

my_proc = proc { "Bill" }
my_method("Hello", &my_proc)
```

⇒
```
Hello, Bill!
```

When you call my_method(), the & converts my_proc to a block and passes that block to the method.

"Now you know how to convert a block to a Proc and back again," Bill observes. "Let's look at a real-life example of a callable object that starts its life as a lambda and is then converted to a regular block."

The HighLine Example

The HighLine gem helps you automate console input and output.[8] For example, you can tell HighLine to collect comma-separated user input and split it into an array, all in a single call. Here's a Ruby program that lets you input a comma-separated list of friends:

blocks/highline_example.rb
```ruby
require 'highline'

hl = HighLine.new
friends = hl.ask("Friends?", lambda {|s| s.split(',') })
puts "You're friends with: #{friends.inspect}"
```

⇒
```
Friends?
```
⇐
```
Bill,Mirella,Luca
```
⇒
```
You're friends with: ["Bill", "Mirella", "Luca"]
```

You call HighLine#ask() with a string (the question for the user) and a Proc that contains the post-processing code.[9] If you read the code of

---

8. HighLine was written by James Edward Gray II. You can install it with gem install highline.
9. You might wonder why HighLine requires a Proc argument rather than a simple block. Actually, you *can* pass a block to ask(), but that mechanism is reserved for a different HighLine feature.

HighLine#ask(), you'll see that it passes the Proc to an object of class Question, which stores the Proc as an instance variable. Later, after collecting the user's input, the Question passes the input to the stored Proc.

If you want to do something else to the user's input—say, change it to uppercase—you just create a different Proc:

```
name = hl.ask("Name?", lambda {|s| s.capitalize })
puts "Hello, #{name}"
```

⇒ Name?
⇐ **bill**
⇒ Hello, Bill!

This is an example of *Deferred Evaluation (86)*.

Procs vs. Lambdas

"We've learned a bunch of different ways to turn a block into a Proc: Proc.new(), lambda(), the & operator...," Bill says. "In all cases, the resulting object is a Proc." You wait patiently for him to go on as he yawns loudly and stretches his arms.[10]

"Confusingly, though," Bill finally continues, "Procs created with lambda() actually differ in some respects from Procs created any other way. The differences are subtle but important enough that people refer to the two kinds of Procs by distinct names: Procs created with lambda() are called *lambdas*, while the others are simply called *procs*."[11]

Bill adds a word of warning. The difference between procs and lambdas is probably the most confusing feature of Ruby, with lots of special cases and arbitrary distinctions. There's no need to go into all the gory details, but you need to know, at least roughly, the important differences.

There are two differences between procs and lambdas. One has to do with the **return** keyword, and the other concerns the checking of arguments. Let's start with **return**.

---

10. Bill is going through some technical details that you might or might not care about right now. This is your chance to take a short nap. Or, in book-speak, you can skip over this section on your first read through this book and go straight to Section 3.5, *Methods Revisited*, on page 92. Be sure to return to this section when you want to dig deeper into Procs and lambdas.

11. Ruby 1.9 introduces a Proc#lambda?() method that returns true if the Proc is a lambda. Previous versions of Ruby didn't provide a direct way to tell a lambda from a regular proc.

Procs, Lambdas, and return

The first difference between lambdas and procs is that the **return** keyword means different things. In a lambda, **return** just returns from the
lambda:

```
blocks/proc_vs_lambda.rb
```
```
def double(callable_object)
  callable_object.call * 2
end


l = lambda { return 10 }
double(l) # => 20
```

In a proc, **return** behaves differently. Rather than return from the proc,
it returns from the scope where the proc itself was defined:

```
def another_double
  p = Proc.new { return 10 }
  result = p.call
  return result * 2  # unreachable code!
end


another_double # => 10
```

If you're aware of this behavior, you can steer clear of buggy code like:

```
def double(callable_object)
  callable_object.call * 2
end


p = Proc.new { return 10 }
# This fails with a LocalJumpError:
# double(p)
```

The previous program tries to return from the scope where p is defined.
Since you can't return from the top-level scope, the program fails. You
can avoid this kind of mistake if you avoid using explicit **return**s:

```
p = Proc.new { 10 }
double(p)    # => 20
```

Now on to the second important difference between procs and lambdas.

Procs, Lambdas, and Arity

The second difference between procs and lambdas concerns the way
they check their arguments. For example, a particular proc or lambda
might have an *arity* of two, meaning that it accepts two arguments:

```
p = Proc.new {|a, b| [a, b]}
p.arity # => 2
```

Now, what happens if you call this callable object with three arguments or a single argument? The long answer to this question is complicated and littered with special cases.[12] The short answer is that, in general, lambdas tend to be less tolerant than procs (and regular blocks) when it comes to arguments. Call a lambda with the wrong arity, and it fails with an ArgumentError. On the other hand, a proc fits the argument list to its own expectations:

```
p = Proc.new {|a, b| [a, b]}
p.call(1, 2, 3)   # => [1, 2]
p.call(1)         # => [1, nil]
```

If there are too many arguments, a proc drops the excess arguments. If there are too few arguments, it assigns nil to the missing arguments.

Procs vs. Lambdas: The Verdict

Bill is confident that you now know the differences between procs and lambdas. But you're wondering which kind of Proc you should use in your own code.

Generally speaking, lambdas are more intuitive than procs because they're more similar to methods. They're pretty strict about arity, and they simply exit when you call **return**. For this reason, many Rubyists use lambdas as a first choice, unless they need the specific features of procs.

Kernel#proc

"What about Proc objects created with Kernel#proc()?" you ask. "Are these procs or lambdas?" You can ask Ruby itself:

```
callable = proc { return }
callable.call  # fails in Ruby 1.9
```

Distressingly, the previous code will either succeed or fail, depending on the version of Ruby you're using. In Ruby 1.8, Kernel#proc() is actually a synonym for Kernel#lambda(). Because of loud protest from programmers, Ruby 1.9 made proc() a synonym for Proc.new() instead.

"See?" Bill laments. "I *told* you it was a big mess."

---

12. Paul Cantrell wrote a program to explore all special cases. You can find this program at http://innig.net/software/ruby/closures-in-ruby.rb.

The Stubby Lambda

To make things more complicated, Ruby 1.9 introduces yet another syntax for defining lambdas—the so-called "stubby lambda" operator:

```
p = ->(x) { x + 1 }
```

Notice the little arrow. The previous code is the same as the following:

```
p = lambda {|x| x + 1 }
```

The stubby lambda is an experimental feature, and it might or might not make its way into Ruby 2.0.

Methods Revisited

For the sake of completeness, you might want to take one more look at the last member of the callable objects' family: methods. If you're not convinced that methods, like lambdas, are just callable objects, look at this code:

`blocks/methods.rb`

```
class MyClass
  def initialize(value)
    @x = value
  end

  def my_method
    @x
  end
end

object = MyClass.new(1)
m = object.method :my_method
m.call                          # => 1
```

By calling Object#method(), you get the method itself as a Method object, which you can later execute with Method#call(). A Method object is similar to a lambda, with an important difference: a lambda is evaluated in the scope it's defined in (it's a closure, remember?), while a Method is evaluated in the scope of its object.

You can detach a method from its object with Method#unbind(), which returns an UnboundMethod object. You can't execute an UnboundMethod, but you can turn it back into a Method by binding it to an object.

```
unbound = m.unbind
another_object = MyClass.new(2)
m = unbound.bind(another_object)
m.call                           # => 2
```

This technique works only if another_object has the same class as the method's original object—otherwise, you'll get an exception. "Good luck finding a good reason to use this exotic stuff in real life!" Bill says, smirking.

Finally, you can convert a Method object to a Proc object by calling Method#to_proc, and you can convert a block to a method with define_method(). Bill looks up from his examples and makes a pronouncement: "It's time for a wrap-up!"

Callable Objects Wrap-Up

Callable objects are snippets of code that you can evaluate, and they carry their own scope along with them. They can be the following:

- *Blocks* (they aren't really "objects," but they are still "callable"): Evaluated in the scope in which they're defined.

- *Procs*: Objects of class Proc. Like blocks, they are evaluated in the scope where they're defined.

- *Lambdas*: Also objects of class Proc but subtly different from regular procs. They're closures like blocks and procs, and as such they're evaluated in the scope where they're defined.

- *Methods*: Bound to an object, they are evaluated in that object's scope. They can also be unbound from their scope and rebound to the scope of another object.

Different callable objects exhibit subtly different behaviors. In methods and lambdas, **return** returns from the callable object, while in procs and blocks, **return** returns from the callable object's original context. Different callable objects also react differently to calls with the wrong arity. Methods are stricter, lambdas are almost as strict (save for some corner cases), and procs and blocks are more tolerant.

These differences notwithstanding, you can still convert from one callable object to another, such as by using Proc.new(), Method#to_proc(), or the & operator.

3.6 Writing a Domain-Specific Language

Where you and Bill write some code, at long last.

"Enough talking about blocks," Bill says. "It's time to focus on today's job. Let's call it the RedFlag project."

Bill describes RedFlag as a monitor utility for the people in the sales department. It should send the sales folks a message when an order is late or total sales are too low—basically, whenever one of many different things happens. Sales wants to monitor dozens of different events, and the list is bound to change every week or so.

Luckily for you and Bill, sales has full-time programmers, so you don't have to write the events yourselves. You can just write a simple domain-specific language that the sales guys can use to define events, like this:[13]

```
event "we're earning wads of money" {
  recent_orders = ...   # (read from database)
  recent_orders > 1000
}
```

To define an event, you give it a descriptive name and a block of code. If the block returns true, then you get an alert via mail. If it returns false, then nothing happens. The system should check all the events every few minutes.

It's time to write RedFlag 0.1!

Your First DSL

You and Bill put together a working RedFlag DSL in no time:

blocks/monitor_blocks/redflag.rb

```
def event(name)
  puts "ALERT: #{name}" if yield
end

Dir.glob('*events.rb').each {|file| load file }
```

The entire DSL is just one method and a single line of code. The last line loads the files with names ending in events.rb, thereby executing the code in those files. This code is supposed to call back into RedFlag's event() method. To test the DSL, you create a file named test_events.rb.

---

13. If you need a crash course in domain-specific languages (or DSLs for friends), read Appendix B, on page 235.

```
blocks/monitor_blocks/test_events.rb
event "an event that always happens" do
  true
end

event "an event that never happens" do
  false
end
```

You save both files in the same folder and run redflag.rb:

⇒ `ALERT: an event that always happens`

"Success!" Bill exclaims, clapping his hands in excitement. "If we schedule this program to run every few minutes, we have a functional first version of RedFlag. Let's show it to the boss."

Sharing Among Events

Your boss is amused by the simplicity of the RedFlag DSL, but she's not completely convinced. "The people who write the events will want to share data among events," she observes. "Can I do this with your DSL? For example, can two separate events access the same variable?" she asks the two of you.

"Of course they can!" you and Bill reply in unison. "We have a *Flat Scope (81)*." To prove that, you whip up a new test file:

```
blocks/monitor_blocks/more_test_events.rb
def monthly_sales
  110    # TODO: read the real number from the database
end

target_sales = 100

event "monthly sales are suspiciously high" do
  monthly_sales > target_sales
end

event "monthly sales are abysmally low" do
  monthly_sales < target_sales
end
```

The two events in this file share a method and a local variable. You run redflag.rb, and it prints what you expected:

⇒ `ALERT: monthly sales are suspiciously high`

"OK, this works," the boss concedes. But she doesn't like the idea of variables and methods like monthly_sales() and target_sales cluttering the top-level scope. "Let me show you what I'd like the DSL to look like instead," she says. Without further ado, the boss grabs the keyboard and starts churning out code like nobody's business.

3.7 Quiz: A Better DSL

Where you're unexpectedly left alone to develop a new version of the RedFlag DSL.

Your boss wants you to add a setup instruction to the RedFlag DSL:

`blocks/monitor_framework/test_events.rb`

```
event "the sky is falling" do
  @sky_height < 300
end

event "it's getting closer" do
  @sky_height < @mountains_height
end

setup do
  puts "Setting up sky"
  @sky_height = 100
end

setup do
  puts "Setting up mountains"
  @mountains_height = 200
end
```

In this new version of the DSL, you're free to mix events and setup blocks (*setups* for short). The DSL stills checks events, and it also executes all the setups before each event. If you run redflag.rb on the previous test file, you expect this output:

```
⇒  Setting up sky
   Setting up mountains
   ALERT: the sky is falling
   Setting up sky
   Setting up mountains
   ALERT: it's getting closer
```

A setup can also set variables by using variable names that begin with an @ sign, like @sky_height and @mountains_height. Events can then read these variables. Your boss thinks that this feature will encourage programmers to write clean code: all shared variables are initialized together in a setup and then used in events—so it's easy to keep track of variables.[14]

Still amazed by your boss' technical prowess, you and Bill get down to business.

Runaway Bill

You and Bill compare the current RedFlag DSL with the new version your boss has suggested. The current RedFlag executes blocks immediately. The new RedFlag should execute the setups and the events in a specific order. You start by rewriting the event() method:

```
def event(name, &block)
  @events[name] = block
end
```

The new event() converts blocks to Procs and stores them in a hash. The hash is a top-level instance variable, so it's visible from outside the event() method.[15] At this point, you can write a similar method to handle setups, and then you can write the code that executes events and setups in the correct sequence.

As you ponder your next step, Bill slaps his forehead. "I forgot about tonight's dinner at the Javaholics Anonymous club!" he exclaims. "I'm sorry, pal; I need to leave early today." Before you can say "No way!" Bill has slipped out the door with surprising agility.

Now it's up to you alone. Can you complete the new RedFlag DSL and get the expected output from the test file?

Quiz Solution

You can find many different solutions to this quiz. Here is one:

`blocks/monitor_framework/redflag.rb`
```
def event(name, &block)
  @events[name] = block
end

def setup(&block)
  @setups << block
end
```

---

14. If you're used to the test/unit library, you might notice that the boss' ideas owe a lot to that.
15. See the sidebar on page 79.

```
Dir.glob('*events.rb').each do |file|
  @setups = []
  @events = {}
  load file
  @events.each_pair do |name, event|
    env = Object.new
    @setups.each do |setup|
      env.instance_eval &setup
    end
    puts "ALERT: #{name}" if env.instance_eval &event
  end
end
```

Both event() and setup() convert the block to a proc with the & operator. Then they store away the proc, in @events and @setups, respectively. These two top-level instance variables are shared by event(), setup(), and the main code.

Your main code loads the files that end with event.rb. For each file, it initializes @events and @setups, and then it loads the file. The code in the file calls back into event() and setup(), adding elements to @events and @setups.

With all the events and setups loaded, your program iterates through the events. For each event, it calls all the setup blocks first and then calls the event itself. Both the setup blocks and the event are converted from procs to blocks with the & operator, and they're evaluated in the context of an Object that acts as a *Clean Room (85)*. The instance variables in the setups and events are actually instance variables of the Object. This is the trick that allows setups to define variables for events. You also run each event in its own Clean Room, so events cannot share instance variables. (On the other hand, events can share *local* variables, because they share the same *Flat Scope (81)*.)

At this point, you can almost hear Bill's voice resounding in your head like the voice of Obi-Wan Kenobi: "Those top-level instance variables, @events and @setups, are like global variables in disguise. Why don't you get rid of them?"

An Even Better DSL

To get rid of the global variables (and Bill's voice in your head), you can use a *Shared Scope (82)*:

blocks/monitor_final/redflag.rb

```
lambda {
  setups = []
  events = {}
```

```ruby
  Kernel.send :define_method, :event do |name, &block|
    events[name] = block
  end

  Kernel.send :define_method, :setup do |&block|
    setups << block
  end

  Kernel.send :define_method, :each_event do |&block|
    events.each_pair do |name, event|
      block.call name, event
    end
  end

  Kernel.send :define_method, :each_setup do |&block|
    setups.each do |setup|
      block.call setup
    end
  end
}.call

Dir.glob('*events.rb').each do |file|
  load file
  each_event do |name, event|
    env = Object.new
    each_setup do |setup|
      env.instance_eval &setup
    end
    puts "ALERT: #{name}" if env.instance_eval &event
  end
end
```

The Shared Scope is contained in a lambda that is called immediately. The code in the lambda defines the RedFlag methods as *Kernel Methods (27)* that share two local variables: setups and events.[16] Now those ugly global variables are gone. The boss will be delighted!

You could improve RedFlag even more. For example, you could push the concept of a Clean Room a bit further, creating an object of your own Clean Room class rather than a generic Object. The instance methods in the Clean Room will then be visible to all the events and setups. With a playful grin, you add a comment to the code and leave this additional feature to Bill, your runaway pal.

What a day it has been! You learned a lot about blocks, and you even wrote your own little DSL. It's time to sneak out of the office and deposit yourself in a nearby pub.

---

16. Old versions of Ruby cannot take a block as the argument to another block. If you experience trouble running this program, then it's probably time to upgrade!

## Chapter 4

Thursday: Class Definitions

As you well know, writing object-oriented programs means spending a good chunk of your time defining classes. In Java and C#, defining a class is like making a deal between you and the compiler. You say, "Here's how my objects are supposed to behave," and the compiler replies, "OK, they will." Nothing really happens until you create an object of that class and then call that object's methods.

In Ruby, class definitions are different. When you use the `class` keyword, you aren't dictating how objects will behave in the future. On the contrary, you're actually *running code*.

If you buy into this notion—that a Ruby class definition is actually regular code that runs—you'll be able to cast some powerful spells. Two such spells that you'll learn about in this chapter are *Class Macros (115)* (methods that modify classes) and *Around Aliases (133)* (methods that wrap additional code around other methods). To help you make the most of these spells, this chapter also describes *eigenclasses* (also known as *singleton classes*), one of Ruby's most elegant features. Eigenclasses are an advanced topic, so understanding them will win you bragging rights among Ruby gurus.

This chapter also comes with a public service announcement: keep in mind that a class is just a souped-up module, so anything you learn about classes also applies to modules. Although I won't repeat this PSA in every section of this chapter, remember that whenever you read about a "class definition," you can also think to yourself "module definition."

4.1 Class Definitions Demystified

Where you and Bill tread familiar ground: the Bookworm application and the Ruby object model.

Today you stumble sleepily into the office, craving your Thursday morning coffee, only to be ambushed by an overexcited Bill. "Hey, buddy!" he shouts, waving his hands. "Do you remember Bookworm, the application that we refactored Monday? Everybody likes our refactorings, and the boss is asking for more!"[1]

"Today we'll be working on Bookworm again," Bill explains. "But first, we need to pin down some theory about class definitions. Let's start right where we left off Monday: in the Ruby object model."

Inside Class Definitions

As you take your first sip of coffee, Bill has already switched to lecture mode. "You probably think of a class definition as the place where you define methods. In truth, you can put any code you want in a class definition." To demonstrate what he's jabbering on about, Bill jumps up and scrawls all over your whiteboard:

```ruby
class MyClass
  puts 'Hello!'
end
```

⇒ Hello!

Bill goes on to explain that class definitions also return the value of the last statement, just like methods and blocks do. He fills up more of your whiteboard:

```ruby
result = class MyClass
  self
end
```

```ruby
result # => MyClass
```

This last example emphasizes a compelling point: in a class (or module) definition, the class itself takes the role of the current object **self**.[2] "Classes and modules are just objects, right?" Bill asks—to no one in particular. "So, why couldn't a class be **self**?" Keep this point about class definitions and **self** in mind, because the concept will become useful a bit later.

---

1. You and Bill worked on Bookworm in Chapter 1, *Monday: The Object Model*, on page 3.
2. You learned about this behavior of **self** in Section 1.5, *Class Definitions and self*, on page 30.

While he's on the topic of **self**, Bill takes the opportunity to tell you about a related concept: that of the current class.

The Current Class

As you know, wherever you are in a Ruby program, you always have a current object: **self**. Likewise, you always have a *current class* (or module). When you define a method, that method becomes an instance method of the current class.

Although you can get a reference to the current object through **self**, there's no equivalent keyword to get a reference to the current class. However, it's not difficult to keep track of the current class just by looking at the code. Whenever you open a class with the **class** keyword (or a module with the **module** keyword), that class becomes the current class:

```ruby
class MyClass
  # The current class is now MyClass...
  def my_method
    # ...so this is an instance method of MyClass
  end
end
```

However, the **class** keyword has a limitation: it needs the name of a class. Unfortunately, in some situations you may not know the name of the class that you want to open. For example, think of a method that takes a class and adds a new instance method to it:

```ruby
def add_method_to(a_class)
  # TODO: define method m() on a_class
end
```

How can you open the class if you don't know its name? You need some way other than the **class** keyword to change the current class. Enter the class_eval() method.

class_eval()

Module#class_eval() (also known by its alternate name, module_eval()) evaluates a block in the context of an existing class:

`class_definitions/class_eval.rb`

```ruby
def add_method_to(a_class)
  a_class.class_eval do
    def m; 'Hello!'; end
  end
end

add_method_to String
"abc".m   # => "Hello!"
```

The Current Class and Special Cases

In Section 4.1, *The Current Class*, on the preceding page, Bill lectured you about the Ruby interpreter always keeping track of the current class. And when he said *always*, he really meant it. To illustrate Bill's point, look at this (admittedly contrived) example:

class_definitions/current_class.rb

```
class MyClass
  def method_one
    def method_two; 'Hello!'; end
  end
end

obj = MyClass.new
obj.method_one
obj.method_two   # => "Hello!"
```

Which class does method_two() belong to? Or, to ask the same question in a different way, which class is the current class when method_two() is defined? In this case, the current class cannot be the same as **self**, because **self** is not a class. Instead, the role of the current class is taken by the class of **self**: MyClass.

The same principle applies if you're at the top level of your program. In that situation, the current class is Object, the class of main. That's why, if you define a method at the top level, that method becomes an instance method of Object.

In case you're wondering, Module#class_eval() is very different from Object#instance_eval(), which you learned about earlier in Section 3.4, *instance_eval()*, on page 83. instance_eval() only changes **self**, while class_eval() changes both **self** and the current class.[3] By changing the current class, class_eval() effectively reopens the class, just like the **class** keyword does.

Module#class_eval() is actually more flexible than **class**. You can use class_eval() on any variable that references the class, while **class** requires a constant. Also, **class** opens a new scope, losing sight of the current bindings, while class_eval() has a *Flat Scope (81)*. As you learned in

---

3. This is not the whole truth: instance_eval() does also change the current class, but you'll have to wait for the sidebar on page 120 to learn how exactly. For now, you can safely ignore the problem and assume that instance_eval() only changes **self**.

> ### Deciding Between instance_eval() and class_eval()
>
> If you want to open an object that is not a class, then you can use instance_eval(). If you want to open a class definition and define methods with **def**, then class_eval() should be your pick. But what if you want to open an object that happens to be a class (or module) to do something else than using **def**? Should you use instance_eval() or class_eval() then?
>
> If all you want is to change **self**, then both instance_eval() and class_eval() will do the job nicely. However, you should pick the method that best communicates your intentions. If you're thinking "I want to open this object, and I don't particularly care it's a class," then instance_eval() is fine. If you're thinking "I want an *Open Class (7)* here," then class_eval() is almost certainly a better match.

Section 3.3, *Scope Gates*, on page 78, this means you can reference variables from the outer scope in a class_eval() block.

Bill takes a huge slurp from his coffee mug. "Permit me to summarize what we just covered," he offers.

Current Class Wrap-up

You just learned a few things about class definitions:

- In a class definition, the current object **self** is the class being defined.

- The Ruby interpreter always keeps a reference to the *current class* (or module). All methods defined with **def** become instance methods of the current class.

- In a class definition, the current class is the same as **self**—the class being defined.

- If you have a reference to the class, you can open the class with class_eval() (or module_eval()).

"I know what you're going to ask now," Bill exclaims. "How on Earth could this stuff ever be useful in real life?"[4] To prove that all this theory

---

4. Actually, there's a good chance that you were *not* going to ask that. But you know Bill. He loves monologues.

about the current class can come very useful, Bill shows you a trick called *Class Instance Variables*.

Class Instance Variables

The Ruby interpreter assumes that all instance variables belong to the current object **self**. This is also true in a class definition:

```
class_definitions/class_instance_variables.rb
```

```
class MyClass
  @my_var = 1
end
```

"In a class definition," Bill reminds you, "the role of **self** belongs to the class itself, so the instance variable @my_var belongs to the class. Don't get confused! Instance variables of the class are different from instance variables of that class's objects." Bill returns to your now nearly illegible whiteboard to add yet another example:

```
class MyClass
  @my_var = 1

  def self.read; @my_var; end
  def write; @my_var = 2; end
  def read; @my_var; end
end

obj = MyClass.new
obj.write
obj.read            # => 2
MyClass.read        # => 1
```

The previous code defines two instance variables. Both happen to be named @my_var, but they're defined in different scopes, and they belong to different objects. To see how this works, you have to remember that classes are just objects, and you have to track **self** through the program. One @my_var is defined with obj as **self**, so it's an instance variable of the obj object. The other @my_var is defined with MyClass as **self**, so it's an instance variable of the MyClass object—a *Class Instance Variable*.

Spell: Class Instance Variable

If you come from Java, you may be tempted to think that Class Instance Variables are similar to Java's "static fields." Instead, they're just regular instance variables that happen to belong to an object of class Class. Because of that, a Class Instance Variable can be accessed only by the class itself—not by an instance or by a subclass.

Class Variables

If you want to store a variable in a class, you have more options than just using a *Class Instance Variable (106)*. You can also use a *class variable*, identified by an @@ prefix:

```
class C
  @@v = 1
end
```

Class variables are different from Class Instance Variables, because they can be accessed by subclasses and by regular instance methods. (In that respect, they're more similar to Java's static fields.)

```
class D < C
  def my_method; @@v; end
end

D.new.my_method  # => 1
```

Unfortunately, class variables have a nasty habit of surprising you. Here's an example:

```
@@v = 1

class MyClass
  @@v = 2
end

@@v  # => 2
```

You get this result because class variables don't really belong to classes—they belong to class *hierarchies*. Since @@v is defined in the context of main, it belongs to main's class Object. . . and to all the descendants of Object. MyClass inherits from Object, so it ends up sharing the same class variable.

As technically sound as this behavior is, it's still likely to trip you. Because of unwelcome surprises like the one shown earlier, most Rubyists nowadays shun class variables in favor of Class Instance Variables.

"We've touched on many things," Bill summarizes. "The current class, class definitions, **self**, class_eval(), Class Instance Variables. . . let's go back to Bookworm and put these features together."

Working on Bookworm Again

The Bookworm source contains very few unit tests, so it's up to you and Bill to write tests as you refactor. Sometimes this proves to be difficult, as is the case with this class:

```
class_definitions/bookworm_classvars.rb
```
```ruby
class Loan
  def initialize(book)
    @book = book
    @time = Time.now
  end

  def to_s
    "#{@book.upcase} loaned on #{@time}"
  end
end
```

Loan stores the title of a book and the time when it was loaned—that is, the time when the object was created. You'd like to write a unit test for the to_s() method, but to write that test, you'd have to know the exact time when the object was created. This is a common problem with code that relies on Time or Date: such code returns a different result every time it runs, so you don't know what result to test for.

"I think I have a solution to this problem," Bill announces. "It's a bit involved, so it will require some attention on your part. Here it is." Back to the whiteboard he goes:[5]

```ruby
class Loan
  def initialize(book)
    @book = book
▶   @time = Loan.time_class.now
  end

▶ def self.time_class
▶   @time_class || Time
▶ end

  def to_s
    # ...
```

Loan.time_class() returns a class, and Loan#initialize() uses that class to get the current time. The class is stored in a *Class Instance Variable (106)* named @time_class. If @time_class is nil, the *Nil Guard (227)* in time_class() returns the Time class as a default.

---

5. Bill borrowed this idea from Rake's ftptools.rb and test_ftp.rb files.

In production, Loan always uses the Time class, because @time_class() is always nil. By contrast, the unit tests can rely on a fake time class that always returns the same value. The tests can assign a value to the private @time_class variable by using either class_eval() or instance_eval(). Any of the two methods will do here, because they both change **self**. In this case, Bill decides that instance_eval() is more appropriate:

```ruby
class FakeTime
  def self.now; 'Mon Apr 06 12:15:50'; end
end

require 'test/unit'

class TestLoan < Test::Unit::TestCase
  def test_conversion_to_string
    Loan.instance_eval { @time_class = FakeTime }
    loan = Loan.new('War and Peace')
    assert_equal 'WAR AND PEACE loaned on Mon Apr 06 12:15:50', loan.to_s
  end
end
```

Bill is quite proud of his own coding prowess. "After this," he says, "I think we deserve a break—and a quiz!"

4.2 Quiz: Class Taboo

Where you write an entire program without ever using a certain popular keyword.

"Did you ever play Taboo?" Bill asks.[6] "The rules are simple: you're given a secret sentence and a list of words that you cannot use (they are "taboo"). You must help a teammate guess the secret sentence. You can give your teammate as many suggestions as you want, but you must never pronounce a taboo word. If you do that, you lose immediately."

Bill asks you to play taboo with Ruby code. You have only one taboo word, the **class** keyword. Here's your secret sentence:"

```ruby
class MyClass < Array
  def my_method
    'Hello!'
  end
end
```

---

6. See http://www.boardgames.com/taboo.html.

You have to write a piece of code that has exactly the same effect as the previous one, without ever using the **class** keyword. Are you up to the challenge? (Just one hint: look at the documentation for Class#new().)

Quiz Solution

Since a class is just an instance of Class, you can create it by calling Class#new(). Class#new() also accepts an argument (the superclass of the new class) and a block that is evaluated in the context of the newborn class:

```
c = Class.new(Array) do
  def my_method
    'Hello!'
  end
end
```

Now you have a variable that references a class, but the class is still anonymous. Do you remember the discussion about class names in Section 1.3, *Constants*, on page 14? The name of a class is just a constant, so you can assign it yourself:

```
MyClass = c
```

Interestingly, Ruby is cheating a little here. When you assign an anonymous class to a constant, Ruby understands that you're trying to give a name to the class, and it does something special: it turns around to the class and says, "Here's your new name." Now the constant references the Class, and the Class also references the constant. If it weren't for this trick, a class wouldn't be able to know its own name, and you couldn't write this:

```
c.name    # => "MyClass"
```

With a sense of pride, you turn to Bill to show him your solution to the quiz—but he's already busy browsing the Bookworm source. It's time to get back to the task at hand.

4.3 Singleton Methods

Where it's your turn to teach Bill a few tricks.

It's late morning, and you and Bill are deep in the flow. You're zipping through the Bookworm source, deleting some useless lines here, changing a confusing name there, and generally polishing the code. . . until you bump into a particularly troublesome refactoring.

The Paragraph class wraps a string and then delegates all calls to the wrapped string—all of them, that is, except for one method, Paragraph# title?(), which returns true if a Paragraph is all uppercase.

```
class_definitions/paragraph.rb
```

```ruby
class Paragraph
  def initialize(text)
    @text = text
  end

  def title?; @text.upcase == @text; end
  def reverse; @text.reverse; end
  def upcase; @text.upcase; end
  #...
```

Paragraph objects are created in a single place in the Bookworm source code. Also, Paragraph#title?() is called only once in the whole application, from a method named index():

```ruby
def index(paragraph)
  add_to_index(paragraph) if paragraph.title?
end
```

"Dang!" Bill exclaims. "The stupid Paragraph class really doesn't hold its own weight. We could scrap it entirely and just use regular Strings, if it weren't for the title?() method."

"Why don't we *Monkeypatch (9)* the String class and add the title?() method right there?" you offer. "I don't like that solution either," Bill mumbles. "A method with that name would make sense only on strings that represent a paragraph, not on each and every string. What a conundrum!"

It hurts you to see your pal suffering, so you spring into action. It takes you a few minutes to Google a solution to Bill's worries.

Introducing Singleton Methods

As it turns out, Ruby allows you to add a method to a single object. For example, here's how you can add title?() to a specific string:

```
class_definitions/singleton_methods.rb
```

```ruby
str = "just a regular string"

def str.title?
  self.upcase == self
end
```

```
str.title?                    # => false
str.methods.grep(/title?/)    # => ["title?"]
str.singleton_methods         # => ["title?"]
```

The previous code adds a method named title?() to str. No other object
gets the method—not even other Strings. A method like this one, which
is specific to a single object, is called a *Singleton Method*.

Spell: Singleton Method

"OK," Bill quips, "but how can Singleton Methods help us solve our
problem?"

Singleton Methods in Action

Thanks to Singleton Methods, you can now fix your problem with the
Bookworm source. You can send any old String to index() if you enhance
that String with a title?() Singleton Method:

`class_definitions/paragraph.rb`

```
paragraph = "any string can be a paragraph"

def paragraph.title?
  self.upcase == self
end

index(paragraph)
```

Now you can use plain strings in Bookworm and delete the Paragraph
class.

"Dude, you rock!" Bill exclaims. "I knew about Singleton Methods, but
I never realized you could use them this way."

"Wait a minute," you reply. "You *knew* about them? What did you think
they were useful for?"

Bill explains that Singleton Methods aren't just useful for enhancing
a specific object, like you just did. They're also the basis for one of
Ruby's most common features. "What if I told you that you've been
using Singleton Methods all along, without ever knowing it?" Bill asks,
rhetorically.

The Truth About Class Methods

Bill looks at you conspiratorially. "Remember what we talked about
on Monday?[7] Classes are just objects, and class names are just con-

---

7.   Bill is talking about the stuff that you learned in Section 1.3, *The Truth About Classes*,
on page 9.

Duck Typing

Some people are horrified by *Singleton Methods (112)*, thinking that if each object can have its own methods, no matter which class it belongs to, then your code is going to become a twisted tangle of spaghetti.

If you reacted that way yourself, then you're probably used to static languages. In a static language such as Java, you say that an object has type T because it belongs to class T (or because it implements interface T). In a dynamic language such as Ruby, the "type" of an object is not strictly related to its class. Instead, the "type" is simply the set of methods to which an object can respond.

People refer to this second, more fluid notion of a type as *duck typing*. This name comes from this motto: "If it walks like a duck and quacks like a duck, then it must be a duck." In other words, you don't care that an object is an instance of class Duck. You just care that it responds to walk( ) and quack( ), whether they're regular methods, *Singleton Methods (112)*, or even *Ghost Methods (50)*.

If you hang around Ruby for a while, you will get used to duck typing—and after learning a few cool dynamic tricks, you might even wonder how you could have lived without it in the first place.

stants." If you remember this concept, then you'll see that calling a method on a class is the same as calling a method on an object:

```
an_object.a_method
AClass.a_class_method
```

See? The first line calls a method on an object referenced by a variable, and the second line calls a method on an object (that also happens to be a class) referenced by a constant. It's the same syntax.

"But, wait! There's more," Bill adds, leaning forward. "Remember how I told you that you've been using *Singleton Methods (112)* all along?" That's really what class methods are: they're *Singleton Methods of a class*. In fact, if you compare the definition of a Singleton Method and the definition of a class method, you'll see that they're the same:

```
def obj.a_singleton_method; end
def MyClass.another_class_method; end
```

If you're writing code in a class definition, you can also take advantage of the fact that **self** is the class itself. Then you can use **self** in place of the class name to define a class method:

```
class MyClass
  def self.yet_another_class_method; end
end
```

So, you always define a Singleton Method in the same way:

```
def object.method
  # Method body here
end
```

In the definition shown previously, object can be an object reference, a constant class name, or **self**. The syntax might look different in the three cases—but in truth, the underlying mechanism is always the same. Nice design, don't you think?

As Bill is quick to point out, you're not finished with class methods yet. There's a very useful and common spell that relies on class methods exclusively, and it deserves its own discussion.

Class Macros

"I'm going to introduce you to a very common spell," Bill announces. He starts with an example that comes straight from the core of Ruby.

The attr_accessor() Example

Ruby objects don't have attributes. If you want something that looks like an attribute, you have to define two *Mimic Methods (224)*, a reader and a writer:

```
class_definitions/attr.rb
class MyClass
  def my_attribute=(value)
    @my_attribute = value
  end

  def my_attribute
    @my_attribute
  end
end

obj = MyClass.new
obj.my_attribute = 'x'
obj.my_attribute        # => "x"
```

Writing methods like these (also called *accessors*) gets boring very quickly. As an alternative, you can generate accessors by using one of the methods in the Module#attr_*() family. Module#attr_reader() generates the reader, Module#attr_writer() generates the writer, and Module#attr_accessor() generates both:

```ruby
class MyClass
  attr_accessor :my_attribute
end
```

All the attr_*() methods are defined on class Module, so you can use them whenever **self** is a module or a class. A method such as attr_accessor() is called a *Class Macro*. Class Macros look like keywords, but they're just regular class methods that are meant to be used in a class definition.

Spell: Class Macro

"Now that you know about Class Macros," Bill sums up, "I think I know a place in Bookworm's source code where we can make good use of them."

Class Macros Applied

"Look at the Book class!" Bill exclaims, pointing at the Bookworm source code. "It has methods named GetTitle(), title2(), and LEND_TO_USER(). "Talk about badly chosen names. By Ruby's conventions, they should be named title(), subtitle(), and lend_to(), respectively."

"Not so fast, buddy," you jump in. "There are other projects that use the Book class, and we have no control over these projects. We can't just rename the methods. That would break the callers!"

Bill concedes that you're right but explains that you can rename the methods if you invent a *Class Macro (115)* that deprecates the old names:

`class_definitions/deprecated.rb`

```ruby
class Book
  def title # ...

  def subtitle # ...

  def lend_to(user)
    puts "Lending to #{user}"
    # ...

  def self.deprecate(old_method, new_method)
    define_method(old_method) do |*args, &block|
      warn "Warning: #{old_method}() is deprecated. Use #{new_method}()."
      send(new_method, *args, &block)
    end
  end
```

```
    deprecate :GetTitle, :title
    deprecate :LEND_TO_USER, :lend_to
    deprecate :title2, :subtitle
end
```

The deprecate() method takes the old name and the new name of a method and defines a *Dynamic Method (45)* that catches calls to the old name. The Dynamic Method forwards the calls to the renamed method—but first it prints a warning on the console to notify the callers that the old name has been deprecated:

```
b = Book.new
b.LEND_TO_USER("Bill")
```

⇒
```
Warning: LEND_TO_USER() is deprecated. Use lend_to().
Lending to Bill
```

Bill is proud of his solution. "*Class Macros (115)* are cool, aren't they? But if you really want to understand Class Macros, as well as Singleton Methods in general, you have to look deeper into the Ruby object model."

4.4 Eigenclasses

Where you and Bill place the final piece in the object model puzzle.[8]

"Now we're going to tackle the difficult topic of *eigenclasses*," Bill commences. "They are the UFOs of the Ruby world: even if you never see one in person, you can find scattered hints of their existence all over the place. Let's start our investigation by collecting some evidence."

The Mystery of Singleton Methods

In Section 1.5, *Method Lookup*, on page 24, you learned how Ruby finds methods by going *right* into the receiver's class and then *up* the class hierarchy. For example:

```
class MyClass
  def my_method; end
end

obj = MyClass.new
obj.my_method
```

---

8.   This section and Section 4.5, *Quiz: Module Trouble*, on page 129, contain advanced material that might take a while for you to digest. If you want, you can snooze through Bill's detailed explanations and skip straight to Section 4.6, *Aliases*, on page 131. Be sure to come back to these sections later!

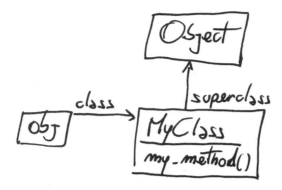

Figure 4.1: WHERE IS THE SINGLETON METHOD?

Bill draws Figure 4.1. "When you call my_method()," he demonstrates, "Ruby goes right into MyClass and finds the method there."

So far, so good. Now, what happens if you define a *Singleton Method (112)* on obj?

```
def obj.my_singleton_method; end
```

If you look at Figure 4.1, you'll notice that there's no obvious home for my_singleton_method() there. The Singleton Method can't live in obj, because obj is not a class. It can't live in MyClass, because if it did, all instances of MyClass would share it. And it cannot be an instance method of MyClass's superclass, Object. So then, where do Singleton Methods live?

Class methods are a special kind of Singleton Method—and just as baffling:

```
def MyClass.my_class_method; end
```

If you look at Figure 4.2, on the next page, you'll find that, again, my_class_method() doesn't seem to live anywhere in Bill's diagram. Bill has an explanation ready.

Eigenclasses Revealed

"When you ask an object for its class," Bill lectures, "Ruby doesn't always tell you the whole truth. Instead of the class that you see, an object can have its own special, hidden class. That's called the *eigenclass* of the object."

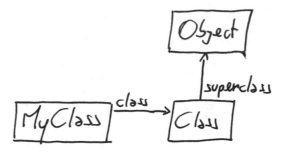

Figure 4.2: WHERE IS THE CLASS METHOD?

Methods like Object#class() keep the eigenclass carefully hidden, but you can work around them. Ruby has a special syntax, based on the **class** keyword, that places you in the scope of the eigenclass:

```
class << an_object
  # your code here
end
```

If you want to get a reference to the eigenclass, you can return **self** out of the scope:

```
obj = Object.new
eigenclass = class << obj
  self
end

eigenclass.class   # => Class
```

"That sneaky eigenclass was trying to hide, but we managed to find it!" Bill exclaims.

Bill's example also shows that an eigenclass is a class—but a very special one. For starters, it's invisible until you resort to the exotic **class** syntax shown earlier. Also, eigenclasses have only a single instance (that's why they're also called *singleton classes*), and they can't be inherited. More important, *an eigenclass is where an object's Singleton Methods live*:

```
def obj.my_singleton_method; end
eigenclass.instance_methods.grep(/my_/)  # => ["my_singleton_method"]
```

To fully understand the consequences of this last point, you have to look deeper into Ruby's object model.

Eigen... what?

The name *eigenclass* has an eventful history. Each Ruby programmer seems to have a pet name for these entities. Most people still call them *singleton classes*, but this name confusingly recalls the (unrelated) Singleton design pattern. Other people call them "metaclasses," meaning "the class of a class." This is still a fashionable name for eigenclasses of classes, but it doesn't really fit eigenclasses of objects.

Yukihiro "Matz" Matsumoto, the author of Ruby, hasn't announced an official name yet—but he seems to like the mathematician-friendly name *eigenclass*. The German word *eigen* roughly means "one's own," so the common translation of *eigenclass* is something like "an object's own class." This book sticks with Matz's vocabulary, but be aware that the term *eigenclass* is not as widely used as *singleton class*.

I also faced another terminology problem while writing this book: what do I call the methods of an eigenclass? Neither *eigenmethods* nor *eigenclass methods* is easy on the eye. After a lot of arguing and coffee drinking, I decided to stick with *Singleton Methods*, which is still the most common name for these things.

Method Lookup Revisited

"On Monday," Bill reminds you, "we talked about the Ruby object model and method lookup.[9] Back then, we had to leave some parts of the object model unexplored. Eigenclasses are the missing link we needed." He promises to demonstrate how, once you understand eigenclasses, all the bits and pieces in the object model finally fall into place.

Lookup Reviewed

To look into the object model, you need a practical example to focus on. Bill quickly writes what he calls a "lab rat" program:

```
class C
  def a_method
    'C#a_method()'
  end
end
```

---

9. That happened in Section 1.5, *What Happens When You Call a Method?*, on page 22.

Eigenclasses and instance_eval()

Now that you know about eigenclasses, you can fill in one missing snippet of knowledge about the instance_eval() method. In Section 4.1, *class_eval()*, on page 103, you learned that instance_eval() changes **self**, and class_eval() changes both **self** and the current class. However, instance_eval() also changes the current class: it changes it to the *eigenclass* of the receiver. This example uses instance_eval() to define a *Singleton Method (112)*:

class_definitions/instance_eval.rb

```
s1, s2 = "abc", "def"

s1.instance_eval do
  def swoosh!; reverse; end
end

s1.swoosh!                # => "cba"
s2.respond_to?(:swoosh!)  # => false
```

You'll rarely, if ever, see instance_eval() used purposefully to change the current class. The standard meaning of instance_eval() is this: "I want to change **self**."

```
class D < C; end

obj = D.new
obj.a_method    # => "C#a_method()"
```

Can you draw a picture of obj and its ancestors chain? If you do, it will probably look like Figure 4.3, on the facing page. (For now, you don't have to bother with eigenclasses or modules.)

You know that method lookup goes "one step to the right, then up." When you call obj.a_method(), Ruby goes *right* into obj's class D. From there, it climbs *up* the ancestors chain until it finds a_method() in class C. "Now," Bill announces, "let's add eigenclasses to the mix."

Eigenclasses and Method Lookup

To make your life easier as you experiment with eigenclasses, Bill writes a helper method that returns the eigenclass of any object.

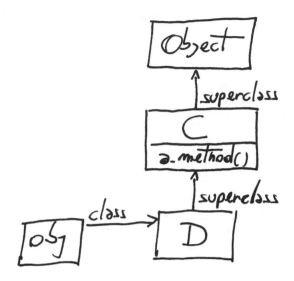

Figure 4.3: A SNIPPET OF THE OBJECT MODEL FOR BILL'S "LAB RAT" PROGRAM

```ruby
class Object
  def eigenclass
    class << self; self; end
  end
end
```

```ruby
"abc".eigenclass    # => #<Class:#<String:0x331df0>>
```

As you try the eigenclass() method, you also notice that the names that Ruby assigns to eigenclasses are a bit of a mouthful. In your diagrams, you and Bill decide to identify eigenclasses with a simple # prefix. By this convention, #obj is the eigenclass of obj, #C is the eigenclass of C, and so on.

Armed with the eigenclass() method and your new naming convention, you can now proceed with your fearless exploration of the object model. You go back to Bill's "lab rat" program and define a *Singleton Method (112)*:

```ruby
class << obj
  def a_singleton_method
    'obj#a_singleton_method()'
  end
end
```

Class Method Syntaxes

You already know two ways to define a class method. Either you get in the class's scope and use **self** or you use the name of the class:

```
class MyClass
  def self.my_method; end
end

def MyClass.my_other_method; end
```

Now you have a third way to define a class method. Since class methods are just Singleton Methods that live in the class's eigenclass, you can just open the eigenclass and define the method in there:

```
class MyClass
  class << self
    def my_method; end
  end
end
```

Which syntax should you use in your daily coding? This is usually a matter of personal taste. The **self** form is arguably more readable for most people, but some coders prefer to acknowledge the eigenclass explicitly. The "class name" syntax is usually frowned upon by expert Rubyists, because it duplicates the class name, making it more difficult to refactor.

"Let's experiment!" Bill exclaims. "We know that an eigenclass is a class, so it must have a superclass. Which is the superclass of the eigenclass?"

```
obj.eigenclass.superclass   # => D
```

The superclass of obj's eigenclass is D.[10] As you finish sipping your coffee, Bill adds this newfound knowledge to his diagram of the "lab rat" object model. The result is shown in Figure 4.4, on the next page.

Now you can see how Singleton Methods fit into the normal process of method lookup. If an object has an eigenclass, Ruby starts looking for methods in the eigenclass rather than the conventional class, and that's

---

10. Some older versions of Ruby disagree with this. Instead, they report that the superclass of any eigenclass is always #Class. This is a bug in the Ruby interpreter and has since been fixed. To be sure you don't stumble into the bug, run this code on Ruby 1.9.

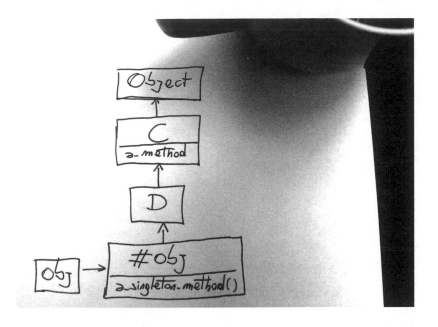

Figure 4.4: METHOD LOOKUP AND EIGENCLASSES

why you can call Singleton Methods such as obj#a_singleton_method(). If Ruby can't find the method in the eigenclass, then it goes up the ancestors chain, ending in the superclass of the eigenclass—which is the object's class. From there, everything is business as usual.

"Now you understand how Singleton Methods work," Bill notes. "But what about class methods? Yes, they're just a special case of Singleton Methods, but they deserve a closer look."

Eigenclasses and Inheritance

"Your head might start spinning right about now," Bill warns you. "We're going to look at the connections between classes, eigenclasses, and superclasses." This area of the object model can be confusing, but once it clicks in your mind, it will all look very obvious and elegant. If you're stuck, just look at the pictures, or fire up irb and experiment on your own.

Bill gets back to the keyboard and adds a class method to the "lab rat" program.

> ### Meta Squared
>
> Eigenclasses are classes, and classes are objects, and objects have eigenclasses.... Can you see where this train of thought is going? Like any other object, an eigenclass must have its own eigenclass:
>
> ```
> class << "abc"
>   class << self
>     self  # => #<Class:#<Class:#<String:0x33552c>>>
>   end
> end
> ```
>
> If you ever find a practical use for eigenclasses of eigenclasses, let the world know!

```ruby
class C
  class << self
    def a_class_method
      'C.a_class_method()'
    end
  end
end
```

Now you can explore the resulting object model:[11]

```ruby
C.eigenclass              # => #<Class:C>
D.eigenclass              # => #<Class:D>
D.eigenclass.superclass   # => #<Class:C>
C.eigenclass.superclass   # => #<Class:Object>
```

Bill grabs a scrap of paper and draws the diagram in Figure 4.5, on the facing page. This is a somewhat complicated diagram, so you should understand its notation before you delve into it. The arrows marked with *S* link classes to their superclasses, and the arrows marked with *C* link objects (including classes) to their classes, which in this case are all eigenclasses. Bill stresses that the arrows marked with a *C* do *not* point at the same classes that the class() method would return, because the class() method doesn't know about eigenclasses. (For example, obj.class() would return D, even if the class of obj is actually its eigenclass, #obj.)[12]

---

11. Because of a bug in the Ruby interpreter, you can get different results if you run this code on versions of Ruby that are earlier than 1.9.

12. Bill's diagram goes up to Object and #Object. In a few minutes, you'll see a diagram that goes higher up the chain—into BasicObject, #BasicObject, and beyond. Meanwhile, if you're a completist, you can draw the Kernel module between Object and BasicObject. On

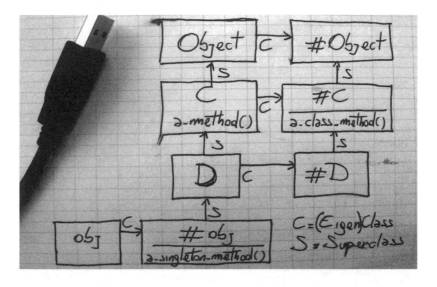

Figure 4.5: EIGENCLASSES OF CLASSES

Apparently, Ruby organizes classes, eigenclasses, and superclasses in a very purposeful pattern. The superclass of #D is #C, which is also the eigenclass of C. By the same rule, the superclass of #C is #Object. Bill tries to sum it all up, making things even more confusing: "The superclass of the eigenclass is the eigenclass of the superclass. It's easy!"

"OK," you say, "but there must be a reason for Ruby arranging classes, superclasses, and eigenclasses this way." Bill confirms, "Sure, there is. Thanks to this arrangement, you can call a class method on a subclass:"

```
D.a_class_method        # => "C.a_class_method()"
```

Even if a_class_method() is defined on C, you can also call it on D. This is probably what you expect, but it's only possible because method lookup starts in #D and goes up to #D's superclass #C, where it finds the method.

"Ingenious, isn't it? Now we can finally grasp the entire object model," Bill announces.

---

the other hand, you probably don't want to include #Kernel in this diagram. Although modules can have eigenclasses like any other object, the eigenclass of Kernel is not part of obj's or #D's ancestor chains.

The Great Unified Theory

"The Ruby object model is a beautiful place," Bill notes, with a dreamy expression on his face. "There are classes, eigenclasses, and modules. There are instance methods, class methods, and Singleton Methods."

At first glance, it all looks very complex. Look closer, and the complexity fades away. If you put eigenclasses together with regular classes and modules, you end up with the seven rules of the Ruby object model:

1. There is only one kind of object—be it a regular object or a module.

2. There is only one kind of module—be it a regular module, a class, an eigenclass, or a proxy class.[13]

3. There is only one kind of method, and it lives in a module—most often in a class.

4. Every object, classes included, has its own "real class," be it a regular class or an eigenclass.

5. Every class has exactly one superclass, with the exception of Basi-cObject (or Object if you're using Ruby 1.8), which has none. This means you have a single ancestors chain from any class up to BasicObject.

6. The superclass of the eigenclass of an object is the object's class. The superclass of the eigenclass of a class is the eigenclass of the class's superclass. (Try repeating that three times, fast! Then look back at Figure 4.5, on the preceding page, and it will all make sense.)

7. When you call a method, Ruby goes "right" in the receiver's real class and then "up" the ancestors chain. That's all there is to know about the way Ruby finds methods.

Any Ruby programmer can stumble on a difficult question about the object model. "Which method in this complicated hierarchy gets called first?" Or maybe, "Can I call this method from that object?" When this happens to you, review the seven rules listed earlier, maybe draw a quick diagram of the object model, and you'll find the answer in no time at all.

---

13. Proxy classes are actually somewhat different from the rest, because they're only used internally by the Ruby interpreter to mix modules in the ancestors chain. You can read about them in Section 1.5, *Modules and Lookup*, on page 25.

Congratulations! You now understand the entire Ruby object model!

Class Attributes

Bill's detailed explanation has left you a bit perplexed. "OK," you say, "I can see how eigenclasses are useful to understanding the object model. But how do I use them in practice?"

Bill answers with an example involving *Class Macros (115)*. "Do you remember the attr_accessor( ) method?[14] It generates attributes for any object:

`class_definitions/class_attr.rb`

```
class MyClass
  attr_accessor :a
end

obj = MyClass.new
obj.a = 2
obj.a          # => 2
```

But what if you want to define an attribute on a *class* instead?" You might be tempted to reopen Class and define the attribute there:

```
class MyClass; end

class Class
  attr accessor :b
end

MyClass.b = 42
MyClass.b      # => 42
```

This works, but it adds the attribute to *all* classes. If you want an attribute that's specific to MyClass, you need a different technique. Define the attribute in the eigenclass:

```
class MyClass
  class << self
    attr_accessor :c
  end
end

MyClass.c = 'It works!'
MyClass.c               # => "It works!"
```

---

14. See Section 4.3, *The attr_accessor() Example*, on page 114.

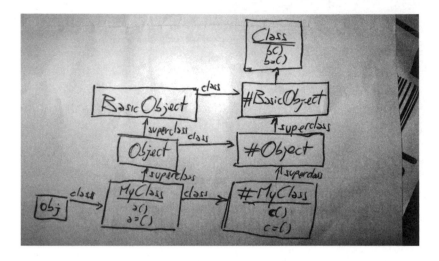

Figure 4.6: CLASS ATTRIBUTES LIVE IN THE CLASS'S EIGENCLASS.

To understand how this works, remember that an attribute is actually a pair of methods.[15] If you define those methods in the eigenclass, they become class methods, as if you'd written this:

```
def MyClass.c=(value)
  @c = value
end

def MyClass.c
  @c
end
```

As usual, Bill grabs the nearest available scrap of paper (probably an important specification document for some high-profile development project) and scribbles a diagram all over it. "That's how you define an attribute on a class," he sums up, pointing at Figure 4.6. "You can also see another interesting detail in this diagram. The superclass of #Basic-Object is none other than good old Class. This fact explains why you can call MyClass#b() and MyClass#b=()."

Clearly happy with his own explanation, Bill leans back in his comfy chair. "Cool stuff, huh? Now, let's try a little quiz!"

---

15. Read the discussion of *Mimic Methods (224)* for more details.

4.5 Quiz: Module Trouble

Where you learn that eigenclasses and modules mix well with each other.

Bill decides it's time for a story: "Every single day, somewhere in the world, a Ruby programmer tries to define a class method by including a module. I tried it myself, but it didn't work:"

class_definitions/module_trouble.rb

```
module MyModule
  def self.my_method; 'hello'; end
end

class MyClass
  include MyModule
end

MyClass.my_method   # NoMethodError!
```

"You see," Bill continues, "when a class includes a module, it gets the module's instance methods—*not* the class methods. Class methods stay out of reach, in the module's eigenclass."

"So, how did you find a solution?" you ask. "Oh, I didn't," Bill replies, blushing. "I just asked for the solution on a mailing list, like everybody else does. But maybe *you* can find a solution." Think about the object model and eigenclasses. How would you modify the code that you just looked at so that it works as expected?

Quiz Solution

The solution to this quiz is simple and subtle at the same time. First, define my_method() as a regular instance method of MyModule. Then include the module in the *eigenclass* of MyClass.

class_definitions/module_trouble_solution.rb

```
module MyModule
▶   def my_method; 'hello'; end
end

class MyClass
▶   class << self
▶     include MyModule
▶   end
end

MyClass.my_method   # => "hello"
```

my_method() is an instance method of the eigenclass of MyClass. As such, my_method() is also a class method of MyClass. This technique is called a *Class Extension*.

"Brilliant!" Bill gushes. "What about trying the same trick on a regular object instead of a class?"

Class Methods and include()

Reviewing Class Extensions, you can define class methods by mixing them into the class's eigenclass. Class methods are just a special case of Singleton Methods, so you can generalize this trick to any object. In the general case, this is called an *Object Extension*. In the following example, obj is extended with the instance methods of MyModule:

class_definitions/module_trouble_object.rb

```
module MyModule
  def my_method; 'hello'; end
end

obj = Object.new
class << obj
  include MyModule
end

obj.my_method            # => "hello"
obj.singleton_methods    # => [:my_method]
```

If you think that opening the eigenclass is a clumsy way to extend a class or an object, Bill is ready to show you an alternative technique.

Object#extend

Class Extensions (130) and *Object Extensions (130)* are common enough that Ruby provides a method just for them, named Object#extend():

class_definitions/module_trouble_extend.rb

```
module MyModule
  def my_method; 'hello'; end
end

obj = Object.new
obj.extend MyModule
obj.my_method        # => "hello"

class MyClass
  extend MyModule
end
MyClass.my_method    # => "hello"
```

Object#extend() is simply a shortcut that includes a module in the receiver's eigenclass. You can always do that yourself, if you so choose.

"Enough talking about eigenclasses today," Bill announces. "I don't want to get a meta-headache, and I have a hunch that we'll meet up with eigenclasses again tomorrow. For now, let's go back to refactoring Bookworm."

4.6 Aliases

Where you and Bill learn that a method by any other name is still a method.

As the day draws to a close, you and Bill find yourself stuck. Many methods in Bookworm rely on an open source library that retrieves a book's reviews from Amazon's website. Here's one example:

```
def deserves_a_look?(book)
  amazon = Amazon.new
  amazon.reviews_of(book).size > 20
end
```

This code works in most cases, but it doesn't manage exceptions. If a remote call to Amazon fails, Bookworm itself should log this problem and proceed. You and Bill could easily add exception management to each line in Bookworm that calls deserves_a_look?()—but there are tens of such lines, and you don't want to change all of them.

Bill sums up the problem: "We have a method that we can't modify directly, because it's in a library. We want to wrap additional functionality around this method so that all clients get the additional functionality automatically." There's a simple solution to this problem—but to get there, you need to know about *method aliases* first.

Method Aliases

You can give an alternate name to a Ruby method by using the **alias** keyword:

`class_definitions/alias.rb`

```
class MyClass
  def my_method; 'my_method()'; end
  alias :m :my_method
end

obj = MyClass.new
obj.my_method   # => "my_method()"
obj.m           # => "my_method()"
```

In **alias**, the new name for the method comes first, and the original name comes second. You can provide the names either as symbols or as plain names without a leading colon. (Most Rubyists would use a symbol.)

Note that **alias** is a keyword, not a method. That's why there's no comma between the two method names. ("That darn comma trips me up every time," Bill admits.) Ruby also provides Module#alias_method(), a method equivalent to **alias**. Continuing with the previous example:

```
class MyClass
  alias_method :m2, :m
end

obj.m2              # => "my_method()"
```

Aliases are common everywhere in Ruby, including the core libraries. For example, String#size() is an alias of String#length().[16]

"The **alias** keyword looks easy," Bill admits, "but it comes with its own challenges."

Around Aliases

What happens if you **alias** a method and then redefine it?

You can try this with a simple program:

`class_definitions/around_alias.rb`
```
class String
  alias :real_length :length

  def length
    real_length > 5 ? 'long' : 'short'
  end
end

"War and Peace".length        # => "long"
"War and Peace".real_length # => 13
```

The previous code redefines String#length(), but the alias still refers to the original method. This gives you insight into how method redefinition works. When you redefine a method, you don't really change the method. Instead, you define a new method and attach an existing name

---

16. From the "Useless Ruby Trivia" department: the aliasing record in the Ruby core libraries might well go to the Integer() class, which calls the same method no less than six different ways (to_int(), to_i(), floor(), ceil(), round(), and truncate()).

to that new method. You can still call the old version of the method as long as you have another name that's still attached to it.

According to Bill, this idea of aliasing a method and then redefining it is the basis of an interesting trick—one that deserves its own examples.

The RubyGems Example

The RubyGems library redefines a *Kernel Method (27)*:

`gems/rubygems-update-1.3.3/lib/rubygems/custom_require.rb`
```ruby
module Kernel
  alias gem_original_require require

  def require(path) # :doc:
    gem_original_require path
  rescue LoadError => load_error
    if load_error.message =~ /#{Regexp.escape path}\z/ and
       spec = Gem.searcher.find(path) then
      Gem.activate(spec.name, "= #{spec.version}")
      gem_original_require path
    else
      raise load_error
    end
  end
end
```

The new Kernel#require() calls the old Kernel#require(). If the old require() fails to locate a file, the new require() then looks for the file among the installed gems and eventually loads it—again, delegating to the old require().

Bill points at the code. "See how the new require() is wrapped around the old require()? That's why this trick is called an *Around Alias*." You can write an Around Alias in three simple steps:

Spell: Around Alias

1. You alias a method.

2. You redefine it.

3. You call the old method from the new method.

Around Alias is a common spell.[17] Just to make sure you got it right, Bill suggests you check out a second example of an Around Alias.

---

17. Rails programmers use Around Aliases a lot but indirectly. See Section 7.2, *alias_method_chain()*, on page 180.

The JCode Example

Before Ruby 1.9 introduced support for Unicode, people had to cope with problems like this:

```
# The successor string of "olè" should be "olé". But:
"olè".succ!   # => "omè"
```

If you want Unicode support in Ruby 1.8, you need a library. Some such libraries rely on the *Decorator* pattern. They define their own string class that wraps Ruby strings (call it UnicodeString). A Unicode-String overrides methods that worry about Unicode, such as succ(), and forwards all other method calls to the wrapped String. The problem with this approach is that you have to painstakingly wrap all your Strings into UnicodeStrings.

To avoid this chore, the JCode standard library shuns Decorators in favor of an *Around Alias (133)*:

```
class String
  alias original_succ! succ!
  private :original_succ!

  def succ!
    if # a custom encoding is enabled...
      # find successor of encoded string
    else
      original_succ!
    end
  end

  # ...
```

(Note that you can have different visibilities for different aliases. It's the method name, not the method itself, that is either public or private.)

Now String#succ works as expected for Unicode strings:

```
$KCODE = "UTF8"
require 'jcode'
"olè".succ!   # => "olé"
```

Et voilà!

Two Words of Warning

You must be aware of two potential pitfalls when you use *Around Alias (133)*, although neither is very common in practice.

First, Around Aliases are a form of *Monkeypatching (9)*, and as such, they can break existing code. Look back at the last section. Although

JCode redefines String#succ, it stops shy of redefining String#length—probably because that would break libraries that expect the "length" of a string to be its size in bytes. Instead, JCode defines a separate String#jlength() method to calculate the length of a Unicode string in characters. As usual, the more powerful the tricks you pull, the more testing of code you need to do!

The second potential problem has to do with loading. You should never load an Around Alias twice, unless you want to end up with an exception when you call the method. Can you see why?

As you ponder this last wrinkle, Bill is already getting busy with the Bookworm source.

Solving the Amazon Problem

"Remember where our discussion of aliases originated?" Bill asks. "We wanted to wrap logging and exception handling around the Amazon# reviews_of() method." You can do that with an *Around Alias (133)*:

`class_definitions/bookworm_aliases.rb`

```
class Amazon
  alias :old_reviews_of :reviews_of

  def reviews_of(book)
    start = Time.now
    result = old_reviews_of book
    time_taken = Time.now - start
    puts "reviews_of() took more than #{time_taken} seconds" if time_taken > 2
    result
  rescue
    puts "reviews_of() failed"
    []
  end
end
```

As you admire this smart piece of code, Bill hits you with an unexpected quiz.

4.7 Quiz: Broken Math

Where you find that one plus one doesn't always equal two.

Bill has one last quiz for you today.[18] "As you know," he observes, "most Ruby operators are actually *Mimic Methods (224)*." For example, the +

---

18. The idea for this quiz comes straight from the *Pickaxe* [TFH08] book.

operator on integers is syntactic sugar for a method named Fixnum#+(). When you write 1 + 1, the parser internally converts it to 1.+(1).

"The cool thing about methods is that you can redefine them. So, here's your challenge: break the rules of math by redefining Fixnum#+() so that it always returns the correct result plus one." For example:

```
1 + 1    # => 3
```

Quiz Solution

You can solve this quiz with an *Open Class (7)*. Just reopen Fixnum, and redefine +() so that (x + y) becomes (x + y + 1). Be careful. This is not as easy as it seems. The new version of +() relies on the old version of +(), so you need an *Around Alias (133):*[19]

`class_definitions/broken_math.rb`

```ruby
class Fixnum
  alias :old_plus :+

  def +(value)
    self.old_plus(value).old_plus(1)
  end
end

class BrokenMathTest < Test::Unit::TestCase
  def test_math_is_broken
    assert_equal 3, 1 + 1
    assert_equal 1, -1 + 1
    assert_equal 111, 100 + 10
  end
end
```

Now you have the power to wreak havoc on Ruby's basic arithmetics. Enjoy this code responsibly!

Calling It a Day

You and Bill did a lot of refactoring today, and you also talked about an awful lot of stuff. Bill sums it all up for you:

- You looked at the effects of class definitions on **self** (the default receiver of the methods you call) and on the *current class* (the default home of the methods you define).

---

19. This test breaks under Ruby 1.9 if you're using the test-unit gem. If this happens to you, use the Test::Unit standard library instead.

> ### Don't Forget Modules!
>
> Even if a class is just a special case of a module, many program-mers think of classes as "more important" than modules. Old habits tend to linger, and most of us are used to seeing classes as the stars of the object-oriented show. Even Bill focused on classes for most of today's examples.
>
> However, all the concepts you learned today can be general-ized from classes to modules. So, when Bill says that "you always have a current class," that class might actually be a module; when he says that "you can define the instance variable of a class," that doesn't stop you from defining the instance variable of a module; when he says that you have "eigenclasses," those could also be "eigenmodules," and so on.

- You made acquaintance with Singleton Methods and eigenclasses, gaining new insights into the object model and method lookup.

- You added a few new tricks to your bag, including *Class Instance Variables (106)*, *Class Macros (115)*, and *Around Aliases (133)*.

While Bill is busy enumerating Ruby features, you quietly slip out of the office. There'll be more time to talk tomorrow, and you need to take a break!

## Chapter 5

Friday: Code That Writes Code

In the previous chapters, you saw many wonderful metaprogramming spells—but it's possible that the "m" word has only become fuzzier for you. The fact is, the original definition of metaprogramming as "writing code that writes code" doesn't fit every technique described in this book. As you master these techniques, you'd be well within your rights to go back to the basics and ask, "Now, what *is* metaprogramming again?"

Rather than look for an updated, Wikipedia-worthy definition, for now I'll just chicken out and avoid answering your question. After all, when it comes to metaprogramming, it's not like there's a single approach that you can define in a short sentence. Metaprogramming is more like a heterogeneous bag of tricks that all happen to revolve around the Ruby object model. And like any other bag of tricks, metaprogramming really shines when you mix tricks together, either from the same bag or from an entirely different one.

Today you'll learn a few new tricks you can add to that bag, including one that quite literally "writes code." But even better, you'll see how you can seamlessly blend many tricks to solve a difficult coding challenge.

5.1 Leading the Way

Where your boss challenges you and Bill to write better code than she can.

Friday, at last! After such an eventful week, you're looking forward to a relaxing final day before the weekend. Wouldn't you know, as soon as you enter the office, your boss approaches you and your pal Bill.

"You guys did a good job this week," she says. "You're really leading the way as our resident Ruby experts. Looking over your code, I got so excited about metaprogramming that I decided to learn it myself. But last night I got stuck on a difficult coding problem. Can you help me?" she asks.

Having a boss who used to be a programmer and still likes to get her hands dirty can sometimes be a problem. But you can hardly say no when your boss is asking for your help.

The Boss' Challenge

"A few days ago," your boss recounts, "I learned about the attr_accessor() method.[1] Now I use it all the time to generate my objects' attributes." While she was at it, your boss also came up with the idea of writing her own *Class Macro (115)*, similar to attr_accessor(), which generates a *validated* attribute. "I call it attr_checked()," she says.

She explains how this attr_checked() method should work, pointing out that it should take the name of the attribute, as well as a block. The block is used for validation. If you assign a value to the attribute and the block doesn't return true for that value, then you get a runtime exception.

Your boss' first requirement is an attr_checked() Class Macro, and she explains her secondary requirement: "I don't want this attr_checked() method to be available to each and every class, because I don't like the idea of cluttering standard classes with my own methods. Instead, a class should gain access to attr_checked() only when it includes a CheckedAttributes module." She provides this example:

```
class Person
▶   include CheckedAttributes

    attr_checked :age do |v|
      v >= 18
    end
end

me = Person.new
me.age = 39    # OK
me.age = 12    # Exception!
```

---

1. The attr_accessor() method appeared in Section 4.3, *The attr_accessor() Example*, on page 114.

Your boss stops and looks you straight in the eye. "Do you think you can write CheckedAttributes and attr_checked() for me?" she asks.[2]

A Development Plan

After a careful analysis of the problem (OK, more like a quick chat at the coffee machine), you and Bill agree that the boss' challenge is a bit too much to handle in a single burst of coding. Instead, you'll get to a solution in small steps. For once, instead of engaging in pair programming, Bill proposes sharing roles: he'll manage the development, and you'll write the code. Before you can utter "No way," he quickly lists the steps you'll take:

1. Write a *Kernel Method (27)* named add_checked_attribute() using eval() to add a super-simple validated attribute to a class.

2. Refactor add_checked_attribute() to remove eval().

3. Validate attributes through a block.

4. Change add_checked_attribute() to a *Class Macro (115)* named attr_checked() that's available to all classes.

5. Write a module adding attr_checked() to selected classes through a hook.

"Weren't we supposed to work as a pair?" you protest. "I don't even understand these steps!"

"No worries, buddy," Bill quips, condescendingly. "You really only need to learn two things before you start developing: one is a method named eval(), and the other is the concept of a Hook Method." He vows to tell you everything you need to know about eval(), because eval() is necessary for the first development step. You will deal with Hook Methods later.

With that, Bill slides into "teaching mode" again. You have no option but to sigh and follow along.

---

2. The boss might have been inspired by the attr_validator() method in the Facets library. Facets is a large collection of useful Ruby snippets (collected and mostly written by Thomas Sawyer) and also a great source of coding ideas. You can install Facets with gem install facets.

5.2 Kernel#eval

Where you learn that, when it comes right down to it, code is just text.

"You already know about instance_eval() and class_eval()," Bill says, grabbing the keyboard.[3] "Now let me introduce you to the third member of the *eval* family—a *Kernel Method (27)* that's simply named eval()." In a sense, Kernel#eval() is the most straightforward of the three *eval* methods. Instead of a block, it takes a string that contains Ruby code— *Spell: String of Code* a *String of Code* for short. Kernel#eval() executes the code in the string and returns the result:

ctwc/simple_eval.rb

```
array = [10, 20]
element = 30
eval("array << element")  # => [10, 20, 30]
```

Executing a literal string of Ruby code is a pretty pointless exercise, but the power of eval() becomes apparent when you compute your Strings of Code on the fly. You can see an example of this in the popular Capistrano library.

The Capistrano Example

Capistrano is a framework for automating the deployment of Ruby applications.[4] Based on Rake, the default Ruby build system, Capistrano borrows Rake's basic idea: you define tasks in a "build file" and then execute those tasks from a command line. Capistrano also provides a few predefined tasks, such as this one:

gems/capistrano-2.5.5/lib/capistrano/recipes/deploy.rb

```
namespace :deploy do
  task :update do
    # ...
  end
end
```

Tasks can be organized into Namespaces. This particular task belongs to the *deploy* Namespace. On a command line, you would call it *deploy: update*. Earlier versions of Capistrano didn't have Namespaces. Back then, *deploy:update* was simply named *update*. But what if you want to execute an old build file (one that uses the non-namespaced *update*

---

3. instance_eval() and class_eval() are covered in Section 3.4, *instance_eval()*, on page 83, and Section 4.1, *class_eval()*, on page 103, respectively.
4. Capistrano was written by Jamis Buck. Install it with gem install capistrano.

task) on a recent version of Capistrano? To cater to this scenario, Capistrano provides a backward-compatibility feature:

`gems/capistrano-2.5.5/lib/capistrano/recipes/compat.rb`

```ruby
map = { "update"   => "deploy:update",
        "restart"  => "deploy:restart",
        "cleanup"  => "deploy:cleanup",
        # ...
}

map.each do |old, new|
  # ...
  eval "task(#{old.inspect}) do
    warn \"[DEPRECATED] `#{old}' is deprecated. Use `#{new}' instead.\"
    find_and_execute_task(#{new.inspect})
  end"
end
```

The map hash translates the old task names into the new namespaced ones. For each key-value pair in the hash, Capistrano evaluates a *String of Code (142)* like this one:

```ruby
task("update") do
  warn "[DEPRECATED] 'update' is deprecated. Use 'deploy:update' instead."
  find_and_execute_task("deploy:update")
end
```

This code defines a task named *update* that warns you to update the old build file and then falls back to the *deploy:update* task. Thanks to this trick, Capistrano can still work with your old build files, but at the same time, it encourages you to update those files by using the new task names.

Most Strings of Code feature some kind of string substitution, as is the case here. For an alternate way to use eval(), you can evaluate arbitrary Strings of Code from an external source, effectively building your own simple Ruby interpreter. Let's check out an example.

The irb Example

You already know about irb, the default Ruby command-line interpreter. At its core, irb is just a simple program that parses the standard input or a file and passes each line to eval(). (This type of program is sometimes called a *Code Processor*.) Here's the line that calls eval(), deep within irb's source code:

Spell: Code Processor

`ctwc/irb/workspace.rb`

```ruby
eval(statements, @binding, file, line)
```

Binding Objects

If you want to use eval() to its fullest, you should learn about the Binding class. A Binding is a whole scope packaged as an object. The idea is that you can create a Binding to capture the local scope and carry it around. Later, you can execute code in that scope by using the Binding object in conjunction with eval(), instance_eval(), or class_eval().

You can create a Binding with the Kernel#binding() method:

```
ctwc/bindings.rb
class MyClass
  def my_method
    @x = 1
    binding
  end
end

b = MyClass.new.my_method
```

You can evaluate code in the captured scope by passing the Binding as an additional argument to one of the eval*() methods:

```
eval "@x", b        # => 1
```

Ruby also provides a predefined constant named TOPLEVEL_BINDING, which is just a Binding of the top-level scope. You can use it to access the top-level scope from anywhere in your program:

```
class AnotherClass
  def my_method
    eval "self", TOPLEVEL_BINDING
  end
end

AnotherClass.new.my_method    # => main
```

In a sense, you can see Binding objects as a "purer" form of closures than blocks, because these objects contain a scope but don't contain code.

"Wait a minute, Bill," you protest. "I can see that the statements argument is a line of Ruby code, but what about those three additional arguments?" Amazingly, Bill admits that you're right, noting that you haven't yet talked about eval()'s optional arguments. "Let's go through each argument in turn."

The first optional argument to eval() is a Binding object, and irb can change this argument to evaluate code in different contexts.[5] This happens, for example, when you open a nested irb session on a specific object. (Did you know you can do that? If you didn't, look at the sidebar on the following page.) irb sets the @binding variable to evaluate your commands in the context of that object, similar to what instance_eval() does.

"What about file and line, the remaining two optional arguments to eval()?" you ask, wondering if Bill even remembers that you are sitting there. These arguments are used to tweak the stack trace in case of exceptions. Bill demonstrates this by writing a Ruby program that raises an exception:

`ctwc/exception.rb`

```
# this file raises an Exception on the second line
x = 1 / 0
```

You can process this program with irb by typing irb exception.rb at the prompt. If you do that, you'll get an exception on line 2 of exception.rb:

```
⇒ ZeroDivisionError: divided by 0
        from exception.rb:2:in '/'
```

When irb calls eval(), it calls it with the filename and line number it's currently processing. That's why you get the right information in the exception's stack trace. Just for fun, you can hack irb's source and remove the last two arguments from the call to eval() (remember to undo the change afterward):

`ctwc/irb/workspace.rb`

```
▶ eval(statements, @binding) # , file, line)
```

Run irb exception.rb now, and the exception reports the file and line where eval() is called:

```
⇒ ZeroDivisionError: divided by 0
        from /opt/local/lib/ruby/1.8/irb/workspace.rb:53:in '/'
```

---

5. Binding objects are described in the sidebar on the preceding page.

<u>**Nested irb Sessions**</u>

While using irb, you can open a nested session that puts you in the context of a specific object and allows you to execute code there, pretty much like instance_eval() does. Just use the irb command:

```
irb(main):001:0> s = "abc"
=> "abc"
irb(main):002:0> irb s
irb#1(abc):001:0> reverse
=> "cba"
irb#1(abc):002:0> exit  # leave the current context
irb(main):003:0>
```

Look at the irb prompt. The object in parentheses is the current **self**, and the *#1* postfix means you're sitting one level deep into a nested irb session. While this nested session lasts, the object you passed to the irb command is the top-level **self**.

This kind of hacking of the stack trace is especially useful when you write Code Processors.[6]

Strings of Code vs. Blocks

In Section 5.2, *Kernel#eval*, on page 142, you learned that eval() is a special case in the eval*() family: it evaluates a *String of Code (142)* instead of a block, like both class_eval() and instance_eval() do. However, this is not the whole truth. Although it's true that eval() always requires a string, instance_eval() and class_eval() can take either a String of Code or a block.

This shouldn't come as a big surprise. After all, code in a string is not that different from code in a block. Strings of Code can even access local variables like blocks do:[7]

```
array = ['a', 'b', 'c']
x = 'd'
array.instance_eval "self[1] = x"

array    # => ["a", "d", "c"]
```

---

6. However, these days it's considered good form to use the extra context parameters everywhere you evaluate a *String of Code (142)* so you can get a better stack trace in case of an exception. See http://olabini.com/blog/2008/01/ruby-antipattern-using-eval-without-positioning-information/.

7. See Section 3.3, *Closures*, on page 74.

Here Documents

A *String of Code (142)* can easily span multiple lines. You can define a multiline string with the usual double quotes, but some people prefer a different, more specific syntax. This alternate syntax, known as a *here document*, opens a string definition with a double less-than sign (<<) followed by a "termination sequence" of characters. The string will end on the first line that contains only the termination sequence:

```
s = <<END
  This is a "multi-line" string
    wishing you a great #{Time.now.year + 1}
END

puts s
```

⇒
```
This is a "multi-line" string
  wishing you a great 2010
```

Apart from the syntax style, there is no difference between a string defined as a here document and a regular double-quoted string.

Because a block and a String of Code are so similar, in many cases you have the option of using either one. Which one should you choose? The short answer is that you should probably go for a block whenever you can, because Strings of Code have a number of downsides. It's worth talking about them.

The Trouble with eval()

"Strings of Code are powerful, no doubt about that," Bill pipes up. "But with great power comes great responsibility—and danger."

To start with, Strings of Code don't always play well with your editor's features, such as syntax coloring and autocompletion. Even when they *do* get along with everyone, Strings of Code tend to be difficult to read and modify. Also, Ruby won't report a syntax error in a String of Code until that string is evaluated, potentially resulting in brittle programs that fail unexpectedly at runtime.

Thankfully, these annoyances are minor compared to the biggest issue with eval(): security. This particular problem calls for a more detailed explanation.

Code Injection

"Why is security a major problem when you use eval()?" you ask, raising your hand like you're in a classroom. Bill is only too happy to continue with the lesson. "Assume that, like most people," he says, "you have trouble remembering what each of the umpteen methods of Array does." As a speedy way to refresh your memory, you can write an eval()-based utility that allows you to call a method on a sample array and view the result (call it the *array explorer*):

`ctwc/array_explorer.rb`

```ruby
def explore_array(method)
  code = "['a', 'b', 'c'].#{method}"
  puts "Evaluating: #{code}"
  eval code
end

loop { p explore_array(gets()) }
```

The infinite loop on the last line collects strings from the standard input and feeds these strings to explore_array(). In turn, explore_array() turns the strings into method calls on a sample array. For example, if you feed the string *"revert()"* to explore_array(), the method will evaluate the string *"['a', 'b', 'c'].revert()"*. It's time to test-drive this utility:

```
⇐  find_index("b")
⇒  Evaluating: ['a', 'b', 'c'].find_index("b")
   1
⇐  map! {|e| e.next }
⇒  Evaluating: ['a', 'b', 'c'].map! {|e| e.next }
   ["b", "c", "d"]
```

Now imagine that, being a sharing kind of person, you decide to make this program widely available on the web. You knock out some quick CGI coding, and—presto!—you have a website where people can call array methods and see the results. (To follow the current web-naming fashion, you might call this site "Arroo" or maybe "MeThood.") Your wonderful site takes the Internet by storm, until a sneaky user feeds it a string like this:

```
⇐  object_id; Dir.glob("*")
⇒  ['a', 'b', 'c'].object_id; Dir.glob("*") => [your own private information here]
```

This input represents an inconsequential call to the array, followed by a command that lists all the files in your program's directory. Oh, the horror! Your malicious user can now execute arbitrary code on your computer—code that does something terrible like wipe your hard disk clean or, worse, read your saccharine electronic love letters. This kind of exploit is called a *code injection* attack.

Defending Yourself from Code Injection

The obvious next question for Bill is, "How can I protect my code from code injection?" You might parse all *Strings of Code (142)* to identify operations that are potentially dangerous. This approach may prove ineffective, though, because there are so many possible ways to write malicious code. Trying to outsmart a determined hacker can be dangerous to both your computer and your ego.

When it comes to code injection, some strings are safer than others. Only strings that derive from an external source can contain malicious code, so you might simply limit your use of eval() to those strings that you wrote yourself. Again, this is easier said than done, because in a live system it can be surprisingly difficult to track which strings come from where.

With all these challenges, some programmers advocate banning eval() altogether. Programmers tend to be paranoid about anything that might possibly go wrong, so this eval() ban turns out to be a pretty popular choice.[8] If you do away with eval(), you'll have to look for alternate techniques on a case-by-case basis. Remember the Array Explorer utility from Section 5.2, *Code Injection*, on the preceding page? You can rewrite it without eval() by using a *Dynamic Dispatch (41)*:

```
ctwc/array_explorer_safe.rb
def explore_array(method, *arguments)
  ['a', 'b', 'c'].send(method, *arguments)
end
```

Still, there are times when you might just miss eval(). For example, the latest, safer version of the Array Explorer requires you to pass the method name and the method arguments separately. Unfortunately, this separation would probably make your web interface less convenient. Also, the safer version of explore_array() cannot call methods that accept a block, such as find(). If you absolutely need to support blocks, you'll find you have to allow arbitrary code back into the system.

It's not easy to hit the sweet spot between too much eval() and no eval() at all. If you don't want to abstain from eval() completely, Ruby does

---

8. Actually, we're not paranoid. It's the government putting something in the tap water that makes us *feel* that way.

provide some features that make it somewhat safer. Let's take a look at them.

Tainted Objects and Safe Levels

Continuing on the topic of security, Bill introduces you to the concept of tainted objects. Ruby automatically marks potentially unsafe objects— in particular, objects that come from external sources—as *tainted*. Tainted objects include strings that your program reads from web forms, files, the command line, or even a system variable. Every time you create a new string by manipulating tainted strings, the result is itself tainted. Here's an example program that checks whether an object is tainted by calling its tainted?() method:

```
ctwc/tainted_objects.rb
```

```
# read user input
user_input = "User input: #{gets()}"
puts user_input.tainted?
```

⇐ x = 1
⇒ true

If you had to check every string for taintedness, then you wouldn't be in a much better position than if you had simply tracked unsafe strings on your own. But Ruby also provides the notion of *safe levels*, which complement tainted objects nicely. When you set a safe level (which you can do by assigning a value to the $SAFE global variable), you disallow certain potentially dangerous operations.

You can choose from five safe levels, from the default 0 ("hippie commune," where you can hug trees and format hard disks) to 4 ("military dictatorship," where you can't even exit the program freely). A safe level of 2, for example, disallows most file-related operations. Note that any safe level greater than 0 also causes Ruby to flat-out refuse to evaluate tainted strings:

```
$SAFE = 1
user_input = "User input: #{gets()}"
eval user_input
```

⇐ x = 1
⇒ SecurityError: Insecure operation - eval

To fine-tune safety, you can explicitly remove the taintedness on Strings of Code before you evaluate them (you can do that by calling Object# untaint()) and then rely on safe levels to disallow dangerous operations such as disk access.

> ### Kernel#eval() and Kernel#load()
>
> Ruby has methods like Kernel#load() and Kernel#require() that take the name of a source file and execute code from that file. If you think about it, evaluating a file is not that different from evaluating a string. This means load() and require() are somewhat similar to eval(). Although these methods are not really part of the *eval() family, you can think of them as first cousins.
>
> You can usually control the content of your files, so you don't have as many security concerns with load() and require() as you do with eval(). Still, safe levels higher than 1 do put some limitations on importing files. For example, a safe level of 2 or higher prevents you from using load() with a tainted filename.

By using safe levels carefully, you can write a controlled environment for eval().[9] Such an environment is called a *Sandbox*. Let's take a look at a sandbox taken from a real-life library.

Spell: Sandbox

The eRB Example

The eRB standard library[10] is the default Ruby template system. This library is a *Code Processor (143)* that you can use to embed Ruby into any file, such as this template containing a snippet of HTML:

`ctwc/template.rhtml`

```
<p><strong>Wake up!</strong> It's a nice sunny <%= Time.new.strftime("%A") %>.</p>
```

The special <%= ... > tag contains embedded Ruby code. When you pass this template through eRB, the code is evaluated:

`ctwc/erb_example.rb`

```
require 'erb'
erb = ERB.new(File.read('template.rhtml'))
erb.run
```

⇒ `<p><strong>Wake up!</strong> It's a nice sunny Friday.</p>`

---

9. Safe levels are typically used in combination with other techniques, such as threads and *Clean Rooms (85)*. For more information about safe levels, see *Programming Ruby* [TFH08].
10. eRB was written by Masatoshi Seki.

Somewhere in eRB's source, there must be a method that takes a snippet of Ruby code extracted from the template and passes it to eval(). Sure enough, here it is:

```
class ERB
  def result(b=TOPLEVEL_BINDING)
    if @safe_level
      proc {
        $SAFE = @safe_level
        eval(@src, b, (@filename || '(erb)'), 1)
      }.call
    else
      eval(@src, b, (@filename || '(erb)'), 1)
    end
  end

  # ...
```

The @src instance variable carries the content of a code tag, and the @safe_level instance variable contains the safe level required by the user. If no safe level is set, the content of the tag is simply evaluated. Otherwise, eRB builds a quick *Sandbox (151)*: it makes sure that the global safe level is exactly what the user asked for and also creates a *Clean Room (85)* to execute the code in a separate scope. (Note that the safe level is changed only within the proc, and it goes back to its former value after the proc has been called.)

"Now," Bill says, finally wrapping up his long explanation, "you know about eval() and how dangerous it can be. But eval() is great at getting code up and running quickly. That's why you can use this method as a first step to solve your original problem: writing the attribute generator for the boss."

5.3 Quiz: Checked Attributes (Step 1)

Where you take your first step toward solving the boss' challenge, with Bill peeking over your shoulder.

Bill interrupts your daydreaming about the weekend by asking you to think back to the development plan the two of you worked out (outlined in Section 5.1, *A Development Plan*, on page 141). "For the first step of the plan, we have to write an eval()-based method that adds a super-simple checked attribute to a class," Bill begins. "Let's call this method add_checked_attribute(). It should generate a reader method and a writer method, pretty much like attr_accessor() does."

The add_checked_attribute() method should differ from attr_accessor() in three ways. First, while attr_accessor() is a *Class Macro (115)*, add_checked_attribute() is supposed to be a simple *Kernel Method (27)*. Second, attr_accessor() is written in C, while add_checked_attribute() should use plain Ruby (and a *String of Code (142)*). Finally, the method add_checked_attribute() should add basic validation to the attribute. You're supposed to keep validation *really* basic for now: the attribute will raise a runtime exception only when you assign it either nil or false. You'll deal with more flexible validation down the road.

These requirements are expressed more clearly in a test suite:

ctwc/checked_attributes/eval.rb

```ruby
require 'test/unit'

class Person; end

class TestCheckedAttribute < Test::Unit::TestCase
  def setup
    add_checked_attribute(Person, :age)
    @bob = Person.new
  end

  def test_accepts_valid_values
    @bob.age = 20
    assert_equal 20, @bob.age
  end

  def test_refuses_nil_values
    assert_raises RuntimeError, 'Invalid attribute' do
      @bob.age = nil
    end
  end

  def test_refuses_false_values
    assert_raises RuntimeError, 'Invalid attribute' do
      @bob.age = false
    end
  end
end

# Here is the method that you should implement.
# (We called the class argument "clazz", because
# "class" is a reserved keyword.)
def add_checked_attribute(clazz, attribute)
  # ...
end
```

Can you implement add_checked_attribute() and pass the test?

Before You Solve This Quiz...

You need to generate an attribute like attr_accessor() does, so you'll probably appreciate a short review of attr_accessor().[11] When you tell attr_accessor() that you want an attribute named, say, :my_attr, it generates two *Mimic Methods (224)* like these:

```
def my_attr
  @my_attr
end

def my_attr=(value)
  @my_attr = value
end
```

Quiz Solution

Here's a solution:

```
def add_checked_attribute(clazz, attribute)
▶   eval "
▶     class #{clazz}
▶       def #{attribute}=(value)
▶         raise 'Invalid attribute' unless value
▶         @#{attribute} = value
▶       end
▶
▶       def #{attribute}()
▶         @#{attribute}
▶       end
▶     end
▶   "
end
```

Here's the *String of Code (142)* that gets evaluated when you call add_checked_attribute(String, :my_attr):

```
class String
  def my_attr=(value)
    raise 'Invalid attribute' unless value
    @my_attr = value
  end

  def my_attr()
    @my_attr
  end
end
```

---

11. We talked about attr_accessor() in Section 4.3, *The attr_accessor() Example*, on page 114.

The String class is treated as an *Open Class (7)*, and it gets two new methods. These methods are almost identical to those that would be generated by attr_accessor(), with an additional check that raises an exception if you call my_attr=() with either nil or false.

"We hit the road running!" Bill exclaims. "But remember our plan. We only used eval() to pass the unit tests quickly; we don't want to stick with eval() for the real solution. This takes us to step 2."

5.4 Quiz: Checked Attributes (Step 2)

Where you make your code eval()-free.

Bill glances at the development plan. "Now," he announces, "we want to refactor add_checked_attribute() and replace eval() with regular Ruby methods."

You may be wondering why the obsession with removing eval(). How can add_checked_attribute() be a target for a code injection attack if it's meant to be used only by you and your teammates? The problem is, you never know whether this method might be exposed to the world some time in the future. Besides, if you rewrite the same method without using *Strings of Code (142)*, it will only get clearer and more elegant. These considerations are reason enough to go forward and drop eval() altogether.

Can you refactor add_checked_attribute() with the same method signature and the same unit tests but using standard Ruby methods in place of eval()? Be forewarned that to solve this quiz, you'll have to do some research. You'll probably need to dig through the Ruby standard libraries for methods that can replace the operations in the current String of Code. You'll also need to manage scope carefully so that the attribute is defined in the context of the right class. (Hint: Remember *Flat Scopes (81)?*)

Quiz Solution

To define methods in a class, you need to get into that class's scope. The previous version of add_checked_attribute() did that by using an *Open Class (7)* inside a String of Code. If you remove eval(), you cannot use the **class** keyword anymore, because **class** won't accept a variable for the class name. Instead, you can get into the class's scope with class_eval().

```
ctwc/checked_attributes/no_eval.rb
```

```
    def add_checked_attribute(clazz, attribute)
▶     clazz.class_eval do
▶       # ...
▶     end
    end
```

You're in the class now, and you can define the reader and writer methods. Previously, you did that by using the **def** keyword in the String of Code. Again, you can no longer use **def**, because you won't know the names of the methods until runtime. In place of **def**, you can use *Dynamic Methods (45)*:

```
    def add_checked_attribute(clazz, attribute)
      clazz.class_eval do
▶       define_method "#{attribute}=" do |value|
▶         # ...
▶       end
▶
▶       define_method attribute do
▶         # ...
▶       end
      end
    end
```

The previous code defines two *Mimic Methods (224)* that are supposed to read and write an instance variable. How can the code do this without evaluating a String of Code? If you browse through Ruby's documentation, you'll find two methods that manipulate instance variables: Object#instance_variable_get() and Object#instance_variable_set(). Let's use them:

```
    def add_checked_attribute(clazz, attribute)
      clazz.class_eval do
        define_method "#{attribute}=" do |value|
▶         raise 'Invalid attribute' unless value
▶         instance_variable_set("@#{attribute}", value)
        end

        define_method attribute do
▶         instance_variable_get "@#{attribute}"
        end
      end
    end
```

"That's it!" Bill exclaims. "We now have a method that enters a class scope and defines instance methods that manipulate instance variables, and there's no string-based eval() to speak of! Now that our code is both working and eval( )-free, we can move on to the third step in our development plan."

5.5 Quiz: Checked Attributes (Step 3)

Where you sprinkle some flexibility over today's project.

"To solve the boss' challenge, we still need to implement a few important features," Bill observes. One of these features is described in the third step of your development plan (in Section 5.1, *A Development Plan*, on page 141). Bill explains that, right now, your generated attribute raises an exception if you assign it nil or false. But it's supposed to support flexible validation through a block.

Because this step changes the interface of add_checked_attribute( ), it also calls for an update of the test suite. Bill replaces the two test cases that checked for nil or false attributes with a single new test case:

ctwc/checked_attributes/block.rb

```
require 'test/unit'

class Person; end

class TestCheckedAttribute < Test::Unit::TestCase
  def setup
►   add_checked_attribute(Person, :age) {|v| v >= 18 }
    @bob = Person.new
  end

  def test_accepts_valid_values
    @bob.age = 20
    assert_equal 20, @bob.age
  end

► def test_refuses_invalid_values
►   assert_raises RuntimeError, 'Invalid attribute' do
►     @bob.age = 17
►   end
► end
end

► def add_checked_attribute(clazz, attribute, &validation)
    # ... (The code here doesn't pass the test. Modify it.)
  end
```

Can you modify add_checked_attribute( ) so that it passes the new tests?

Quiz Solution

You can pass the tests and solve the quiz by changing a couple of lines
in add_checked_attribute():

```
▶ def add_checked_attribute(clazz, attribute, &validation)
    clazz.class_eval do
      define_method "#{attribute}=" do |value|
▶       raise 'Invalid attribute' unless validation.call(value)
        instance_variable_set("@#{attribute}", value)
      end

      define_method attribute do
        instance_variable_get "@#{attribute}"
      end
    end
  end
```

"Step 3 was quick," Bill notes. "On to step 4!"

5.6 Quiz: Checked Attributes (Step 4)

Where you pull a Class Macro (115) from your bag of tricks.

Bill looks back at the development plan in Section 5.1, *A Development
Plan*, on page 141. "The fourth step," he announces, "asks us to change
the Kernel Method to a *Class Macro (115)* that's available to all classes."
What this means is that instead of an add_checked_attribute() method,
you and Bill want an attr_checked() method that the boss can use in a
class definition. Also, instead of taking a class and an attribute name,
this new method should take only the attribute name, because the class
is already available as **self**. Bill offers to update the test case:

`ctwc/checked_attributes/macro.rb`

```
require 'test/unit'

class Person
▶   attr_checked :age do |v|
▶     v >= 18
▶   end
  end

class TestCheckedAttributes < Test::Unit::TestCase
    def setup
▶     @bob = Person.new
    end

    def test_accepts_valid_values
      @bob.age = 20
```

```
      assert_equal 20, @bob.age
    end

  def test_refuses_invalid_values
    assert_raises RuntimeError, 'Invalid attribute' do
      @bob.age = 17
    end
  end
end
```

Can you write the attr_checked() method and pass the tests?

Quiz Solution

Think back to the discussion of class definitions in Section 4.1, *Class Definitions Demystified*, on page 102. If you want to make attr_checked() available to any class definition, you can simply make it an instance method of either Class or Module. Let's go for the first option:

`ctwc/checked_attributes/macro.rb`

```
► class Class
►   def attr_checked(attribute, &validation)
      define_method "#{attribute}=" do |value|
        raise 'Invalid attribute' unless validation.call(value)
        instance_variable_set("@#{attribute}", value)
      end

      define_method attribute do
        instance_variable_get "@#{attribute}"
      end
►   end
► end
```

This code doesn't even need to call to class_eval(), because when the method executes, the class is already taking the role of **self**.

"That's great!" Bill blurts out. "One more step, and we'll be done." For this last step, however, you need to learn about a feature that you and Bill haven't talked about yet: Hook Methods. You decide to take a donut break, during which Bill does a brain dump on Hook Methods.

5.7 Hook Methods

Where Bill decides it's time for another lesson in advanced coding.

The object model is an eventful place. Lots of things happen there as your code runs: classes are inherited, modules are mixed into classes, and methods are defined, undefined, and removed. Imagine if you could "catch" these events like you catch a mouse-click event on a graphical interface. You'd be able to execute code whenever a class is inherited or whenever a class gains a new method.

Well, it turns out you can do all these things. This program prints a notification on the screen when a class inherits from String:

```
ctwc/hooks.rb
class String
  def self.inherited(subclass)
    puts "#{self} was inherited by #{subclass}"
  end
end

class MyString < String; end
```

⇒ String was inherited by MyString

The inherited() method is an instance method of Class, and Ruby calls it when a class is inherited. By default, Class#inherited() does nothing, but you can override it with your own code as in the earlier example.

Spell: Hook Method A method such as Class#inherited() is called a *Hook Method* because you can use it to hook into a particular event.

More Hooks

Ruby provides a motley bunch of hooks that cover the most newsworthy events in the object model. Just as you override Class#inherited() to plug into the life cycle of classes, you can plug into the life cycle of modules by overriding Module#included():

```
module M
  def self.included(othermod)
    puts "M was mixed into #{othermod}"
  end
end

class C
  include M
end
```

⇒ M was mixed into C

You can also execute code when a module extends an object by overriding Module#extend_object(). Finally, you can execute method-related events by overriding Module#method_added(), method_removed(), or method_undefined().[12]

```ruby
module M
  def self.method_added(method)
    puts "New method: M##{method}"
  end

  def my_method; end
end
```

⇒   New method: M#my_method

Module#included() is probably the most widely used hook, thanks to a common metaprogramming spell that's worthy of an example of its own.

The Merb Example

Merb is a popular framework for web applications. Like many other web frameworks, Merb centers around the concepts of "controllers" and "actions."[13] As an example, Bill defines a Merb controller that caches the result of an action:

ctwc/merb_example.rb

```ruby
class MyController < Merb::Controller
  include Merb::Cache::CacheMixin

  cache :my_action

  def action
    # ...
```

CacheMixin is a module provided by Merb. When you include CacheMixin in a controller, that controller gains access to a method named cache() that you can use to enable the caching of a specific action.

"Wait!" you shout, on a donut-induced sugar high. "The cache() method is a *Class Macro (115)*, so it must be a class method of MyController." But

---

12. These hooks only work for regular instance methods, which live in the object's class. They don't work for *Singleton Methods (112)*, which live in the object's eigenclass. To catch Singleton Method events, you can use Kernel#singleton_method_added(), singleton_method_removed(), and singleton_method_undefined().

13. Merb is currently being merged with the Rails 3 framework—but as this book is being published, you can still install the original Merb (written by Ezra Zygmuntowicz, Yehuda Katz, and others) with gem install merb. This command will also install the merb-cache gem that Bill is using as his example (written by Ben Burkert). If you're not familiar with Ruby web frameworks, all you need to know here is that a *controller* is a class, and an *action* is an instance method of the controller.

Plugging Into Standard Methods

The notion of hooks extends beyond specialized methods like Class#inherited() or Module#method_added(). Because most operations in Ruby are just regular methods, you can easily twist them into improvised Hook Methods.

For example, in Section 5.7, *Hook Methods*, on page 159, you learned how to override Module#included() to execute code when a module is included. But you can also plug into the same event, so to speak, from the other side: because you include a module with the include() method, instead of overriding Module#included(), you can override Module#include() itself.

For example:

```ruby
module M; end

class C
  def self.include(*modules)
    puts "Called: C.include(#{modules})"
    super
  end

  include M
end
```
⇒ `Called: C.include(M)`

There is an important difference between overriding Module#included() and overriding Module#include(). Module#included() exists solely to be used as a Hook Method, and its default implementation is empty. But Module#include() has some real work to do: it must actually include the module. That's why our hook's code also should call the base implementation of Module#include() through **super**. If you forget **super**, you'll still catch the event, but you won't include the module anymore!

As an alternative to overriding, you can turn a regular method into a Hook Method by using an *Around Alias (133)*. You can find an example of this technique in Section 4.6, *The RubyGems Example*, on page 133.

when a class includes a module, it usually gets a bunch of instance methods and no class methods at all. "How can a mixin like CacheMixin bend the rules and define class methods on the class that includes it?"

The answer, according to Bill, is the *Class Extension (130)* spell, where you define class methods by including a module in the *eigenclass* instead of in the class itself. If you do that, the methods in the module become instance methods in the eigenclass, which also makes them class methods in the class.

"But wait!" you shout (again). "CacheMixin was included by MyController, not by MyController's eigenclass." "That's true," Bill is ready to admit. "But CacheMixin itself pulled a little trick the moment it was included. Let's peek into the source:"

`gems/merb-cache-1.0.11/lib/merb-cache/merb_ext/controller.rb`

```
module Merb::Cache::CacheMixin
  def self.included(base)
    base.extend(ClassMethods)
  end

  module ClassMethods
    def cache(*actions)
      # ...
```

Merb::Cache::CacheMixin acts both as a mixin and as a *Namespace (17)* for an inner module. This inner module, appropriately named Class-Methods, defines Class Macros such as cache(). When you include CacheMixin, you trigger a chain of events:

- Ruby calls a *Hook Method (160)*: the included() method.

- The hook turns back to the including class (which is sometimes called the *inclusor*, or the *base* in this case) and extends it with the ClassMethods module.

- The extend() method includes the methods from ClassMethods in the inclusor's eigenclass.

As a result, cache() and other instance methods get mixed into the eigenclass, effectively becoming class methods of the inclusor. How's that for a complicated code concoction?

Class Extension Mixins

You've just seen an example of a mixin that defines class methods (as opposed to instance methods) on its inclusors. This technique mixes together two previous spells: *Class Extensions (130)* and *Hook Methods (160)*. You can call this technique a *Class Extension Mixin*.

It's time to review the steps you can take to cast this spell on your own:

1. You define a module. Let's call it MyMixin.

2. You define an inner module of MyMixin (usually named ClassMethods) that defines some methods. These methods ultimately become class methods.

3. You override MyMixin#included() to extend() inclusors with ClassMethods.

Here's how you can put it all together:

```ruby
module MyMixin
  def self.included(base)
    base.extend(ClassMethods)
  end

  module ClassMethods
    def x
      "x()"
    end
  end
end
```

You can also apply your own variations to this spell. For example, you can define additional methods directly in MyMixin, outside the ClassMethods submodule. These methods would then become instance methods of the including class. This way, you'd get new instance methods *and* new class methods just by including a single module. On the other hand, if you don't need to define instance methods on the including class, you can drop the inner module altogether and define all the methods in the mixin itself:

```ruby
module MyMixin
  def self.included(base)
    base.extend(self)
  end

  def x
    "x()"
  end
end
```

No matter how you twist the execution, the basic idea stays the same: you want a mixin that adds class methods (usually *Class Macros (115)*) to its inclusors.

Bill interrupts your thoughts. "Now that you know about Hook Methods, we can take the final step in our development plan and solve today's challenge for good."

5.8 Quiz: Checked Attributes (Step 5)

Where you finally earn Bill's respect and the title of Master of Metaprogramming.

"In case you need to refresh your memory," Bill offers helpfully, "here's the code that we wrote in the previous step of our development:"

```ruby
class Class
  def attr_checked(attribute, &validation)
    define_method "#{attribute}=" do |value|
      raise 'Invalid attribute' unless validation.call(value)
      instance_variable_set("@#{attribute}", value)
    end

    define_method attribute do
      instance_variable_get "@#{attribute}"
    end
  end
end
```

The previous code defines a *Class Macro (115)* named attr_checked(). This Class Macro is an instance method of Class, so it's available to all classes. Your final task is to restrict access to attr_checked(): it should be available only to those classes that include a module named CheckedAttributes. The test suite for this step is pretty much the same one you used in step 4, with a single additional line:

```
ctwc/checked_attributes/module.rb
```

```ruby
require 'test/unit'

class Person
  include CheckedAttributes

  attr_checked :age do |v|
    v >= 18
  end
end

class TestCheckedAttributes < Test::Unit::TestCase
  def setup
    @bob = Person.new
  end
```

```ruby
  def test_accepts_valid_values
    @bob.age = 18
    assert_equal 18, @bob.age
  end

  def test_refuses_invalid_values
    assert_raises RuntimeError, 'Invalid attribute' do
      @bob.age = 17
    end
  end
end
```

Can you remove attr_checked() from Class, write the CheckedAttributes module, and solve the boss' challenge?

Quiz Solution

You can write CheckedAttributes as an *Class Extension Mixin (164)* that defines attr_checked() as a class method on its inclusors:

```ruby
▶  module CheckedAttributes
▶    def self.included(base)
▶      base.extend ClassMethods
▶    end
▶
▶    module ClassMethods
       def attr_checked(attribute, &validation)
         define_method "#{attribute}=" do |value|
           raise 'Invalid attribute' unless validation.call(value)
           instance_variable_set("@#{attribute}", value)
         end

         define_method attribute do
           instance_variable_get "@#{attribute}"
         end
       end
     end
▶    end
▶  end
```

Your boss will be delighted. These are the same Class Macro and module that she challenged you to write this morning. If you can write code like this, you're on your way to mastering the art of metaprogramming!

The Way of Metaprogramming

"You learned a lot this week, my friend," Bill says, smiling for the first time in what seems like a week. "Now you know enough to walk the metaprogramming path on your own. Before we take off for the weekend, let me tell you one last story."

"A master developer," Bill begins, "sits on top of a mountain, meditating..."

## Chapter 6

Epilogue

A master developer was meditating on top of a steep mountain. So deep was his meditation, so profoundly interwoven his code and his soul, that he began to snore gently.

A disciple climbed the mountain and interrupted the master's concentration. "I am struggling terribly, Master," he said. "I've studied many advanced techniques, but I still don't know how to apply them correctly. Tell me, what's the essence of metaprogramming?"

"Look at this small tree by my side," the Master replied, languidly waving his hand. "See how delicately it bends toward the ground, as if feeding on its own roots? Thus must your code be: simple and plain, and closing in on itself like a circle."

"I am still confused, Master," said the disciple, even more worried than before. "They always taught me that self-modifying code is bad. How will I know that I am wielding this art properly?"

"Look over your code with a pure heart and a clean mind," the master coached the disciple. "You will know when the code gets obscure. Exercise your knowledge to shed light, not to obfuscate and confuse."

"But Master," the disciple argued, "I lack experience. I need simple rules to know right from wrong."

The master began to get annoyed. "You're smart enough to learn, Dude," he said, "but are you smart enough to forget what you have learned? There's no such thing as metaprogramming. It's just programming all the way through. Now get lost, and let me meditate in peace."

At those words, the disciple was enlightened.

Part II

Metaprogramming in Rails

Good artists copy, great artists steal.
► Pablo Picasso

Chapter 7

The Design of ActiveRecord

In the first part of this book, you spent a week brushing elbows with another coder and making your way through the internals of Ruby. You also filled your toolbox with magic metaprogramming tricks like *Dynamic Methods (45)* and *Class Macros (115)*.

So, you've got the know-how and the tools. But now you might be wondering how to combine the knowledge and tools into real-life code. How can you keep your *Open Classes (7)* under control? When should you use a *Ghost Method (50)* rather than a *Dynamic Method (45)*? How do you test your *Class Macros (115)*? To answer these kinds of questions, you need more than knowledge and tools. You need *experience*.

You can't get experience simply by reading a book, but you *can* get a lot of value out of looking at the work of experienced coders. This chapter, together with the two that follow, takes you on a tour through the source code of Ruby on Rails, the quintessential Ruby project.[1] Rather than an exhaustive exploration of Rails, this tour is like a sightseeing excursion on one of those open, double-decker buses. I'll trace a few scenic routes through the Rails source code and in the process show you how some of the best Ruby programmers apply metaprogramming spells to solve real problems.

A last word of warning before we start: in this chapter, I'll focus on the good sides of metaprogramming, not on the headaches that metaprogramming might give you. If you wonder whether too much meta-

---

1. Ruby on Rails (or just "Rails," for short) was written by David Heinemeier Hansson, together with a small army of core developers and contributors. The official Rails site is http://rubyonrails.org.

programming can make your code unmanageable, please be patient. I'll try to address those worries in the next two chapters.

7.1 Preparing for the Tour

Chances are, you already know that Rails is a Model-View-Controller (MVC) framework for developing database-backed web applications in Ruby. Rails is so popular that many people get into Ruby just so that they can use Rails.

Even if you don't know much about Rails and its features, you can still follow along on this tour. I'll focus on the Rails source code, not on the features. Whenever features *are* important to understand the source code, I'll take the time to demonstrate them. However, if you are completely new to Rails and MVC frameworks, you might want to read a quick introduction to the topic before reading the rest of this chapter.[2] I'll also assume that you have RubyGems installed on your system and that you know what a "gem" is.[3]

While touring the Rails source code, I'll show you the snippets of code that are important to focus on. However, you might also want to keep the source code handy to explore it on your own. To do that, you need to install Rails.

Installing Rails

Because Rails is always evolving, it's quite possible that the source code has changed significantly by the time you read this chapter. Luckily, you can easily install the same version of Rails that I used to write this book, by simply running the following command:

⇒ `gem install rails -v 2.3.2`

Running this command installs all the gems that make up Rails 2.3.2. The rails gem just contains helpers such as code generators and Rake tasks, as well as the glue code that binds together the other gems. Those gems are the ones that do the real work. The most important Rails components are ActiveRecord (the "M" in Model-View-Controller, which maps application objects to database tables), ActionPack (which

---

2. You can find such an introduction, by Amy Hoy, at http://slash7.com/articles/2005/2/22/mvc-the-most-vexing-conundrum. If you want to dig deeper, the canonical book on Rails is *Agile Web Development with Rails* [TH05].
3. If you don't, take a look at http://rubygems.org/read/book/1.

contains both the view and the controller), and ActiveSupport (utilities and core extensions for generic problems such as time calculations, type conversions, and logging).[4]

After installing Rails, you'll find the Rails source code in your gems directory. To locate this directory on your system, you can ask Ruby-Gems for its environment information by running the gem environment command. You'll get output like this:

⇒
```
- RUBYGEMS VERSION: 1.3.1
- RUBY VERSION: 1.9.1 (2009-07-16 patchlevel 243) [i386-darwin10]
- INSTALLATION DIRECTORY: /opt/local/lib/ruby1.9/gems/1.9.1
[...]
- GEM PATHS:
   - /opt/local/lib/ruby1.9/gems/1.9.1
[...]
```

Look at the GEM PATHS. Those are the paths where RubyGems installs your gems. Usually it's only a single path, where you'll find a gems directory that contains all your gems' source code in subdirectories named like activerecord-2.3.2. When referring to specific source files, I'll give you the files' paths relative to the GEM PATHS (like: gems/activerecord-2.3.2/lib/active_record.rb).

The Rails Source Code

As of version 2.3, Rails and its core libraries contain almost 100,000 lines of code (including white lines and comments). You can cram a lot of information into just a few lines of Ruby code—let alone tens of thousands. Also, you can barely find a Rails source file that doesn't make heavy use of metaprogramming spells and other sophisticated idioms and techniques. All things considered, the Rails source code contains enough information to be intimidating.

These challenges shouldn't stop you from browsing through this wonderful piece of code. For all its power, size, and cleverness, the Rails source code is remarkably clear and beautifully written. Start slowly, don't get discouraged as you piece together the basics, and soon you might enter the growing list of Rails contributors.

---

4. A typical Rails installation also includes a few more gems. Some of these, like rake and rack, are installed automatically with Rails. If you want to run ActiveRecord programs on your system, you also need to install a database adapter like sqlite3-ruby. But you can probably follow along just fine by just reading the examples, without running them.

Also, don't forget the unit tests. When you're confronted with a confusing piece of code, reach for its tests and find out how it's supposed to be used. Once you understand their intentions, most perplexing lines of code will suddenly make sense.

Now you have the Rails source code and the tools you need to explore it. Let's dive into the first stop on our tour: a quick look at ActiveRecord, the most iconic of the Rails components.

7.2 The Design of ActiveRecord

ActiveRecord is the part of Rails that takes care of mapping Ruby objects to database tables. This functionality is called *object-relational mapping*, and it allows you to get the best of both the relational database (used for persistence) and object-oriented programming (used for business logics).

You can use ActiveRecord either in a Rails application or in a regular program. In a Rails application, you use ActiveRecord in the model—the "M" of MVC that contains domain objects and business logic. The idea is that you work with regular Ruby objects to manage your business logic, and you use ActiveRecord to make sure that those objects are persisted in your database.

Let's see a quick example of a stand-alone program that uses Active-Record, just enough to kick start our tour.

A One-Page ActiveRecord Example

Assume that you already have a file-based SQLite database that follows ActiveRecord's conventions. This database contains a table named ducks, which has a field named name. You want to map the records in the ducks table to objects of class Duck in your code.

You can start by requiring ActiveRecord and opening a connection to the database:[5]

`rails/ar_example.rb`
```
require 'activerecord'
ActiveRecord::Base.establish_connection :adapter => "sqlite3",
                                        :database => "dbfile"
```

---

5. In a Rails application, you wouldn't need to worry about opening the connection. The application reads the names of the adapter and the database from a configuration file and calls establish_connection() for you. You're using ActiveRecord on its own here, so you have to open the connection yourself.

Ruby Editors and IDEs

Once you start looking at a large library such as Rails, you'll probably want a good editor to move faster through the library's source code. However, if you're looking for the Ruby equivalent of Eclipse or Visual Studio, you'll probably come out disappointed. Traditionally, the Ruby community tends to shun integrated development environments (IDEs) in favor of simpler text editors such as TextMate* (for the Mac) or Komodo Edit.[†]

How can modern programmers live without automated refactorings, code generation, and all the modern bells and whistles? Apart from a certain amount of snobbery, there are pragmatic reasons for the average Rubyist's condescension toward IDEs. Because Ruby code tends to be brief and terse, an IDE's management and navigation features are not always as essential as in more verbose languages. Also, given Ruby's extremely dynamic nature, some of the features of full-fledged IDEs (like automated refactorings and code analysis) are less effective in Ruby than they are in a static language such as Java or C#. Finally, popular text editors such as TextMate come with enough features to compete with full-fledged IDEs and benefit by staying slimmer and lighter than an IDE.

Still, it's worth noting that the Ruby support in some IDEs is getting good enough to convince some Rubyists to drop TextMate in favor of something larger. NetBeans[‡] is a free IDE with excellent Ruby support. Aptana RadRails,[§] also free, is an Eclipse-based IDE for Rails development. RubyMine[¶] is an excellent commercial IDE from JetBrains, built on top of the company's extremely popular IntelliJ Java IDE.

---

*. TextMate is at http://macromates.com/.
†. Komodo Edit is at http://www.activestate.com/komodo.
‡. NetBeans is at http://ruby.netbeans.org.
§. RadRails is at http://www.aptana.com/rails.
¶. RubyMine is at http://www.jetbrains.com/ruby.

ActiveRecord::Base is the most important class in ActiveRecord. Not only does it contain class methods that do important stuff like opening database connections, it's also the base class of all mapped classes, such as Duck:

```
class Duck < ActiveRecord::Base
  validates_length_of :name, :maximum => 6
end
```

The validates_length_of() method is a *Class Macro (115)*. In this example, it ensures that a Duck's name cannot exceed six characters. If you try to save a Duck with a longer name to the database, you'll get an exception (if you use the save!() method) or a silent failure (if you use the more discreet save() method).[6]

By convention, ActiveRecord automatically maps Duck objects to the ducks table. By looking at the database schema, it also finds out that Ducks have a name, and it defines a *Ghost Method (50)* to access that field. Thanks to these conventions, you can use the Duck class right away:

```
my_duck = Duck.new
my_duck.name = "Donald"
my_duck.valid?          # => true
my_duck.save!
```

I've checked that my_duck is valid (its name is six characters at most) and saved it to the database. Reading it back, you get this:

```
some_duck = Duck.find(:first)
some_duck.id            # => 1
some_duck.name          # => "Donald"
some_duck.delete
```

That's enough code to give you a sense for how ActiveRecord is supposed to be used. Now let's see what's happening under the hood.

ActiveRecord::Base

At first sight, the classes and methods in ActiveRecord can be disorienting. If you look at the previous example, you will probably expect to find a validates_length_of() class method in ActiveRecord::Base. However, the documentation for the class contains no trace of that method. Search around, and you'll find validates_length_of() in the ActiveRecord::

---

6. ActiveRecord validation happens in the business model, not the database. The database can still contain ducks with very long names, for example, because they were there before you added validation to the Duck class.

Validations module. This is a common problem for newcomers to Rails. It's often difficult to understand which methods are available and where they're defined.

However, there is a simple logic behind this seemingly complicated structure. Let's see what happens in the Rails source code by going back to the first line in the example: require 'activerecord'. This line loads the activerecord.rb file, a simple stub that, in turn, loads the similarly named active_record.rb (this is just so that you can write either require 'activerecord' or require 'active_record'). This second file loads all the ActiveRecord bits and pieces—some twenty modules defined in a *Namespace (17)* named ActiveRecord:

gems/activerecord-2.3.2/lib/active_record.rb

```ruby
module ActiveRecord
  autoload :Base, 'active_record/base'
  autoload :Batches, 'active_record/batches'
  autoload :Calculations, 'active_record/calculations'
  autoload :Callbacks, 'active_record/callbacks'
  # ...
  autoload :Timestamp, 'active_record/timestamp'
  autoload :Transactions, 'active_record/transactions'
  autoload :Validations, 'active_record/validations'
  # ...
end
```

ActiveRecord loads each module through autoload(). This core *Kernel Method (27)* is a convenient helper when you have a lot of files and you don't want to load more files than you really need. Kernel#autoload() takes a module name and a filename and ensures that the file is loaded automatically the first time you refer to the module. For example, as soon as you reference the ActiveRecord::Base class, autoload() loads activerecord/base.rb, which, in turn, defines the class:

gems/activerecord-2.3.2/lib/active_record/base.rb

```ruby
module ActiveRecord
  class Base
    class << self # Class methods
      def find(*args) # ...
      def first(*args) # ...
      def last(*args) # ...
      # ...
    end

    public
      def id # ...
      def save # ...
```

```
      def save! # ...
      def delete # ...
      # ...
    end
end
```

ActiveRecord::Base defines a long list of class methods, like find() and first().[7] It also defines a list of instance methods, like save() and delete(). However, these are just a small part of ActiveRecord::Base's class and instance methods. Let's see why.

ActiveRecord::Validations

In Section 7.2, *A One-Page ActiveRecord Example*, on page 174, you looked at validation methods such as valid?() and validates_length_of(). To find out where those methods come from, go to the end of the base.rb file. There, you'll find code that reopens ActiveRecord::Base to include a bunch of modules:

gems/activerecord-2.3.2/lib/active_record/base.rb

```
module ActiveRecord
  Base.class_eval do
    # ...
    include Validations
    include Locking::Optimistic, Locking::Pessimistic
    include AttributeMethods
    include Dirty
    include Callbacks, Observing, Timestamp
    # ...
  end
end
```

Both valid?() and validates_length_of() are defined by the ActiveRecord:: Validations module:

gems/activerecord-2.3.2/lib/active_record/validations.rb

```
module ActiveRecord
  module Validations
    def self.included(base)
      base.extend ClassMethods
      base.class_eval do
        alias_method_chain :save, :validation
        alias_method_chain :save!, :validation
      end
      base.send :include, ActiveSupport::Callbacks
      # ...
    end
```

---

7. class << self means that the methods defined here are class methods. If you're perplexed by this syntax, go read Section 4.4, *Eigenclasses*, on page 116.

```
    module ClassMethods
      def validates_each(*attrs)  # ...
      def validates_confirmation_of(*attr_names)  # ...
      def validates_length_of(*attrs) # ...
      # ...
    end

    def save_with_validation(perform_validation = true) # ...
    def save_with_validation!   # ...
    def valid?    # ...
    # ...
  end
end
```

There is a lot going on in ActiveRecord::Validations, so let's look at the example one piece at a time. First, ActiveRecord::Validations defines instance methods like valid?(). So, when ActiveRecord::Base includes ActiveRecord::Validations, it earns a few new instance methods. ActiveRecord::Validations also adds class methods to ActiveRecord::Base, because it's a *Class Extension Mixin (164)*. This spell uses a *Hook Method (160)* (the included() method) to extend its including class with the ClassMethods module, effectively turning the methods in ClassMethods to class methods on ActiveRecord::Base.

Skip the class_eval() part for now—I'll take you back there in a minute. ActiveRecord::Validations.included() also causes its including class to include the ActiveSupport::Callbacks module. Note that this code can't call base.include() directly, because include() is a private method—so it cuts through the encapsulation red tape with a *Dynamic Dispatch (41)*.[8]

Now ActiveRecord::Base also includes ActiveSupport::Callbacks. If you look at the source of ActiveSupport::Callbacks (in callbacks.rb), you'll see that this module is itself a Class Extension Mixin, and it also plays the same trick with include() and Dynamic Dispatch as ActiveRecord::Validations, thus forcing ActiveRecord::Base to pile up even more methods and include even more modules.

It's time to leave this long trail of consecutive module inclusions to look back at the lines I skipped in ActiveRecord::Validations, marked in the following listing with small arrows.

---

8. In the Ruby world, private() is generally considered a suggestion rather than a prescription. That's a staple of Ruby's philosophy. There are rules, but if you know what you're doing, you can break most of them. As Matz, the author of Ruby, would say, Ruby treats you like a grown-up developer.

```
gems/activerecord-2.3.2/lib/active_record/validations.rb
```

```
module ActiveRecord
  module Validations
    def self.included(base)
      base.extend ClassMethods
▶     base.class_eval do
▶       alias_method_chain :save, :validation
▶       alias_method_chain :save!, :validation
▶     end
      base.send :include, ActiveSupport::Callbacks
      # ...
    end

    def save_with_validation(perform_validation = true) # ...
    def save_with_validation!   # ...
    # ...
```

To understand these lines, I need to take a short detour into the Active-Support library and the alias_method_chain() method.

alias_method_chain()

To understand how alias_method_chain() is useful, look at this:

```
rails/amc_example.rb
```

```
class MyClass
  def greet
    puts "Hello!"
  end
end

MyClass.new.greet
```

⇒ Hello!

Now suppose you want to wrap logging behavior around MyClass#greet(). You can do that with an *Around Alias (133)*:

```
class MyClass
  def greet_with_log
    puts "Calling method..."
    greet_without_log
    puts "...Method called"
  end

  alias_method :greet_without_log, :greet
  alias_method :greet, :greet_with_log
end

MyClass.new.greet
```

⇒ Calling method...
   Hello!
   ...Method called

I defined a new method called greet_with_log() and aliased it to greet(). The code that used to call greet() still works, but it gets the new logging behavior as well. I also defined an alias to the original greet(), so you can still greet without logging if you want:

```
MyClass.new.greet_without_log
```

⇒ Hello!

To sum it all up, the original method greet() is now called greet_without_log(). If you want logging, you can call either greet_with_log() or greet(), which are actually aliases of the same method.

This kind of Around Alias is very common in Rails. You provide the original method (say, operation()) and the enhanced method (say, operation_with_feature()), and you end up with three methods: operation(), operation_with_feature(), and operation_without_feature(). The first two do include the feature; the third doesn't.

Instead of duplicating these aliases all around, Rails provides a generic metaprogramming method that does all the aliasing for you. It's named Module#alias_method_chain(), and it's provided by the ActiveSupport library:

```
gems/activesupport-2.3.2/lib/active_support/core_ext/module/aliasing.rb
module Module
  def alias_method_chain(target, feature)
    # Strip out punctuation on predicates or bang methods since
    # e.g. target?_without_feature is not a valid method name.
    aliased_target, punctuation = target.to_s.sub(/([?!=])$/, ''), $1
    yield(aliased_target, punctuation) if block_given?

    with_method, without_method =
      "#{aliased_target}_with_#{feature}#{punctuation}",
      "#{aliased_target}_without_#{feature}#{punctuation}"

    alias_method without_method, target
    alias_method target, with_method

    case
      when public_method_defined?(without_method)
        public target
      when protected_method_defined?(without_method)
        protected target
      when private_method_defined?(without_method)
        private target
    end
  end
end
```

Look at the way alias_method_chain() works. First, it strips out the final exclamation mark or question mark from the name of the method to put it at the end of the new aliases. Then (after maybe yielding to a block so that the caller can override the default naming), it calculates names for all the aliases. Next, it aliases the methods. And finally, it sets the visibility on operation_without_feature() so that it's the same visibility as the original operation().

Now that you know how alias_method_chain() works, look again at the ActiveRecord::Validations module:

`gems/activerecord-2.3.2/lib/active_record/validations.rb`

```
module ActiveRecord
  module Validations
    def self.included(base)
      base.extend ClassMethods
►     base.class_eval do
►       alias_method_chain :save, :validation
►       alias_method_chain :save!, :validation
►     end
      base.send :include, ActiveSupport::Callbacks
      # ...
    end

    def save_with_validation(perform_validation = true) # ...
    def save_with_validation!   # ...
    # ...
```

These lines reopen the ActiveRecord::Base class and hack its save() and save!() methods to add validation. This aliasing ensures that you will get automatic validation whenever you save an object to the database. If you want to save without validating, you can call the aliased versions of the original methods: save_without_validation() and save_without_validation!().

Enough of the Rails source code for now. Here's a recap of what's been covered so far.

One Last Look at ActiveRecord::Base

ActiveRecord::Base is the main ActiveRecord class. Besides defining its own instance methods and class methods, it includes additional modules like ActiveRecord::Validations. Each of these modules adds its own instance methods and class methods to ActiveRecord::Base, and some modules force ActiveRecord::Base to include additional modules, defining even more methods. The modules also take the liberty of tweaking ActiveRecord::Base's methods with tricks like alias_method_chain(), which—you guessed it—define even more methods. What's more, most Rails plug-ins expand on this architecture and cause ActiveRecord::Base to include more modules, yielding yet more methods.

With all these method definitions going on, you won't be too surprised that ActiveRecord::Base() is a very large class. In a plain-vanilla Rails installation without plug-ins, this class has more than 200 instance methods and a staggering 450 class methods. ActiveRecord::Base() is the ultimate *Open Class (7)*!

This is an unusual design, to say the least. What can we take away by learning about it?

7.3 Lessons Learned

When it comes to lessons learned, everybody is different. Personally, I learned three important guidelines by looking at ActiveRecord's design. Here they are.

Leave Java Behind

When I looked at Ruby for the first time, I'd been a Java programmer for years. The Ruby approach, and ActiveRecord in particular, left me shocked. No Java coder in his or her right mind would ever write a library that consists almost solely of a single huge class with many hundreds of methods. Such a library would be madness—impossible to understand and maintain!

And yet, that's exactly what ActiveRecord's design is like. But wait, it gets worse. Many of the modules that comprise ActiveRecord don't think twice about modifying their including class with tricks like alias_method_chain(). You might think that with all that patching and tweaking, the main class in ActiveRecord would become a tangled mass of spaghetti. And yet, somehow, it doesn't.

Consider the evidence: not only does ActiveRecord manage to get away with that design and still be extremely popular, but it also proves easy to read and change. Many users modify and *Monkeypatch (9)* ActiveRecord for their own purpose, and the original source code evolves so quickly that Rails books and articles routinely run the risk of getting obsolete before they're even published.[9] As it changes, ActiveRecord

---

9. Of course, that would never happen with *this* book.

also manages to remain extremely high quality—so much so that some people trust it enough to use the nightly builds (the "edge version") in their daily work.

Apparently, design assumptions that are taken for granted in other languages aren't necessarily valid in Ruby. It's not that the good design rules of old suddenly grew obsolete. On the contrary, the basic tenets of design (decoupling, simplicity, no duplication) hold true in Ruby as much as they do in any other language. In Ruby, though, the techniques you wield to achieve those design goals can be surprisingly different.

Look at ActiveRecord::Base again. Granted, it's a huge class. But it's actually designed as an assembly of loosely coupled, relatively simple, easy-to-test, easy-to-reuse modules. In fact, thanks to their dynamically typed nature, ActiveRecord's modules are more decoupled than Java classes and easier to use in isolation. If you only need the validation features, you can include ActiveRecord::Validation in your own class and happily ignore ActiveRecord::Base and all the other modules.

`rails/modules.rb`

```ruby
require 'activerecord'
ActiveRecord::Base  # autoload all modules

class MyClass
  def save; end
  def save!; end
  def new_record?; true; end

  include ActiveRecord::Validations

  attr_accessor :attr
  validates_length_of :attr, :minimum => 4
end

obj = MyClass.new
obj.attr = 'test'
obj.valid?        # => true
obj.attr = 'tst'
obj.valid?        # => false
```

I had to go through some hoops to make this code work. For example, I referenced ActiveRecord::Base to set up the autoloading of ActiveRecord modules, and I stubbed a few methods that ActiveRecord::Validations relies upon. However, that wasn't too much work in exchange for a flexible set of validation *Class Macros (115)*. Also, this technique of using

ActiveRecord modules in isolation makes it easier to poke at a module from an irb shell and find out how it works.

By now, it's clear that modules are a very powerful tool. This brings me to the second important guideline that I learned.

Think in Modules

In most object-oriented languages, classes rule the land. Object orientation means that you call methods on objects, and you decide on the behavior of those methods by writing classes. In Ruby, you don't need a class to define a method. It's enough that you have a module.

A Ruby module is basically a place where you define methods. (In fact, a class is just a souped-up module.) Once you have the methods, you can use them in many different ways. Here are some things that you can do just by including a module:

- Include the module in a class, and the methods become instance methods of the class.

- Include the module in *the eigenclass* of a class, and the methods become class methods.

- Include the module in the eigenclass of any generic object, and the methods become *Singleton Methods (112)* of the object.

But wait—there's more. For example, you can let the module modify the class (or module, or object) that includes it, like Rails does with *Class Extension Mixins (164)* and alias_method_chain(). Modules are a very versatile tool, and the more you become proficient in Ruby, the more you'll learn to use them in original ways. In the next two chapters, you'll see more examples of how modules can help you write clean, beautiful code.

However, modules alone are not enough to justify the extreme flexibility of Ruby. To explain that flexibility, I'll move on to the last of the three important guidelines and reintroduce the "M" word while I'm at it.

Do Things Your Own Way

In most languages, there aren't that many ways to bind components together. Maybe you inherit from a class or you delegate to an object. If you want to get fancy, you can use a library that specializes in managing dependencies, like a dependency injection container.

Now, see how Rails manages its parts. Instead of sticking with the standard ways of doing things, the Rails authors came up with their own mechanism for binding the pieces of their libraries together and implemented it with minimal, unobtrusive code and a bunch of magic metaprogramming spells. The whole scheme looks complicated at first, but once you understand the principles behind it, it looks natural and effortless, as if it was built into the Ruby language itself.

Look at another example of Rails solving a problem its own way. A few versions ago, the Rails code contained many instances of the same idiom: an *Around Alias (133)* was used to add a feature to a method, and the old version of the method was renamed to something like method_without_feature(). Apart from the method names, which changed every time, the code that did this was always the same, duplicated all over the place. In most languages, you cannot avoid that kind of duplication. In Ruby, you can sprinkle some metaprogramming magic over your pattern and extract it into its own method...and thus was born alias_method_chain().

Examples like these are what people are thinking about when they say that Ruby is *expressive*: you don't have to spend many words to say what you want to say. If you want a class to include a bunch of modules that allow you to extend the definitions of its subclasses, you can do it, instead of turning to some complicated framework to manage dependencies. If you want to jump up a level of abstraction and define a method that defines and renames methods based on your own naming convention, you can do just that, instead of duplicating code. There is rarely a great distance between what you mean to do and the code you write.

In this chapter, I've shown the basic structure of ActiveRecord, with a short side trip into the alias_method_chain() utility method. The next chapter continues the tour of ActiveRecord, with a closer look into the ActiveRecord::Base class.

## Chapter 8

Inside ActiveRecord

In the previous chapters I showed you plenty of metaprogramming code snippets, many of them coming from real libraries. However, you might still be wondering how metaprogramming fits into a big, complex system. How many metaprogramming spells can you pile on to your code before it becomes a nightmare to read and maintain?

This chapter attempts to answer that question. I'll go back to ActiveRecord to give you a look at the source code behind two of its most impressive features: dynamic attributes and dynamic finders. These features are backed by some of the most extreme metaprogramming code in all of Rails, so they serve as a good benchmark for deciding how much metaprogramming is good for you. This is by and large a matter of personal opinion, so I'll let the code speak for itself until the end of this chapter. In the last section of the chapter, I'll discuss the reasoning behind some of the choices in the ActiveRecord source, and I'll offer you my own conclusions.

In this chapter I won't attempt to track all the minute details of the Rails source code. Instead, assuming that you have the Rails source somewhere handy, I'll just stop at the main signposts. Even so, you'll have plenty of code to look at!

8.1 Dynamic Attributes

I'll show you an example of ActiveRecord's dynamic attributes in action. Assume that you've created a database table that contains tasks.

`rails/ar_attributes.rb`

```ruby
require 'activerecord'
ActiveRecord::Base.establish_connection :adapter => "sqlite3",
                                        :database => "dbfile"

ActiveRecord::Base.connection.create_table :tasks do |t|
  t.string   :description
  t.boolean  :completed
end
```

Now you can define an empty Task class that inherits from ActiveRecord::Base, and you can use objects of that class to interact with the database:

`rails/ar_attributes.rb`

```ruby
class Task < ActiveRecord::Base; end

task = Task.new
task.description = 'Clean up garage'
task.completed = true
task.save

task.description   # => "Clean up garage"
task.completed?    # => true
```

The previous code calls four *Mimic Methods (224)* to access the object's attributes: two "write" methods (description=() and completed=()), one "read" method (description()), and one "question" method (completed?()). None of these "attribute accessors" comes from the definition of Task. So, where do they come from?

ActiveRecord::Base#method_missing()

You probably guessed that attribute accessors like description=() are actually *Ghost Methods (50)*. Things are actually a tad more complicated than that, as you'll find out if you look at ActiveRecord::Base's method_missing(). Let's do that.

ActiveRecord::Base#method_missing() is initially defined in the Attribute-Methods module, and it gets rolled into ActiveRecord::Base() with the mechanism you saw earlier in Chapter 7, *The Design of ActiveRecord*, on page 171. Here it is, together with a few related methods:

`gems/activerecord-2.3.2/lib/active_record/attribute_methods.rb`

```ruby
module ActiveRecord
  module AttributeMethods
    def method_missing(method_id, *args, &block)
      method_name = method_id.to_s
```

```ruby
    if self.class.private_method_defined?(method_name)
      raise NoMethodError.new("Attempt to call private method", method_name, args)
    end

    # If we haven't generated any methods yet, generate them, then
    # see if we've created the method we're looking for.
    if !self.class.generated_methods?
      self.class.define_attribute_methods
      if self.class.generated_methods.include?(method_name)
        return self.send(method_id, *args, &block)
      end
    end

    if self.class.primary_key.to_s == method_name
      id
    elsif md = self.class.match_attribute_method?(method_name)
      attribute_name, method_type = md.pre_match, md.to_s
      if @attributes.include?(attribute_name)
        __send__("attribute#{method_type}", attribute_name, *args, &block)
      else
        super
      end
    elsif @attributes.include?(method_name)
      read_attribute(method_name)
    else
      super
    end
  end

  def read_attribute(attr_name)
    # ...

  def write_attribute(attr_name, value)
    # ...

  def query_attribute(attr_name)
    # ...

  private

    # Handle *? for method_missing.
    def attribute?(attribute_name)
      query_attribute(attribute_name)
    end

    # Handle *= for method_missing.
    def attribute=(attribute_name, value)
      write_attribute(attribute_name, value)
    end

    # ...
```

This is quite a lot of code, so I'll go over it with you one piece at a time.

Ghost Attributes Incarnated

I'll start by concentrating on the first half of method_missing():

```ruby
def method_missing(method_id, *args, &block)
  method_name = method_id.to_s

  if self.class.private_method_defined?(method_name)
    raise NoMethodError.new("Attempt to call private method", method_name, args)
  end

  # If we haven't generated any methods yet, generate them, then
  # see if we've created the method we're looking for.
  if !self.class.generated_methods?
    self.class.define_attribute_methods
    if self.class.generated_methods.include?(method_name)
      return self.send(method_id, *args, &block)
    end
  end

  # ...
```

When you call a method such as Task#description=() for the first time, the call is delivered to method_missing(). Before it does its job, method_missing() ensures that you're not inadvertently using it to bypass encapsulation and call a private method. Then it calls a magic method named define_attribute_methods().

You'll get a look inside define_attribute_methods() in a minute, but for now all you need to know is that it defines read, write, and question *Dynamic Methods (45)* for all the columns in the database. The next time you call description=(), or any other accessor that maps to a database column, your call isn't handled by method_missing(). Instead, you call a real, nonghost method. (That's a good thing when it comes to performance, as I'll argue at the end of this chapter.)

When you entered method_missing(), description=() was a *Ghost Method (50)*. Now description=() is a regular, flesh-and-blood method, and method_missing() can call it with a *Dynamic Dispatch (41)* and return the result. This process takes place only once for each class that inherits from ActiveRecord::Base. If you enter method_missing() a second time for any reason (for example, because you mistype a method name in irb), the class method generated_methods() returns true, and this code is skipped.

Before I show you the second half of method_missing(), take a peek at define_write_method().

Defining Accessors

Here's the code that defines nonghostly accessors:

gems/activerecord-2.3.2/lib/active_record/attribute_methods.rb

```ruby
# Generates all the attribute related methods for columns in the database
# accessors, mutators and query methods.
def define_attribute_methods
  return if generated_methods?
  columns_hash.each do |name, column|
    unless instance_method_already_implemented?(name)
      if self.serialized_attributes[name]
        define_read_method_for_serialized_attribute(name)
      elsif create_time_zone_conversion_attribute?(name, column)
        define_read_method_for_time_zone_conversion(name)
      else
        define_read_method(name.to_sym, name, column)
      end
    end

    unless instance_method_already_implemented?("#{name}=")
      if create_time_zone_conversion_attribute?(name, column)
        define_write_method_for_time_zone_conversion(name)
      else
        define_write_method(name.to_sym)
      end
    end

    unless instance_method_already_implemented?("#{name}?")
      define_question_method(name)
    end
  end
end
```

The instance_method_already_implemented?() method is there to prevent involuntary *Monkeypatches (9)*, and I'll return to it in Chapter 9, *Meta-programming Safely*, on page 205. Apart from that, the previous code does little but delegate to one of a few other methods that do the real work, like define_read_method() or define_write_method(). As an example, take a look at define_write_method(). I've marked the most important lines with little arrows:

gems/activerecord-2.3.2/lib/active_record/attribute_methods.rb

```ruby
► def define_write_method(attr_name)
►   evaluate_attribute_method attr_name,
►     "def #{attr_name}=(new_value);write_attribute('#{attr_name}', new_value);end",
```

```
▶         "#{attr_name}="
▶     end

▶     def evaluate_attribute_method(attr_name, method_definition, method_name=attr_name)
        unless method_name.to_s == primary_key.to_s
          generated_methods << method_name
        end

        begin
▶         class_eval(method_definition, __FILE__, __LINE__)
        rescue SyntaxError => err
          generated_methods.delete(attr_name)
          if logger
            logger.warn "Exception occurred during reader method compilation."
            logger.warn "Maybe #{attr_name} is not a valid Ruby identifier?"
            logger.warn err.message
          end
        end
      end
```

The define_write_method() method builds a *String of Code (142)* that is evaluated by class_eval(). For example, if you call description=(), then evaluate_attribute_method() evaluates this String of Code:

```
def description=(new_value);write_attribute('description', new_value);end
```

Thus is the description=() method born. A similar process happens for description(), description?(), and the accessors for all the other database columns.

Here's a recap of what I've covered so far. When you access an attribute for the first time, that attribute is a *Ghost Method (50)*. ActiveRecord:: Base#method_missing() takes this chance to turn the Ghost Method into a real method. While it's there, method_missing() also dynamically defines read, write, and question accessors for all the other database columns. The next time you call that attribute, or another database-backed attribute, you find a real accessor method waiting for you, and you don't have to enter method_missing() anymore.

However, this logic doesn't apply to each and every attribute accessor, as you'll discover by looking at the second half of method_missing().

Attributes That Stay Dynamic

As it turns out, there are cases where ActiveRecord doesn't want to define accessors—for example, for attributes that are not backed by a database column, like calculated fields.

rails/ar_attributes.rb

```
my_query = "tasks.*, (description like '%garage%') as heavy_job"
task = Task.find(:first, :select => my_query)
task.heavy_job?  # => true
```

Attributes like heavy_job can be different for each object, so there's no
point in generating *Dynamic Methods (45)* to access them. The second
half of method_missing() deals with these attributes:

```
def method_missing(method_id, *args, &block)
  # ...

  if self.class.primary_key.to_s == method_name
    id
  elsif md = self.class.match_attribute_method?(method_name)
    attribute_name, method_type = md.pre_match, md.to_s
    if @attributes.include?(attribute_name)
      __send__("attribute#{method_type}", attribute_name, *args, &block)
    else
      super
    end
  elsif @attributes.include?(method_name)
    read_attribute(method_name)
  else
    super
  end
end
```

First, this code checks whether you're accessing the object's identifier (which is called id by default, but you can change it). If you're
not, then you're calling either an attribute accessor or a method that
method_missing() doesn't know how to deal with. In the second case,
method_missing() calls **super**, which raises a NoMethodError.

Now, assume that you're calling an attribute accessor. Is that a read
accessor or some other kind of accessor? It's easy for method_missing() to
recognize read accessors. When you created your ActiveRecord object,
ActiveRecord::Base#initialize looked at the columns in the query's result
set and compiled a list of their names in the @attributes instance variable. If you're calling one of those names (for example, description()),
then method_missing() knows that you're reading an attribute and calls
read_attribute() to retrieve the value of the attribute from the database.

The code that recognizes other types of accessors is slightly more complex. match_attribute_method?() applies a regular expression to check
whether the name of the method you called ends with a known extension (such as ? or =) and returns a MatchData object. Then it uses the

extension to build the name of a "handler method," like attribute?() or attribute=(), and it calls the handler with a *Dynamic Dispatch (41)*.[1] In turn, the handlers call query_attribute() or write_attribute(), which finally access the value of the attribute.

You might be asking yourself why the authors of ActiveRecord jumped through all these hoops. Couldn't they have just added a couple of if branches to deal with question accessors and write accessors separately? The authors were seeking the advantage of a system that's extensible. For example, Rails also recognizes a fourth type of attribute accessor that I haven't mentioned yet. This accessor ends with a _before _type_cast extension, like completed_before_type_cast() (that reads the raw value of the completed column without first converting it to a Ruby boolean). Thanks to the flexible method_missing(), the code that supports these accessors just consists of a _before_type_cast item in the list of recognized extensions and an attribute_before_type_cast handler. This mechanism keeps code duplication to a minimum.

Before I leave dynamic attributes behind, it's a good idea to look at one last piece of ActiveRecord code that closely complements our friend method_missing().

ActiveRecord::Base#respond_to?

In Chapter 2, *Tuesday: Methods*, on page 37, you learned that it's often a good idea to redefine respond_to?() together with method_missing() to keep the two methods consistent.

For example, if I can call my_task.description(), then I expect that my_task. respond_to?(:description) returns true. Here is the redefined respond_to?() of ActiveRecord::Base:

```
gems/activerecord-2.3.2/lib/active_record/attribute_methods.rb
def respond_to?(method, include_private_methods = false)
  method_name = method.to_s
  if super
    return true
  elsif !include_private_methods && super(method, true)
    # If we're here than we haven't found among non-private methods
    # but found among all methods. Which means that given method is private.
    return false
```

---

1. This Dynamic Dispatch uses the _send_() method. See the sidebar on page 64 for a discussion of _send_() vs. send().

```
  elsif !self.class.generated_methods?
    self.class.define_attribute_methods
    if self.class.generated_methods.include?(method_name)
      return true
    end
  end

  if @attributes.nil?
    return super
  elsif @attributes.include?(method_name)
    return true
  elsif md = self.class.match_attribute_method?(method_name)
    return true if @attributes.include?(md.pre_match)
  end
  super
end
```

respond_to?() contains similar code to method_missing(), including code that defines accessors if they haven't been defined yet. So, if you happen to call respond_to?() before you call method_missing() for the first time, you'll still get a reliable answer.

Now you know how ActiveRecord's dynamic attribute accessors are implemented. Let's move on to a second, even more metaprogramming-happy feature: dynamic finders.

8.2 Dynamic Finders

To see an example of dynamic finders in action, look back at our Task class. Here are the database table and the ActiveRecord class again:

`rails/ar_attributes.rb`

```
require 'activerecord'
ActiveRecord::Base.establish_connection :adapter => "sqlite3",
                                        :database => "dbfile"

ActiveRecord::Base.connection.create_table :tasks do |t|
  t.string   :description
  t.boolean  :completed
end

class Task < ActiveRecord::Base; end
```

After you have saved a few objects to the database, you'll probably want to retrieve them. ActiveRecord has many features that help you find objects, including a very flexible find() method:[2]

```
task = Task.find(:first, :conditions => {:completed => true})
task.description      # => "Clean up garage"
```

As flexible as it is, find() can be somewhat verbose when you want to specify a lot of options. ActiveRecord offers an elegant alternative to find() with so-called dynamic finders, which let you specify attributes right in the method name:

```
task = Task.find_by_description('Clean up garage')
task.id      # => 1
```

Dynamic finders are also quite flexible themselves:

```
# Find all completed tasks
Task.find_all_by_completed(true)

# Find the first completed task where description == 'Clean up garage'
Task.find_by_description_and_completed('Clean up garage', true)

# Find the first task where description == 'Water plants',
# or create it if it doesn't exist
Task.find_or_create_by_description('Water plants')

# Find the first task where description == 'Get some sleep',
# and raise an exception if it doesn't exist
Task.find_by_description!('Get some sleep')
```

Aren't dynamic finders beautiful? Next, let's look at the code behind them.

ActiveRecord::Base.method_missing()

You probably wouldn't be surprised if I told you that dynamic finders are *Ghost Methods (50)*, so you have to look for a method_missing(). However, this is not the same method_missing() that I talked about in Section 8.1, *ActiveRecord::Base#method_missing()*, on page 188. Dynamic finders are class methods (you call them on model classes like Task), so you have to look for the class's method_missing(), not the instances' method_missing().

---

2. You can read more about find() and its arguments in Section A.3, *Tricks with Method Arguments*, on page 227.

ActiveRecord::Base.method_missing() is a very long and complex method, so take a deep breath before you look at it. Here it is (I removed the comments, and I split a few lines to make them fit on the page):

```
gems/activerecord-2.3.2/lib/active_record/base.rb
module ActiveRecord
  class Base
    class << self # Class methods
      def method_missing(method_id, *arguments, &block)
        if match = DynamicFinderMatch.match(method_id)
          attribute_names = match.attribute_names
          super unless all_attributes_exists?(attribute_names)
          if match.finder?
            finder = match.finder
            bang = match.bang?
            self.class_eval %{
              def self.#{method_id}(*args)
                options = args.extract_options!
                attributes = construct_attributes_from_arguments(
                  [:#{attribute_names.join(',:')}],
                  args
                )
                finder_options = { :conditions => attributes }
                validate_find_options(options)
                set_readonly_option!(options)

                #{'result = ' if bang}if options[:conditions]
                  with_scope(:find => finder_options) do
                    find(:#{finder}, options)
                  end
                else
                  find(:#{finder}, options.merge(finder_options))
                end
                #{'result || raise(RecordNotFound, "Couldn\'t find #{name} with
                  #{attributes.to_a.collect {|pair|
                    "#{pair.first} = #{pair.second]"}.join(\', \')}")' if bang}
              end
            }, __FILE__, __LINE__
            send(method_id, *arguments)
          elsif match.instantiator?
            instantiator = match.instantiator
            self.class_eval %{
              def self.#{method_id}(*args)
                guard_protected_attributes = false

                if args[0].is_a?(Hash)
                  guard_protected_attributes = true
                  attributes = args[0].with_indifferent_access
                  find_attributes = attributes.slice(
                                  *[:#{attribute_names.join(',:')}])
```

```
        else
          find_attributes = attributes =
                construct_attributes_from_arguments(
                  [:#{attribute_names.join(',:')}], args)
        end

        options = { :conditions => find_attributes }
        set_readonly_option!(options)

        record = find(:first, options)

        if record.nil?
          record = self.new { |r|
            r.send(:attributes=, attributes, guard_protected_attributes)
          }
          #{'yield(record) if block_given?'}
          #{'record.save' if instantiator == :create}
          record
        else
          record
        end
      end
    }, __FILE__, __LINE__
    send(method_id, *arguments, &block)
  end
elsif match = DynamicScopeMatch.match(method_id)
  attribute_names = match.attribute_names
  super unless all_attributes_exists?(attribute_names)
  if match.scope?
    self.class_eval %{
      def self.#{method_id}(*args)
        options = args.extract_options!
        attributes = construct_attributes_from_arguments(
          [:#{attribute_names.join(',:')}], args
        )

        scoped(:conditions => attributes)
      end
    }, __FILE__, __LINE__
    send(method_id, *arguments)
  end
else
  super
end
end

# ...
```

This is as scary a piece of code as you're likely to find in all of Rails. Let's try to make some sense of it. The first branch of the large if deals with the simpler dynamic finders, and the second branch deals with more complex variations such as find_or_create_by_description(). The third branch takes care of *dynamic scopes*, yet another ActiveRecord feature that requires Ghost Methods, unrelated to dynamic finders. I'll focus on the first branch and leave the rest for another book.

This code is somewhat similar in concept to the code that you saw in Section 8.1, *Dynamic Attributes*, on page 187. First, method_missing() ensures that your call is legitimate. The method name starts with *find*, all the attributes you mentioned actually exist, and so on. Then, it defines a real, non-ghost version of the method and calls it with a *Dynamic Dispatch (41)*. The added difficulty here is that the dynamic finder code chooses to define the new method by evaluating a huge *String of Code (142)*.

If you call find_all_by_description_and_completed(), the generated String of Code looks like this:

```
def self.find_all_by_description_and_completed(*args)
  options = args.extract_options!
  attributes = construct_attributes_from_arguments(
    [:description,:completed],
    args
  )
  finder_options = { :conditions => attributes }
  validate_find_options(options)
  set_readonly_option!(options)

  if options[:conditions]
    with_scope(:find => finder_options) do
      find(:all, options)
    end
  else
    find(:all, options.merge(finder_options))
  end
end
```

If you call a different dynamic finder, then you'll get a different String of Code. Here's the String of Code for find_by_description!(), with the differences from the previous String of Code marked by small arrows:

```
▶ def self.find_by_description!(*args)
  options = args.extract_options!
  attributes = construct_attributes_from_arguments(
▶   [:description],
    args
  )
  finder_options = { :conditions => attributes }
  validate_find_options(options)
  set_readonly_option!(options)
```

```
▶    result = if options[:conditions]
       with_scope(:find => finder_options) do
▶        find(:first, options)
       end
     else
▶      find(:first, options.merge(finder_options))
     end
▶    result || raise(RecordNotFound, "Couldn't find #{name} with
▶      #{attributes.to_a.collect {|pair|
▶        "#{pair.first} = #{pair.second}"}.join(', ')}")
   end
```

Yes, this String of Code contains a string that contains yet more code. ActiveRecord::Base.method_missing() is code that writes code that writes code! Before I discreetly sneak away from the complexities of this method_missing(), I'll show you its companion method, respond_to?().

ActiveRecord::Base.respond_to?()

ActiveRecord::Base.respond_to? is consistent with ActiveRecord::Base. method_missing(), in the sense that it knows about dynamic finders and other *Ghost Methods (50)*:

`gems/activerecord-2.3.2/lib/active_record/base.rb`

```
module ActiveRecord
  class Base
    class << self # Class methods
      def respond_to?(method_id, include_private = false)
        if match = DynamicFinderMatch.match(method_id)
          return true if all_attributes_exists?(match.attribute_names)
        elsif match = DynamicScopeMatch.match(method_id)
          return true if all_attributes_exists?(match.attribute_names)
        end

        super
      end

      # ...
```

Compared with the headache-inducing method_missing(), respond_to?() is a pretty tame method. It also provides a nice wrap-up of our look at ActiveRecord's source.

8.3 Lessons Learned

As usual, studying the Rails source taught me a couple of lessons. They're admittedly colored by my own personal biases, but they probably deserve to be shared anyway.

Don't Obsess Over Performance

Perhaps you're wondering how metaprogramming affects performance. After all, Ruby is generally considered a slow language, and you don't want to make it even slower by pulling too many tricks. When and how should you optimize your metaprogramming code?

Look at the performance optimizations behind ActiveRecord's dynamic attributes. Most attribute accessors, in particular those that are backed by database tables, start their lives as *Ghost Methods (50)*. When you access an attribute for the first time, ActiveRecord takes the opportunity to define these accessors as real methods, by evaluating a *String of Code (142)*. However, ActiveRecord doesn't do that for all accessors. Some accessors, such as _before_type_cast accessors and accessors to calculated fields, never become real methods, and they remain ghosts forever.

This is just one of a number of different possible designs. The authors of ActiveRecord had no shortage of alternatives, including the following:

- Never define accessors dynamically, relying on Ghost Methods exclusively.

- Define accessors when you create the object, in the initialize() method.

- Define accessors only for the attribute that is being accessed, not for the other attributes.

- Always define all accessors for each object, including _before_type_cast accessors and accessors to calculated fields.

- Define accessors with define_method() instead of a String of Code.

I don't know about you, but I wouldn't have been able to pick among all of these options just by guessing which ones are faster. How did the authors of ActiveRecord settle on the current design? They probably tried a few alternative designs, and they profiled their code in a real-life system to discover where the performance bottlenecks were. . . and *then* they optimized.

If you look at the current optimized source code, you can try to guess some of the motivations behind it. Calling a real method is faster than calling a Ghost Method, so Rails chooses to define real methods to access attributes. On the other hand, defining a method also takes time, so Rails doesn't do that until it's sure that you really want to access at least one attribute on your ActiveRecord objects. Also, define_ method() is known to be slower than **def** on some Ruby implementations (but not on others!), and that might be one reason why the authors of Rails opted to use Strings of Code to define accessors. None of these considerations is obvious, however. As a rule, you should never optimize your code prematurely—whether it's metaprogramming code or not.

The source code behind dynamic attributes proves that metaprogramming can either impair your system's performance or help you optimize it. For example, if you find out that you're slowing down your system by calling too many Ghost Methods, you can get some performance back by defining *Dynamic Methods (45)*. So, when it comes to metaprogramming, performance generally is no more of an issue than it is with any other code.

However, metaprogramming comes with another trade-off that probably deserves more attention than performance, and that is complexity. Let's talk about that.

Draw Your Own Line

Metaprogramming is like magic, but what kind of magic is it? Is it the gentle, tree-fairy type of magic or the dark, necromancer-in-a-dungeon variation? In other words, how much metaprogramming can you wield before you make a mess of your code and your coding job turns from a pleasure to a chore?

Look back at the ActiveRecord code in this chapter, and you'll probably agree that's there is no hard-and-fast answer to these questions. You have to decide for yourself where the line between "just enough metaprogramming" and "too much metaprogramming" is. All I can give you here is my own personal opinion. For me, the mechanism for dynamic attributes in Rails is relatively simple and clean, considering how complex the feature itself is. On the other hand, I think that the code behind dynamic finders relies too much on evaluating complicated strings, and I wouldn't exactly jump at the chance to maintain that code. All things being equal, I think that I'd draw my own line somewhere between the dynamic attributes code and the dynamic finders code.

Of course, things are not always equal. There are a number of context-related considerations that you should consider when deciding how much metaprogramming is appropriate. The following are a few.

Complexity for Beginners vs. Complexity for Experts

Show the dynamic attributes code in ActiveRecord::Base#method_missing() to a Ruby rookie, and his brain will likely explode. In fact, newcomers to Ruby are often intimidated by the freedom that the language (and especially metaprogramming) gives them, compared to the cozy, railroaded feeling of developing a Java or C# application.

After reading through this book, you're probably not as scared anymore. Sure, there's a bunch of *Ghost Methods (50)* turned into *Dynamic Methods (45)* by evaluating a few *Strings of Code (142)* and then called with a *Dynamic Dispatch (41)*—not such a big deal. For an experienced Ruby coder, metaprogramming code can actually look simple and perfectly readable. Remember, though, that not everybody is as familiar with metaprogramming as you are. Resist the temptation to go wild with magic.

Internal Complexity vs. External Complexity

Sure, the code behind ActiveRecord's dynamic attributes could scare a beginner away. But it allows even a first-time Rails developer to write very terse, elegant code in her application. If you stripped all metaprogramming out of ActiveRecord, you'd end up with a tamer code base, but the library itself wouldn't be nearly as simple to use. For example, you'd miss all the magic methods like task.completed=() or Task.find_by_description().

That's another common trade-off of metaprogramming: by making the insides of your code more complex, you make your library simpler for clients.

Complexity by Terseness vs. Complexity by Duplication

Granted, the Strings of Code in ActiveRecord's dynamic finders look scary.[3] Each String of Code can generate different snippets of code, and it's difficult to track which code is generated in which case.

However, if you removed these Strings of Code, then you'd end up with separate but similar method definitions. That would be a lot of duplicated code, which might be easier to read than a single large String of Code but arguably even harder to maintain. One of the basic principles of the Rails philosophy is "don't repeat yourself," and the dynamic finders code makes a choice that's consistent with that principle.

---

3. Unless you're used to scarier stuff like C macros or C++ templates, that is.

Complexity for Humans vs. Complexity for Tools

If you use it sparingly, metaprogramming can make your code more readable for humans—but it will probably make it less readable for programs such as refactoring engines or code analysis tools. Ruby's extremely dynamic nature makes life very hard for such tools, and that's why some IDE features that work great for static languages (such as finding all the calls to a method, renaming a variable, or jumping from a method usage to its definition) are difficult to implement well in Ruby. Add metaprogramming to the mix, and your poor IDE will be even more confused.[4]

That's one of the fundamental trade-offs of metaprogramming (and, to a point, of dynamic languages). You have the freedom to write expressive, terse code, but to read that code, you need a human brain.

I listed a few trade-offs that you should be aware of when you decide how complex your metaprogramming code can be. There are also techniques and tools that you can leverage to deal with that complexity and to avoid some common metaprogramming pitfalls. Some of these tools, such as unit tests and *Monkeypatch (9)* guards, are the focus of the next chapter.

---

4. Still, code analysis tools are far from useless when working with Ruby. Most modern Ruby IDEs include a refactoring engine, even if it's not as reliable as Eclipse's. Also, code analysis tools such as Flog (by Ryan Davis and Eric Hodel, available on http://ruby.sadi.st/ Flog.html) can effectively spot trouble areas in your program.

Chapter 9

Metaprogramming Safely

Metaprogramming gives you the power to write beautiful, concise code. Metaprogramming also gives you the power to shoot yourself in the foot. Throughout this book, you've seen a fair number of hidden traps, confusing features, and perplexing bugs within the Ruby object model— enough to make even grown-up developers quiver as they write their first lines of metaprogramming code.

With experience, however, comes confidence. Once you learn where the major pitfalls of metaprogramming are, you can easily sidestep them. Even better, you can use metaprogramming to make your code safer and more reliable. This chapter looks at a few techniques that can help you get there.

Your first line of defense against metaprogramming bugs is a trusty suite of unit tests. Here's an example of well-tested metaprogramming code in Rails' ActionPack library.

9.1 Testing Metaprogramming

In the previous two chapters I focused on Rails' ActiveRecord, the library that implements the model part of Model-View-Controller. In this chapter I'll look at ActionPack, the library that takes care of the views and the controllers.

Rails controllers are the components that process the client's HTTP requests. They also call model objects to execute business logics, and they return the HTTP response, usually by rendering an HTML template (the view). All controllers are subclasses of ActionController::Base.

Here's a controller:

```
class GreetController < ActionController::Base
  def hello
    render :text => "Hello, world"
  end

  def goodbye
    render :text => "Goodbye, world"
  end
end
```

The methods in a controller are also called *actions*. In a Rails application, a user executes the hello() action by pointing the browser at a URL like http://my_server/my_rails_app/hello and gets back a page containing the string *Hello, world*. Similarly, a user pointing at http://my_server/my_rails_app/goodbye gets back the string *Goodbye, world*.[1] Sometimes you have code that's common to all the actions in a controller, such as logging code or security code. You can extract that code in a *filter* and ask the controller to execute it before each action (a *before filter*) or after each action (an *after filter*). It's time to watch the filter in action.

Controller Filters

You can create a before filter with a *Class Macro (115)*:

```
class GreetController < ActionController::Base
▶  before_filter :check_password

  def hello
    render :text => "Hello, world"
  end

  def goodbye
    render :text => "Goodbye, world"
  end

▶  private
▶    def check_password
▶      raise 'No password' unless 'my_password' == params[:pwd]
▶    end
end
```

The check_password() method raises an error unless the client added a password to the URL (like http://my_server/my_rails_app/hello?pwd=my_

---

1. In a real Rails application, most actions would be more complicated than this. I've kept the example simple because I want to focus on the controllers themselves, not on the role they take in a Rails application. Also, in a real application, controllers usually inherit from ApplicationController, which, in turn, inherits from ActionController::Base.

password). Being a private method, it's not an action—you can't access it directly at http://my_server/my_rails_app/check_password. Instead, the controller itself executes this method before executing either hello() or goodbye(). So, that's how you can use controller filters. You just call before_filter() (or after_filter()) with the name of a method. In the next section, I'll show you the source code for before filters.

The Source Behind Controller Filters

The before_filter() method is defined in the ActionController::Filters module. This module is rolled into ActionController::Base with a *Class Extension Mixin (164)*, just like the ActiveRecord methods that you saw in Chapter 7, *The Design of ActiveRecord*, on page 171:

`gems/actionpack-2.3.2/lib/action_controller/filters.rb`

```ruby
module ActionController
  module Filters
    def self.included(base)
      base.class_eval do
        extend ClassMethods
        include ActionController::Filters::InstanceMethods
      end
    end

    module ClassMethods
      def append_before_filter(*filters, &block)
        filter_chain.append_filter_to_chain(filters, :before, &block)
      end

      alias :before_filter :append_before_filter
      # ...
    end

    module InstanceMethods
      private
        def run_before_filters(chain, index, nesting)
          while chain[index]
            filter = chain[index]
            break unless filter # end of call chain reached

            filter.call(self)
            # ...
          end
        end

      # ...
    end
  end
end
```

If you go to the original source and look at the append_filter_to_chain()
method, you'll see that it creates filters (objects of class ActionController::Filters::Filter) and inserts them in a "filter chain." Before each action,
the controller executes all the before filters in the chain by calling their
call() methods and passing itself.[2]

If you look around the source code, you'll see that all filters inherit from
ActiveSupport::Callbacks::Callback, a utility class in Rails' ActiveSupport
utility library. Here are a few handpicked lines of code from this class:

`gems/activesupport-2.3.2/lib/active_support/callbacks.rb`

```ruby
module ActiveSupport
  module Callbacks
    class Callback
      attr_reader :kind, :method, :identifier, :options

      def initialize(kind, method, options = {})
        @method       = method
        # ...
      end

      def call(*args, &block)
        evaluate_method(method, *args, &block) if should_run_callback?(*args)
        # ...
      end

      # ...

      private
        def evaluate_method(method, *args, &block)
          case method
            when Symbol
              object = args.shift
              object.send(method, *args, &block)
            when String
              eval(method, args.first.instance_eval { binding })
            when Proc, Method
              method.call(*args, &block)
            else
              if method.respond_to?(kind)
                method.send(kind, *args, &block)
              else
                raise ArgumentError,
                  "Callbacks must be a symbol denoting the method to call, "+
```

---

2. I scrapped most of the code in run_before_filters(), and I slightly edited what was left to
make it clearer. The original method also deals with after filters—and with *around filters*,
another kind of controller filter that I carefully tiptoed around in these pages.

```
                    "a string to be evaluated, a block to be invoked, " +
                    "or an object responding to the callback method."
              end
          end
        end
    end
  end
end
```

An ActiveSupport::Callbacks::Callback can wrap a method name, a callable object, or a string. The wrapped object is then evaluated with a *Dynamic Dispatch (41)* (for method names), a *Deferred Evaluation (86)* (for callable objects), or an eval() (for *Strings of Code (142)*).

Note that although procs and methods carry their own context, symbols and Strings of Code don't, so you need a context to evaluate them. In the case of symbols and strings, Rails' callbacks use call()'s first argument as a context. For example, look at the line that evaluates Strings of Code. It uses a *Context Probe (83)* to extract the bindings from the first argument, and then it uses those bindings as a context to evaluate the string.

I tried to distill this code down to its most essential lines, but the source for filters is actually way more complex than that. You won't be surprised, then, to learn that it's extensively tested. Let's look at a couple of these tests.

Testing Controller Filters

Here's part of ActionController's test suite for filters:

`gems/actionpack-2.3.2/test/controller/filters_test.rb`

```ruby
class FilterTest < Test::Unit::TestCase
  class TestController < ActionController::Base
    before_filter :ensure_login

    def show
      render :inline => "ran action"
    end

    private
      def ensure_login
        @ran_filter ||= []
        @ran_filter << "ensure_login"
      end
  end
```

```ruby
  class PrependingController < TestController
    prepend_before_filter :wonderful_life

    private
      def wonderful_life
        @ran_filter ||= []
        @ran_filter << "wonderful_life"
      end
  end

  def test_prepending_filter
    assert_equal [ :wonderful_life, :ensure_login ],
                 PrependingController.before_filters
  end

  def test_running_filters
    assert_equal %w( wonderful_life ensure_login ),
                 test_process(PrependingController).template.assigns["ran_filter"]
  end

end
```

The TestController contains a single before filter. Simply by defining this class, the test guarantees that before_filter() is correctly defined as a *Class Macro (115)* in ActionController::Base.

The test also defines a subclass of TestController called PrependingController, using the prepend_before_filter() Class Macro, which is similar to before_filter(), but it inserts the filter at the beginning of the filter chain, rather than at the end. So, even though :wonderful_life is defined after the :ensure_login filter, it's supposed to be executed first. Both filters append their own names to a @ran_filter array, initialized with a *Nil Guard (227)* by the first filter that's executed.

Now I'll move past the helper classes and on to the tests themselves. Among the many unit tests in FilterTest, I picked two that test the features in PrependingController. The first test, test_prepending_filter(), verifies that the Class Macros add the filters to the chain in the right order. The second test, test_running_filters(), simulates a client call to a controller action. It does that by calling a helper method named test_process(), which I'll show you in a few moments. This method then copies the instance variables of the controller into the response, so the test can just look at the response to find out which filters were executed.

Even if the code in controller filters uses metaprogramming, its unit tests look exactly like the tests you'd write for any regular piece of code. Before you start wondering what these tests have to do with meta-programming at all, I'll show you the test_process() helper method:

gems/actionpack-2.3.2/test/controller/filters_test.rb

```
def test_process(controller, action = "show")
  ActionController::Base.class_eval {
    include ActionController::ProcessWithTest
  } unless ActionController::Base < ActionController::ProcessWithTest
  request = ActionController::TestRequest.new
  request.action = action
  controller = controller.new if controller.is_a?(Class)
  controller.process_with_test(request, ActionController::TestResponse.new)
end
```

FilterTest#test_process() reopens ActionController::Base to include a helper module called ActionController::ProcessWithTest. Then it creates a mock HTTP request, binds it to an action (by default show(), which all controllers inherit from ActionController::Base), creates a new controller, and asks the controller to process that request. If you look at ActionController::ProcessWithTest, you'll see more juicy metaprogramming action:

gems/actionpack-2.3.2/lib/action_controller/test_process.rb

```
module ActionController
  module ProcessWithTest
    def self.included(base)
      base.class_eval { attr_reader :assigns }
    end

    def process_with_test(*args)
      process(*args).tap { set_test_assigns }
    end

    private
    def set_test_assigns
      @assigns = {}
      (instance_variable_names - self.class.protected_instance_variables).
        each do |var|
          name, value = var[1..-1], instance_variable_get(var)
          @assigns[name] = value
          response.template.assigns[name] = value if response
        end
    end
  end
end
```

ActionController::ProcessWithTest is a pretty wild metaprogramming party. It uses a *Class Extension Mixin (164)* and an *Open Class (7)* to define an assigns attribute on its inclusor. It also defines a process_with_test()

method that delegates to ActionController::Base#process(), which, in turn, catches the request and forwards it to the appropriate action.

However, process_with_test() also taps set_test_assigns() in the result before returning it.[3] If you're using Ruby 1.9 or greater, tap() is one of the standard methods in Object. If you're using an earlier version of Ruby, then Rails defines tap() for you:

```
gems/activesupport-2.3.2/lib/active_support/core_ext/object/misc.rb
def tap
  yield self
  self
end unless Object.respond_to?(:tap)
```

Now look at set_test_assigns(). The second line uses two reflection methods: instance_variable_names(), which returns all the instance variables in the controller, and protected_instance_variables(), which returns only those variables that are defined by ActionController::Base.[4] By subtracting the two arrays, this code gets only those instance variables that are defined right in the controller class, excluding the ones that are defined in the controller's superclass.

Then set_test_assigns() iterates through all these instance variables. It gets the value of each variable with instance_variable_get() and stores both the name of the variable (minus the @ at the beginning) and its value in the HTTP response. It also stores the name and value in an @assigns variable to cater to cases where the HTTP response is nil. In the end, this code allows a test class like FilterTest to call a controller action and then make assertions on the controller's instance variables, all in a single line—just like FilterTest#test_running_filters() does.

As you can see, you can use metaprogramming in your unit tests to reach hard-to-test areas of your code (either metaprogramming code or regular code) and ensure that it works as expected. However, there is one particular spell in this book that you should handle with care, even in the presence of good tests.

---

3. The tap() method is a *Self Yield (231)*. You can read more about tap() in Section A.4, *The tap() Example*, on page 232.

4. Both instance_variable_names() and protected_instance_variables() are defined by Rails. You might be wondering why Rails defines a method like Object#instance_variable_names() when Ruby already has Object#instance_variables(). There is some trickery going on here. Object#instance_variables() returns either strings or symbols depending on the version of Ruby that you're using. But Rails' instance_variable_names() always returns strings, making this code compatible with all versions of Ruby.

9.2 Defusing Monkeypatches

In Chapter 1, *Monday: The Object Model*, on page 3, you learned that all classes and modules, including classes and modules in Ruby's core library, can be reopened as *Open Class (7)*:

```
rails/monkeypatch.rb
"abc".capitalize  # => "Abc"

class String
  def capitalize
    upcase
  end
end

"abc".capitalize  # => "ABC"
```

Open Classes are useful but are also dangerous. By reopening a class, you can change its existing features, like the String#capitalize() method shown earlier. This technique (also called a *Monkeypatch (9)*) presents a few problems that you should be aware of.

First, a Monkeypatch is *global*. If you change a method on String, all the strings in your system will see that method. Second, a Monkeypatch is *invisible*. Once you've redefined String#capitalize(), it's difficult to notice that the method was changed. If your code, or a library that you're using, relies on the original behavior of capitalize(), that code will break—and because Monkeypatches are global, you might have trouble spotting where the problem is and finding out which code modified which class.

For all these reasons, you might be tempted to steer clear of Monkeypatches altogether. Doing that, however, takes away most of Ruby's dynamic steam. Instead, as I mentioned in Section 1.2, *Monkey See, Monkey Patch*, on page 9, you can apply a few techniques to make Monkeypatches a bit safer. I'll show you some techniques next, taking examples from the Rails source.

Making Monkeypatches Explicit

One reason why *Monkeypatches (9)* are dangerous is that they're difficult to spot. If you make them a tad more visible, you'll have an easier time tracking them. For example, instead of defining methods straight in the *Open Class (7)*, you can define methods in a module and then include the module in the Open Class. At least this way you'll be able to see the module among the Open Class' ancestors.

Rails' ActiveSupport library uses modules to extend core library classes like String. First it defines additional methods in modules like ActiveSupport::CoreExtensions::String:

```
gems/activesupport-2.3.2/lib/active_support/core_ext/string/filters.rb
module ActiveSupport
  module CoreExtensions
    module String
      module Filters
        def squish # ...
        def squish! # ...
      end
    end
  end
end
```

Then ActiveSupport includes all the extension modules in String:

```
gems/activesupport-2.3.2/lib/active_support/core_ext/string.rb
class String
  include ActiveSupport::CoreExtensions::String::Access
  include ActiveSupport::CoreExtensions::String::Conversions
▶ include ActiveSupport::CoreExtensions::String::Filters
  include ActiveSupport::CoreExtensions::String::Inflections
  include ActiveSupport::CoreExtensions::String::StartsEndsWith
  include ActiveSupport::CoreExtensions::String::Iterators
  include ActiveSupport::CoreExtensions::String::Behavior
  include ActiveSupport::CoreExtensions::String::Multibyte
end
```

Now imagine that you're writing code in your Rails application, and you want to track all the modules that define new methods on String. You can get the complete list of those modules by calling String.ancestors():

```
[String, ActiveSupport::CoreExtensions::String::Multibyte,
ActiveSupport::CoreExtensions::String::Behavior,
▶ ActiveSupport::CoreExtensions::String::Filters,
ActiveSupport::CoreExtensions::String::Conversions,
ActiveSupport::CoreExtensions::String::Access,
ActiveSupport::CoreExtensions::String::Inflections,
Enumerable, Comparable, Object, ActiveSupport::Dependencies::Loadable,
Base64::Deprecated, Base64, Kernel, BasicObject]
```

Although modules don't really solve the problems with Monkeypatches, they do a good job making the patching more visible so that you can at least track Monkeypatches more easily. As I argued in Section 7.3, *Think in Modules*, on page 185, modules are your friends.[5]

---

5. Modules are also useful when you define *Singleton Methods (112)*. Look back at the module-based mechanism in Chapter 7, *The Design of ActiveRecord*, on page 171.

However, modules alone won't protect you from the most dangerous types of Monkeypatches—those that happen by mistake. You saw an example of this in Section 1.2, *Monkey See, Monkey Patch*, on page 9, where you and Bill meant to define a new method and ended up redefining an existing one. Take a look at how Rails attempts to prevent this kind of accident.

Preventing Monkeypatches

In ActiveRecord, there's one place in particular where involuntary *Monkeypatches (9)* are likely to occur: the source code of dynamic attributes that I exposed in Chapter 8, *Inside ActiveRecord*, on page 187.

Imagine having a table with a column called save. ActiveRecord is supposed to generate *Dynamic Methods (45)* like save() and save=() on your model class. But ActiveRecord::Base already has a save() method, so you'd end up overriding the original save() method with an attribute getter!

ActiveRecord avoids this problem by staying on the safe side. Before defining a Dynamic Method, it checks that no method by the same name already exists. This check happens in the instance_method_already_implemented?() method (that's a mouthful, so let's call it imai?() for short). ActiveRecord calls this method before generating each dynamic accessor:

gems/activerecord-2.3.2/lib/active_record/attribute_methods.rb

```ruby
module ActiveRecord
  module AttributeMethods
    def instance_method_already_implemented?(method_name)
      method_name = method_name.to_s
      return true if method_name =~ /^id(=$|\?$|$)/
      @_defined_class_methods ||=
        ancestors.first(ancestors.index(ActiveRecord::Base)).sum([]) { |m|
          m.public_instance_methods(false) |
          m.private_instance_methods(false) |
          m.protected_instance_methods(false)
        }.map(&:to_s).to_set
      @@_defined_activerecord_methods ||=
        (ActiveRecord::Base.public_instance_methods(false) |
         ActiveRecord::Base.private_instance_methods(false) |
         ActiveRecord::Base.protected_instance_methods(false)
        ).map(&:to_s).to_set
```

ActiveRecord defines most of its methods in modules and then uses *Class Extension Mixins (164)* to turn those methods into class methods on ActiveRecord::Base. As an alternative, ActiveRecord could have added the methods straight into ActiveRecord::Base's eigenclass, but modules make the code easier to understand and change.

```
        raise DangerousAttributeError,
            "#{method_name} is defined by ActiveRecord" if
                @@_defined_activerecord_methods.include?(method_name)
            @_defined_class_methods.include?(method_name)
      end

      # ...
```

This is a busy little method. Let's try to understand it. First, this code checks that the attribute accessor that is about to be defined isn't named id(), id=(), or id?(). If it does have one of these names, then imai?() returns true, which means "Don't bother defining this method. It already exists."

Then, imai?() initializes two variables with a couple of *Nil Guards (227)*. Both variables contain a set of method names that have been converted to strings with a *Symbol To Proc (234)*. To understand the two variables, remember that this code is going to be called on a subclass of ActiveRecord::Base.

The first variable, @_defined_class_methods, contains the methods defined by the current model class and all its ancestors, up to and excluding ActiveRecord::Base. The second variable is a class variable called @@_defined_activerecord_methods, which contains the instance methods defined by ActiveRecord::Base itself. Being a class variable, it's shared by all subclasses of ActiveRecord::Base. (Note that all calls to *_instance_ methods() methods have a false argument, which means "Ignore inherited methods.")

Now imai?() knows all the instance methods of this particular subclass of ActiveRecord::Base. If the name of the method being generated clashes with one of the existing methods in ActiveRecord::Base, then you have a dangerous column name in your database (like save). In this case, instance_method_already_implemented?() raises a DangerousAttributeError. If the name of the method clashes with one of the methods in an ActiveRecord::Base's subclass, then imai?() assumes that you overrode the attribute accessor with your own custom code, and it returns true. Otherwise, imai?() returns false, and ActiveRecord generates the accessor for this attribute.

I've gone through one example of code that guards against Monkeypatches while generating dynamic attributes. However, code like this cannot protect you from your own Monkeypatches—those that happen as you define your own methods. Here's one possible strategy to defend against that kind of Monkeypatch.

How Rake Prevents Monkeypatches

Rake, the popular build system, avoids involuntary *Monkeypatches (9)* with a *Class Macro (115)* called Module#rake_extension():[6]

`gems/rake-0.8.7/lib/rake.rb`

```ruby
class Module
  def rake_extension(method)
    if method_defined?(method)
      $stderr.puts "WARNING: Possible conflict with Rake extension:\
#{self}##{method} already exists"
    else
      yield
    end
  end
end
```

Rake uses rake_extension() when it wants to add methods to an *Open Class (7)*. For example, here's how Rake defines methods such as String#ext() and String#pathmap():

```ruby
class String
  rake_extension("ext") do
    def ext(newext='')
      # ...
    end
  end

  rake_extension("pathmap") do
    def pathmap(spec=nil, &block)
      # ...
    end
  end

  # ...
end
```

The idea is that rake_extension() checks first to see whether a method exists before going ahead and defining it. If you're about to mistakenly redefine a method that already exists, rake_extension() raises a warning:

`rails/rake_patch.rb`

```ruby
require 'rake'

class String
  rake_extension("reverse") do
```

---

6. Rake is not really a part of Rails, so I'm cheating a little by talking about it here. However, Rails depends on Rake, so if you installed Rails, you already have the Rake source code in your gems folder.

```
      def reverse
        'my_reverse'
      end
    end
  end
end
```

⇒ WARNING: Possible conflict with Rake extension: String#reverse already exists

The rake_extension() method also protects Rake from accidentally modifying Ruby's core libraries in the future. If a future version of Ruby ever defines a String#pathmap method, rake_extension() will warn you before you get an involuntary Monkeypatch.

Although Rake's approach certainly works, it requires discipline on the programmer's part. If you don't use rake_extension() each and every time you want to define a new method on an *Open Class (7)*, you'll bypass the safety check entirely. In the end, your own careful approach and unit tests are the best defense against involuntary Monkeypatches.

Having navigated large amounts of code here, it's time to wrap up what I've covered in this chapter.

9.3 Lessons Learned

By looking at Rails' source code, its unit tests, and the way it attempts to avoid involuntary Monkeypatches, you learned two very important lessons. Here they are.

Test Your Metaprogramming Code

Metaprogramming code can get complex, but you can manage this complexity with a tool that you already know and love: unit testing. No matter how "meta," code is still code, and unit tests can go a long way in helping you write code that's clean and error-free.

Compared to testing regular code, testing metaprogramming code introduces an additional dimension. Remember, metaprogramming is "code that writes code," so you might have to test it at two different levels: you need to test the code you write, and you should also test the code that your code writes. For example, take a *Class Macro (115)* like before_filter(). If you wrote this Class Macro yourself, then you'd have two features to test for:

- You need to ensure that before_filter() is available in controllers.

- You should check that filters defined with before_filter() are executed before every action.

The good news in the case of before_filter() (and in many other cases) is that by testing the second feature you also indirectly test the first feature. To write a test for before_filter(), you need to define a controller class that uses it—and by defining that class, you also test that before_filter() is available in controllers.

The lesson here is this: test your metaprogramming code even more carefully than you test any other code, but use the same techniques. This lesson, however, is just part of a deeper lesson, which has to do with the meaning of metaprogramming.

Metaprogramming Is Just Programming

When I started learning metaprogramming, it looked like magic. I felt like leaving my usual programming behind to enter a new world—a world that was surprising, exciting, and sometimes a bit scary.

As I finish writing this book, the feeling of magic is still there. However, I realize now that in practice there is no hard line separating metaprogramming from plain old vanilla programming. Metaprogramming is just another powerful set of coding tools that you can wield to write code that's clean, safe, and well tested.

I'll go out on a limb to make a bolder assertion: with Ruby, the distinction between metaprogramming and regular code is fuzzy—and, ultimately, pointless. Once you have an in-depth understanding of the language, you'd have a hard time deciding which techniques and idioms are "meta" and which ones are plain old programming.

In fact, metaprogramming is so deeply engrained in Ruby that you can barely write an idiomatic Ruby program without using a few metaprogramming spells. The language actually *expects* that you'll manipulate the language constructs, tweak the object model, reopen classes, define methods dynamically, and manage scopes with blocks.

As Bill would say in his Zen moments, "There is no such thing as metaprogramming. It's just programming all the way through!"

Part III

Appendixes

Common Idioms

This appendix is a mixed bag of popular Ruby idioms. They aren't really "meta," so they don't fit into the main story of this book. However, they're so common and they're the foundation of so many meta-programming spells that you'll probably want to get familiar with them.

A.1   Mimic Methods

Much of Ruby's appeal comes from its flexible syntax. You can find an example of this flexiblity even in the most basic program:

```
puts 'Hello, world!'
```

Newcomers to Ruby often mistake puts for a language keyword, when it's actually a method. If you usually leave out the parentheses when calling puts() so that it doesn't look like a method, reinsert the parentheses, and puts()'s nature becomes obvious:

```
puts('Hello, world!')
```

Thanks to disguised method calls such as this one, Ruby manages to provide many useful function-like methods while keeping the core of the language relatively small and uncluttered.

This simple idea of dropping parentheses from method calls is used quite often by expert coders. Sometimes you'll want to keep the parentheses because they make a method's nature obvious or maybe because the parser is requiring the parentheses to make sense of a complex line of code. Other times, you'll want to drop the parentheses to make the code cleaner or to make a method look like a keyword, as is the case with puts().

For another example of flexible syntax, think of object attributes, which are actually methods in disguise:

```
common_idioms/mimic_methods.rb
class C
  def my_attribute=(value)
    @p = value
  end

  def my_attribute
    @p
  end
end

obj = C.new
obj.my_attribute = 'some value'
obj.my_attribute    # => "some value"
```

Writing obj.my_attribute = 'some value' is the same as writing obj.my_attribute=('some value'), but it looks cleaner.

What should we call disguised methods such as my_attribute() and my_attribute=()? Let's take a cue from zoology: an animal that disguises itself as another species is said to employ "mimicry." Therefore, a method call that disguises itself as something else, such as puts or obj.my_attribute=, can be called a *Mimic Method*.

Spell: Mimic Method

Mimic Methods are a very simple concept, but the more you look into Ruby, the more you find creative uses for this concept. For example, access modifiers such as private() and protected() are Mimic Methods, as are *Class Macros (115)* such as attr_reader(). Popular libraries provide further examples. Here is one such example.

The Camping Example

The following snippet of code comes from an application written with the Camping web framework.[1] It binds the /help URL to a specific controller action:

```
class Help < R '/help'
    def get
      # rendering for HTTP GET...
```

Class Help seems to inherit from a class named R. But what's that quirky little string right after R? You might assume that Ruby would

---

1. Camping is a library written by "_why the lucky stiff." You can install it with gem install camping.

Attribute Trouble

Object attributes (which I describe in Section A.1, *Mimic Methods*, on page 223) contain a hidden trap for the unsuspecting programmer:

common_idioms/attribute_trouble.rb

```ruby
class MyClass
  attr_accessor :my_attr

  def initialize_attributes
    my_attr = 10
  end
end

obj = MyClass.new
obj.initialize_attributes
obj.my_attr                  # => nil
```

This result is probably not what you expected. The problem is that the code in initialize_attributes() is ambiguous. Ruby has no way of knowing whether this code is an assignment to a local variable called my_attr or a call to a *Mimic Method (224)* called my_attr=(). When in doubt, Ruby defaults to the first option. It defines a variable called my_attr, which immediately falls out of scope.

To steer clear of this problem, use **self** explicitly whenever you assign an attribute to the current object:

```ruby
class MyClass
  def initialize_attributes
    self.my_attr = 10
  end
end

obj.initialize_attributes
obj.my_attr                  # => 10
```

By using **self**, you remove the ambiguity and make it clear to Ruby that you're calling a Mimic Method, not assigning a value to a local variable.

simply refuse this syntax, until you realize that R() is actually a Mimic Method that takes a string and returns an instance of Class. That is the class that Help actually inherits from.[2] Thanks to creative tricks such as this one, Camping feels less like a Ruby web framework and more like a domain-specific language for web development. In general, this is a good thing, as I argue in Appendix B, on page 235.

A.2 Nil Guards

Most Ruby beginners looking through someone else's code are perplexed by this exotic idiom:

```
common_idioms/nil_guards.rb
```

```
a ||= []
```

In this example, the value to the right happens to be an empty array, but it could be any assignable value. The ||= is actually a syntax shortcut for the following:

```
a = a || []
```

To understand this code, you need to understand the details of the "or" operator (||). Superficially, the || operator simply returns true if either of the two operands is true—but there is some subtlety to this. Here's the way that || actually works.

Remember that any value is considered true with the exception of nil and false. If the first operand is true, the || operator simply returns it; if it's false, the || operator returns the second operand instead. This means the result will be true unless both operands are false, which is consistent with the intuitive notion of an "or" operator.

Now you can see that the previous code has the same effect as this:

```
if a != nil
  a = a
else
  a = []
end
```

You can translate this code as this: "If a is nil, then make it an empty array; if it's not, just leave it alone." In such cases, experienced Ruby

---

2. If the notion of a method returning a class sounds strange to you, consider that Ruby classes are just objects. You can find more information about classes as objects in Chapter 1, *Monday: The Object Model*, on page 3.

coders generally consider the || operator more elegant and readable than an **if**. Of course, you're not limited to arrays. You can use the same idiom to initialize just about anything. This idiom is sometimes called a *Nil Guard*, because it's used to make sure that a variable is not nil.

Spell: Nil Guard

Nil Guards are also used quite often to initialize instance variables. Look at this class:

```
class C
  def initialize
    @a = []
  end

  def elements
    @a
  end
end
```

By using a Nil Guard, you can rewrite the same code more succinctly:

```
class C
  def elements
    @a ||= []
  end
end
```

The previous code initializes the instance variable at the latest possible moment, when it's actually accessed. This idiom is called a *Lazy Instance Variable*. Sometimes, as in the earlier example, you manage to replace the whole initialize() method with one or more Lazy Instance Variables.

Spell: Lazy Instance Variable

A.3 Tricks with Method Arguments

When it comes to method arguments, Ruby has a few interesting tricks up its sleeve. Here's a summary of the most popular tricks.

Named Arguments

When you call a method in Ruby, you have to pass the arguments in a specific order. If the order is wrong, then you introduce a bug:

```
def login(name, password, message)
  # ...
end

login('bill', 'just doing some administration', 'pwd2341') # Bug!
```

This kind of mistake is quite common when you have a long list of arguments. Some languages provide a feature called *Named Arguments*, which allows you to set arguments by their names rather than their position. Named Arguments can make your code more explicit and less likely to be wrong.

Ruby doesn't come with this feature, but it sports a different feature with a similar effect. If you call a method with a sequence of key-value pairs (using the "arrow" syntax), all the pairs will be collected into a single hash argument:

```
common_idioms/named_arguments.rb
def my_method(args)
  args
end
```

```
my_method(:a => 'X', :b => 3, :c => 'Y') # => {:c=>"Y", :a=>"X", :b=>3}
```

Spell: Named Arguments

This is Ruby's way of implementing *Named Arguments*. It's actually the same as passing a hash to the method, but the syntax is more concise, because you don't have the confusing curly braces. The receiving method must still take responsibility for extracting the arguments from the hash.

Named arguments can easily be used together with a "block" argument (we described the block argument in Section 3.5, *The & Operator*, on page 87). You can also mix Named Arguments and regular arguments, but regular arguments must come first in a method's signature. Also, remember that Named Arguments are less explicit than regular arguments, because with Named Arguments you cannot see the list of arguments just by looking at the method declaration.

Argument Arrays and Default Values

The * operator collects multiple arguments in a single array:

```
common_idioms/argument_array.rb
def my_method(*args)
  args
end
```

```
my_method(1, '2', 'three')  # => [1, "2", "three"]
```

> ### Symbols As Argument Names
>
> A set of Named Arguments is a simple hash, where the keys are the arguments' names. You can use any object you like as a key, but just as ActiveRecord does, most libraries use symbols for that purpose. This is a good idea for two reasons. First, as we mention in the sidebar on page 42, symbols are conventionally used as the names of programming entities in general, which makes them a good choice for the names of arguments. Second, symbols are immutable, which makes them ideal as hash keys.
>
> This convention is common enough that version 1.9 of Ruby includes a more concise syntax specifically for Named Arguments that use symbols as argument names. On older versions of Ruby, you'd write something like the following:
>
> ```
> login(:name => 'bill', :code => 45, :password => 'pwd2341')
> ```
>
> Starting with Ruby 1.9, you can now write the same method call as follows:
>
> ```
> login(name: 'bill', code: 45, password: 'pwd2341')
> ```

This idiom is called an *Argument Array*. Note that you can have only one Argument Array per method.[3] *Spell: Argument Array*

Ruby also supports default values for arguments:

`common_idioms/default_arguments.rb`

```
def my_method(x, y = "a default value")
  "#{x} and #{y}"
end

my_method("a value")  # => "a value and a default value"
```

You've learned a set of useful techniques. Now, you can learn how to mix them together.

Mixing Argument Idioms

It can be somewhat difficult to mix default values, Argument Arrays, and Named Arguments in the same method, because they all want to

---

3. In Ruby 1.8 and earlier, the Argument Array also had to be the last argument in the method, not considering the final "block" argument.

come last in the arguments list. However, Named Arguments and Argument Arrays get along quite well. Programmers often use them together to write flexible methods that can take many different combinations of arguments. Here's an example of an Argument Array where the last element in the array is also a hash of Named Arguments:

`common_idioms/mixed_arguments.rb`

```
def my_method(*args)
  args
end
```

```
my_method(:x, :y => 1, :z => 'A')  # => [:x, {:y=>1, :z=>"A"}]
```

Let's look at another example of this mixed approach.

The Rails find() Example

ActiveRecord, the popular database access library that's also part of Rails, includes a very powerful find() method.[4] You can call find() with many different combinations of arguments:

```
Person.find(:first)
Person.find(:first, :order => "created_on DESC", :offset => 5)
Person.find(:last, :conditions => [ "user_name = ?", user_name])
Person.find(:all, :offset => 10, :limit => 10)
Person.find(:all, :conditions => [ "name IN (?)", names], :limit => 5)
```

All this flexibility comes at a price: it makes the receiving code more complex. With regular arguments, the receiving method can rest assured that the arguments are actually there (although they might have invalid values). With Argument Arrays and Named Arguments, the method itself has to parse the arguments list and possibly even validate the arguments. ActiveRecord's find() does exactly that and finally delegates to one of a number of more specialized methods:

```
def find(*args)
  options = args.extract_options!
  validate_find_options(options)
  set_readonly_option!(options)

  case args.first
    when :first then find_initial(options)
    when :last  then find_last(options)
    when :all   then find_every(options)
    else             find_from_ids(args, options)
  end
end
```

---

4. ActiveRecord was originally written by David Heinemeier Hansson. You can install it with gem install activerecord.

The find() method accepts both Argument Arrays and Named Arguments. That's how it manages to support both flag-like arguments (such as :first and :all) and Named Arguments with values (such as :order and :offset).

A.4 Self Yield

When you pass a block to a method, you expect the method to call back to the block through **yield**. A useful twist on callbacks is that an object can also pass *itself* to the block. This next example (that comes from the RubyGems package manager) helps explain how this can be useful.

The RubyGems Example

When you create a RubyGems Specification, typically you initialize its attributes like this:

```
spec = Gem::Specification.new
spec.name = "My Gem name"
spec.version = "0.0.1"
# ...
```

Alternately, you can pass a block containing your initialization code to Specification.new():

```
spec = Gem::Specification.new do |s|
  s.name = "My Gem name"
  s.version = "0.0.1"
  # ...
end
```

I prefer this second style, because it makes it clear that all the statements in the block are focusing on the same object. If you track the RubyGems source code, you'll see that Specification.new() passes the block on to initialize(), where the newborn Specification can **yield** itself to the block:

```
module Gem
  class Specification
    def initialize
      yield self if block_given?
      # ...
```

This simple idiom is known as a *Self Yield*. For another, more creative example of this, you can check out the tap() method.

Spell: Self Yield

The tap() Example

In Ruby, it's common to find long chains of method calls such as this:

```
common_idioms/tap.rb
```

```ruby
['a', 'b', 'c'].push('d').shift.upcase.next # => "B"
```

Chains of calls are frowned upon in most languages (and sometimes referred to as "train wrecks"). Ruby's terse syntax makes call chains generally more readable, but they still present a problem: if you have an error somewhere along the chain, it can be difficult to track down the error.

For example, assume that you find a bug in the previous code, and you suspect that the call to shift() is not returning what you expect. To confirm your suspicions, you have to break the chain and print out the result of shift() (or set a breakpoint in your debugger):

```ruby
temp = ['a', 'b', 'c'].push('d').shift
puts temp
x = temp.upcase.next
```

⇒   a

This is a clumsy way to debug your code. If you don't want to split the call chain, you can use the tap() method to slip intermediate operations into the middle of a call chain:

```ruby
['a', 'b', 'c'].push('d').shift.tap {|x| puts x }.upcase.next
```

⇒   a

The tap() method was introduced by Ruby 1.9. If you haven't upgraded to Ruby 1.9 yet, you can easily implement tap() yourself:

```ruby
class Object
  def tap
    yield self
    self
  end
end
```

A.5 Symbol#to_proc()

This exotic spell is popular among black-belt Ruby programmers. When I stumbled upon this spell for the first time, I had trouble understanding the reasoning behind it. It's easier to get there by taking one small step at a time.

Look at this code:

`common_idioms/symbol_to_proc.rb`

```
names = ['bob', 'bill', 'heather']
names.map {|name| name.capitalize }   # => ["Bob", "Bill", "Heather"]
```

Focus on the block—a simple "one-call block" that takes a single argument and calls a single method on that argument. One-call blocks are very common in Ruby, especially (but not exclusively) when you're dealing with arrays.

In a language such as Ruby, which prides itself on being succinct and to the point, even a one-call block looks verbose. Why do you have to go through the trouble of creating a block, with curly braces and all, just to ask Ruby to call a method? The idea of Symbol#to_proc() is that you can replace a one-call block with a shorter construct. Let's start with the smallest piece of information you need, which is the name of the method that you want to call, as a symbol:

```
:capitalize
```

You want to convert the symbol to a one-call block like this:

```
{|x| x.capitalize }
```

As a first step, you can add a method to the Symbol class, which converts the symbol to a Proc object:

```
class Symbol
►   def to_proc
►     Proc.new {|x| x.send(self) }
►   end
end
```

See how this method works? If you call it on, say, the :capitalize symbol, it returns a proc that takes an argument and calls capitalize() on the argument. Now you can use to_proc() and the & operator to convert a symbol to a Proc and then to a block:

```
names = ['bob', 'bill', 'heather']
► names.map(&:capitalize.to_proc)   # => ["Bob", "Bill", "Heather"]
```

You can make this code even shorter. As it turns out, you can apply the & operator to any object, and it will take care of converting that object to a Proc by calling to_proc(). (You didn't think we picked the name of the to_proc() method randomly, did you?) So, you can simply write the following:

```
names = ['bob', 'bill', 'heather']
► names.map(&:capitalize)   # => ["Bob", "Bill", "Heather"]
```

Spell: Symbol To Proc   That's the trick known as *Symbol To Proc*. Neat, huh?

If you're running Ruby 1.9, you don't even need to define the to_proc() method on Symbol, because it's already there. In fact, Ruby 1.9's implementation of Symbol#to_proc also supports blocks with more than one argument, which are required by methods such as inject():

```
# without Symbol#to_proc:
[1, 2, 5].inject(0) {|memo, obj| memo + obj }   # => 8

# with Symbol#to_proc:
[1, 2, 5].inject(0, &:+)  # => 8

# cool!
```

Domain-Specific Languages

Domain-specific languages are a popular topic these days. They overlap somewhat with metaprogramming, so you'll probably want to know a thing or two about them.

B.1 The Case for Domain-Specific Languages

Are you old enough to remember Zork? It was one of the first "text adventures": text-based computer games that were popular in the early 80s. Here are the first few lines from a game of Zork:

```
⇒   West of house
    You are standing in an open field west of a
    white house, with a boarded front door.
    You see a small mailbox here.
⇐   open mailbox
⇒   Opening the small mailbox reveals a leaflet.
⇐   take leaflet
⇒   Taken.
```

Suppose you have to write a text adventure as your next job. What language would you write it in?

You'd probably pick a language that's good at manipulating strings and supports object-oriented programming. But whatever language you chose, you'd still have a gap between that language and the problem you're trying to solve. This probably happens in your daily programming job as well. For example, many large Java applications deal with money, but Money is not a standard Java type. That means each application has to reinvent money, usually as a class.

In the case of our adventure game, you have to deal with entities such as rooms and items. No general-purpose language supports these entities directly. How would you like a language that's specifically targeted to text adventures? Given such a language, you could write code like this:

```
me: Actor
    location = westOfHouse
;

westOfHouse : Room 'West of house'
    "You are standing in an open field west of
     a white house, with a boarded front door."
;

+ mailbox : OpenableContainer 'mailbox' 'small mailbox';

++ leaflet : Thing 'leaflet' 'leaflet';
```

This is not a mocked-up example—it's real code. It's written in a language called TADS, specifically designed for creating "interactive fiction" (today's fancier name for text adventures). TADS is an example of a *domain-specific language* (DSL), a language that focuses on a specific problem domain.

The opposite of a DSL is a *general-purpose language* (GPL) such as C++ or Ruby. You can use a GPL to tackle a wide variety of problems, even if it might be more suited to some problems than others. Whenever you write a program, it's up to you to choose between a flexible GPL or a focused DSL.

Let's assume that you decide to go down the DSL route. How would you proceed then?

Using DSLs

If you want a DSL for your own specific problem, you might get lucky. There are hundreds of DSLs around, focusing on a wide range of domains. The UNIX shell is a DSL for gluing command-line utilities together. Microsoft's VBA was designed to extend Excel and other Microsoft Office applications. The *make* language is a DSL focused on building C programs, and *Ant* is an XML-based equivalent of make for Java programs. Some of these languages are very limited in scope, while others are flexible enough to cross the line into GPL-dom.

What if you can't find a ready-made DSL that fits the domain you're working in? In that case, you can write your own DSL and then use that

DSL to write your program. You could say that this process—writing a DSL and then using it—is another take on metaprogramming. It can be a slippery path, though. You'll probably need to define a grammar for your language with a system such as ANTLR or Yacc, which are themselves DSLs for writing language parsers. As the scope of your problem expands, your humble little language can grow into a GPL before you even realize it. At that point, your leisurely foray into language writing will have escalated into an exhausting marathon.

To avoid these difficulties, you can pick a different route. Rather than writing a full-fledged DSL, you can bend a GPL into something resembling a DSL for your specific problem. The next section shows you how.

B.2 Internal and External DSLs

Let's see an example of a DSL that's actually a GPL in disguise. Here's a snippet of Ruby code that uses the Markaby library to generate HTML:[1]

```ruby
dsl/markaby_example.rb
require 'rubygems'
require 'markaby'

html = Markaby::Builder.new do
  head { title "My wonderful home page" }
  body do
    h1 "Welcome to my home page!"
    b "My hobbies:"
    ul do
      li "Juggling"
      li "Knitting"
      li "Metaprogramming"
    end
  end
end
```

This code is plain old Ruby, but it looks like a specific language for HTML generation. You can call Markaby an *internal DSL*, because it lives within a larger, general-purpose language. By contrast, languages that have their own parser, such as make, are often called *external DSLs*. One example of an external DSL is the Ant build language. Even though the Ant interpreter is written in Java, the Ant language is completely different from Java.

---

1. Markaby was written by "_why the lucky stiff." Install it with gem install markaby.

Let's leave the GPL vs. DSL match behind us and assume that you want to use a DSL. Which DSL should you prefer? An internal DSL or an external DSL?

One advantage of an internal DSL is that you can easily fall back to the underlying GPL whenever you need to do so. However, the syntax of your internal DSL will be constrained by the syntax of the GPL behind it. This is a big problem with some languages. For example, you can write an internal DSL in Java, but the result is probably still going to look pretty much like Java. But with Ruby, you can write an internal DSL that looks more like an *ad hoc* language tailored to the problem at hand. Thanks to Ruby's flexible, uncluttered syntax, the Markaby example shown earlier barely looks like Ruby at all.

That's why Ruby programmers tend to use Ruby where Java programmers would use an external language or an XML file. It's easier to adapt Ruby to your own needs than it is to adapt Java. As an example, consider build languages. The standard build languages for Java and C (Ant and make, respectively) are external DSLs, while the standard build language for Ruby (Rake) is just a Ruby library—an internal DSL.

B.3 DSLs and Metaprogramming

In the introduction to this book, we defined metaprogramming as "writing code that writes code" (or, if you want to be more precise, "writing code that manipulates the language constructs at runtime"). Now that you know about DSLs, you have another definition of metaprogramming: "designing a domain-specific language and then using that DSL to write your program."

This is a book about the first definition, not a book about DSLs. To write a DSL, you have to deal with a number of challenges that are outside the scope of this book. You have to understand your domain, care about your language's user-friendliness, and carefully evaluate the constraints and trade-offs of your grammar. While writing this book, I opted to keep this particular can of worms shut.

Still, metaprogramming and DSLs have a close relationship in the Ruby world. To build an internal DSL, you must bend the language itself, and doing so requires many of the techniques described in this book. Put another way, metaprogramming provides the bricks that you need to build DSLs. If you're interested in internal Ruby DSLs, this book contains information that's important for you.

Appendix C

Spell Book

This appendix is a "spell book"—a quick reference to all the "spells" in the book, in alphabetical order. Most of these spells are metaprogramming related (but the ones from Appendix A, on page 223, are arguably not that "meta").

Each spell comes with a short example and a reference to the page where it's introduced. Go to the associated pages for extended examples and the reasoning behind each spell.

C.1 The Spells

Argument Array

Collapse a list of arguments into an array.

```
def my_method(*args)
  args.map {|arg| arg.reverse }
end

my_method('abc', 'xyz', '123') # => ["cba", "zyx", "321"]
```

For more information, see page 229.

Around Alias

Call the previous, aliased version of a method from a redefined method.

```
class String
  alias :old_reverse :reverse

  def reverse
    "x#{old_reverse}x"
  end
end
```

```
"abc".reverse # => "xcbax"
```

For more information, see page 133.

Blank Slate

Remove methods from an object to turn them into *Ghost Methods (50)*.

```
class C
  def method_missing(name, *args)
    "a Ghost Method"
  end
end

obj = C.new
obj.to_s # => "#<C:0x357258>"

class C
  instance_methods.each do |m|
    undef_method m unless m.to_s =~ /method_missing|respond_to?|^__/
  end
end

obj.to_s # => "a Ghost Method"
```

For more information, see page 61.

Class Extension

Define class methods by mixing a module into a class's eigenclass (a special case of *Object Extension (130)*).

```
class C; end

module M
  def my_method
    'a class method'
  end
end

class << C
  include M
end

C.my_method # => "a class method"
```

For more information, see page 130.

Class Extension Mixin

Enable a module to extend its includer through a *Hook Method (160)*.

```ruby
module M
  def self.included(base)
    base.extend(ClassMethods)
  end

  module ClassMethods
    def my_method
      'a class method'
    end
  end
end

class C
  include M
end

C.my_method # => "a class method"
```

For more information, see page 164.

Class Instance Variable

Store class-level state in an instance variable of the Class object.

```ruby
class C
  @my_class_instance_variable = "some value"

  def self.class_attribute
    @my_class_instance_variable
  end
end

C.class_attribute # => "some value"
```

For more information, see page 106.

Class Macro

Use a class method in a class definition.

```ruby
class C; end

class << C
  def my_macro(arg)
    "my_macro(#{arg}) called"
  end
end

class C
  my_macro :x # => "my_macro(x) called"
end
```

For more information, see page 115.

Clean Room

Use an object as an environment in which to evaluate a block.

```ruby
class CleanRoom
  def a_useful_method(x); x * 2; end
end

CleanRoom.new.instance_eval { a_useful_method(3) }     # => 6
```

For more information, see page 85.

Code Processor

Process *Strings of Code (142)* from an external source.

```ruby
File.readlines("a_file_containing_lines_of_ruby.txt").each do |line|
  puts "#{line.chomp} ==> #{eval(line)}"
end

# >> 1 + 1 ==> 2
# >> 3 * 2 ==> 6
# >> Math.log10(100) ==> 2.0
```

For more information, see page 143.

Context Probe

Execute a block to access information in an object's context.

```ruby
class C
  def initialize
    @x = "a private instance variable"
  end
end

obj = C.new
obj.instance_eval { @x } # => "a private instance variable"
```

For more information, see page 83.

Deferred Evaluation

Store a piece of code and its context in a proc or lambda for evaluation later.

```ruby
class C
  def store(&block)
    @my_code_capsule = block
  end

  def execute
    @my_code_capsule.call
  end
end
```

```
obj = C.new
obj.store { $X = 1 }
$X = 0

obj.execute
$X # => 1
```

For more information, see page 86.

Dynamic Dispatch

Decide which method to call at runtime.

```
method_to_call = :reverse
obj = "abc"

obj.send(method_to_call) # => "cba"
```

For more information, see page 41.

Dynamic Method

Decide how to define a method at runtime.

```
class C
end

C.class_eval do
  define_method :my_method do
    "a dynamic method"
  end
end

obj = C.new
obj.my_method # => "a dynamic method"
```

For more information, see page 45.

Dynamic Proxy

Forward to another object any messages that don't match a method.

```
class MyDynamicProxy
  def initialize(target)
    @target = target
  end

  def method_missing(name, *args, &block)
    "result: #{@target.send(name, *args, &block)}"
  end
end

obj = MyDynamicProxy.new("a string")
obj.reverse # => "result: gnirts a"
```

For more information, see page 55.

Flat Scope

Use a closure to share variables between two scopes.

```
class C
  def an_attribute
    @attr
  end
end

obj = C.new
a_variable = 100

# flat scope:
obj.instance_eval do
  @attr = a_variable
end

obj.an_attribute # => 100
```

For more information, see page 81.

Ghost Method

Respond to a message that doesn't have an associated method.

```
class C
  def method_missing(name, *args)
    name.to_s.reverse
  end
end

obj = C.new
obj.my_ghost_method # => "dohtem_tsohg_ym"
```

For more information, see page 50.

Hook Method

Override a method to intercept object model events.

```
$INHERITORS = []

class C
  def self.inherited(subclass)
    $INHERITORS << subclass
  end
end

class D < C
end
```

```
class E < C
end

class F < E
end

$INHERITORS # => [D, E, F]
```

For more information, see page 160.

Kernel Method

Define a method in module Kernel to make the method available to all objects.

```
module Kernel
  def a_method
    "a kernel method"
  end
end

a_method # => "a kernel method"
```

For more information, see page 27.

Lazy Instance Variable

Wait until the first access to initialize an instance variable.

```
class C
  def attribute
    @attribute = @attribute || "some value"
  end
end

obj = C.new
obj.attribute # => "some value"
```

For more information, see page 227.

Mimic Method

Disguise a method as another language construct.

```
def BaseClass(name)
  name == "string" ? String : Object
end

class C < BaseClass "string" # a method that looks like a class
  attr_accessor :an_attribute # a method that looks like a keyword
end

obj = C.new
obj.an_attribute = 1  # a method that looks like an attribute
```

For more information, see page 224.

Monkeypatch

Change the features of an existing class.

```
"abc".reverse # => "cba"

class String
  def reverse
    "override"
  end
end

"abc".reverse # => "override"
```

For more information, see page 9.

Named Arguments

Collect method arguments into a hash to identify them by name.

```
def my_method(args)
  args[:arg2]
end

my_method(:arg1 => "A", :arg2 => "B", :arg3 => "C") # => "B"
```

For more information, see page 228.

Namespace

Define constants within a module to avoid name clashes.

```
module MyNamespace
  class Array
    def to_s
      "my class"
    end
  end
end

Array.new # => []
MyNamespace::Array.new # => my class
```

For more information, see page 17.

Nil Guard

Override a reference to nil with an "or."

```
x = nil
y = x || "a value" # => "a value"
```

For more information, see page 227.

Object Extension

Define Singleton Methods by mixing a module into an object's eigen-class.

```ruby
obj = Object.new

module M
  def my_method
    'a singleton method'
  end
end

class << obj
  include M
end

obj.my_method # => "a singleton method"
```

For more information, see page 130.

Open Class

Modify an existing class.

```ruby
class String
  def my_string_method
    "my method"
  end
end

"abc".my_string_method # => "my method"
```

For more information, see page 7.

Pattern Dispatch

Select which methods to call based on their names.

```ruby
$x = 0

class C
  def my_first_method
    $x += 1
  end

  def my_second_method
    $x += 2
  end
end

obj = C.new
obj.methods.each do |m|
  obj.send(m) if m.to_s =~ /^my_/
end
```

```
$x # => 3
```

For more information, see page 44.

Sandbox

Execute untrusted code in a safe environment.

```
def sandbox(&code)
  proc {
    $SAFE = 2
    yield
  }.call
end

begin
  sandbox { File.delete 'a_file' }
rescue Exception => ex
  ex    # => #<SecurityError: Insecure operation `delete' at level 2>
end
```

For more information, see page 151.

Scope Gate

Isolate a scope with the **class**, **module**, or **def** keyword.

```
a = 1
defined? a # => "local-variable"

module MyModule
  b = 1
  defined? a # => nil
  defined? b # => "local-variable"
end

defined? a  # => "local-variable"
defined? b  # => nil
```

For more information, see page 78.

Self Yield

Pass **self** to the current block.

```
class Person
  attr_accessor :name, :surname

  def initialize
    yield self
  end
end
```

```
joe = Person.new do |p|
  p.name = 'Joe'
  p.surname = 'Smith'
end
```

For more information, see page 231.

Shared Scope

Share variables among multiple contexts in the same *Flat Scope (81)*.

```
lambda {
  shared = 10

  self.class.class_eval do
    define_method :counter do
      shared
    end

    define_method :down do
      shared -= 1
    end
  end
}.call

counter            # => 10
3.times { down }
counter            # => 7
```

For more information, see page 82.

Singleton Method

Define a method on a single object.

```
obj = "abc"

class << obj
  def my_singleton_method
    "x"
  end
end

obj.my_singleton_method # => "x"
```

For more information, see page 112.

String of Code

Evaluate a string of Ruby code.

```
my_string_of_code = "1 + 1"
eval(my_string_of_code) # => 2
```

For more information, see page 142.

Symbol To Proc

Convert a symbol to a block that calls a single method.

```
[1, 2, 3, 4].map(&:even?)    # => [false, true, false, true]
```

For more information, see page 234.

Appendix D

Bibliography

[Arm07]   Joe Armstrong. *Programming Erlang: Software for a Concurrent World*. The Pragmatic Programmers, LLC, Raleigh, NC, and Dallas, TX, 2007.

[Gra96]   Paul Graham. *ANSI Common Lisp*. Prentice Hall, Englewood Cliffs, NJ, 1996.

[Hal09]   Stuart Halloway. *Programming Clojure*. The Pragmatic Programmers, LLC, Raleigh, NC, and Dallas, TX, 2009.

[OSV08]   Martin Odersky, Lex Spoon, and Bill Venners. *Programming in Scala*. 2008.

[TFH08]   David Thomas, Chad Fowler, and Andrew Hunt. *Programming Ruby: The Pragmatic Programmers' Guide*. The Pragmatic Programmers, LLC, Raleigh, NC, and Dallas, TX, third edition, 2008.

[TH05]   David Thomas and David Heinemeier Hansson. *Agile Web Development with Rails*. The Pragmatic Programmers, LLC, Raleigh, NC, and Dallas, TX, 2005.

[Tho99]   Simon Thompson. *Haskell: The Craft of Functional Programming*. Addison-Wesley, Reading, MA, second edition, 1999.

Index

The Pragmatic Bookshelf

Available in paperback and DRM-free PDF, our titles are here to help you stay on top of your game. The following are in print as of December 2009; be sure to check our website at pragprog.com for newer titles.

Title	Year	ISBN	Pages
Advanced Rails Recipes: 84 New Ways to Build Stunning Rails Apps	2008	9780978739225	464
Agile Coaching	2009	9781934356432	250
Agile Retrospectives: Making Good Teams Great	2006	9780977616640	200
Agile Web Development with Rails, Third Edition	2009	9781934356166	784
Augmented Reality: A Practical Guide	2008	9781934356036	328
Behind Closed Doors: Secrets of Great Management	2005	9780976694021	192
Best of Ruby Quiz	2006	9780976694076	304
Core Animation for Mac OS X and the iPhone: Creating Compelling Dynamic User Interfaces	2008	9781934356104	200
Core Data: Apple's API for Persisting Data on Mac OS X	2009	9781934356326	256
Data Crunching: Solve Everyday Problems using Java, Python, and More	2005	9780974514079	208
Debug It! Find, Repair, and Prevent Bugs in Your Code	2009	9781934356289	232
Deploying Rails Applications: A Step-by-Step Guide	2008	9780978739201	280
Design Accessible Web Sites: 36 Keys to Creating Content for All Audiences and Platforms	2007	9781934356029	336
Desktop GIS: Mapping the Planet with Open Source Tools	2008	9781934356067	368
Developing Facebook Platform Applications with Rails	2008	9781934356128	200
Domain-Driven Design Using Naked Objects	2009	9781934356449	375
Enterprise Integration with Ruby	2006	9780976694069	360
Enterprise Recipes with Ruby and Rails	2008	9781934356234	416
Everyday Scripting with Ruby: for Teams, Testers, and You	2007	9780977616619	320
FXRuby: Create Lean and Mean GUIs with Ruby	2008	9781934356074	240
From Java To Ruby: Things Every Manager Should Know	2006	9780976694090	160
GIS for Web Developers: Adding Where to Your Web Applications	2007	9780974514093	275
Google Maps API, V2: Adding Where to Your Applications	2006	PDF-Only	83

Continued on next page

Title	Year	ISBN	Pages
Grails: A Quick-Start Guide	2009	9781934356463	200
Groovy Recipes: Greasing the Wheels of Java	2008	9780978739294	264
Hello, Android: Introducing Google's Mobile Development Platform	2009	9781934356494	272
Interface Oriented Design	2006	9780976694052	240
Land the Tech Job You Love	2009	9781934356265	280
Learn to Program, 2nd Edition	2009	9781934356364	230
Manage It! Your Guide to Modern Pragmatic Project Management	2007	9780978739249	360
Manage Your Project Portfolio: Increase Your Capacity and Finish More Projects	2009	9781934356296	200
Mastering Dojo: JavaScript and Ajax Tools for Great Web Experiences	2008	9781934356111	568
Modular Java: Creating Flexible Applications with OSGi and Spring	2009	9781934356401	260
No Fluff Just Stuff 2006 Anthology	2006	9780977616664	240
No Fluff Just Stuff 2007 Anthology	2007	9780978739287	320
Pomodoro Technique Illustrated: The Easy Way to Do More in Less Time	2009	9781934356500	144
Practical Programming: An Introduction to Computer Science Using Python	2009	9781934356272	350
Practices of an Agile Developer	2006	9780974514086	208
Pragmatic Project Automation: How to Build, Deploy, and Monitor Java Applications	2004	9780974514031	176
Pragmatic Thinking and Learning: Refactor Your Wetware	2008	9781934356050	288
Pragmatic Unit Testing in C# with NUnit	2007	9780977616671	176
Pragmatic Unit Testing in Java with JUnit	2003	9780974514017	160
Pragmatic Version Control Using Git	2008	9781934356159	200
Pragmatic Version Control using CVS	2003	9780974514000	176
Pragmatic Version Control using Subversion	2006	9780977616657	248
Programming Clojure	2009	9781934356333	304
Programming Cocoa with Ruby: Create Compelling Mac Apps Using RubyCocoa	2009	9781934356197	300
Programming Erlang: Software for a Concurrent World	2007	9781934356005	536
Programming Groovy: Dynamic Productivity for the Java Developer	2008	9781934356098	320
Programming Ruby: The Pragmatic Programmers' Guide, Second Edition	2004	9780974514055	864
Programming Ruby 1.9: The Pragmatic Programmers' Guide	2009	9781934356081	960
Programming Scala: Tackle Multi-Core Complexity on the Java Virtual Machine	2009	9781934356319	250

Continued on next page

Title	Year	ISBN	Pages
Prototype and script.aculo.us: You Never Knew JavaScript Could Do This!	2007	9781934356012	448
Rails Recipes	2006	9780977616602	350
Rails for .NET Developers	2008	9781934356203	300
Rails for Java Developers	2007	9780977616695	336
Rails for PHP Developers	2008	9781934356043	432
Rapid GUI Development with QtRuby	2005	PDF-Only	83
Release It! Design and Deploy Production-Ready Software	2007	9780978739218	368
Scripted GUI Testing with Ruby	2008	9781934356180	192
Ship it! A Practical Guide to Successful Software Projects	2005	9780974514048	224
Stripes ...and Java Web Development Is Fun Again	2008	9781934356210	375
TextMate: Power Editing for the Mac	2007	9780978739232	208
The Definitive ANTLR Reference: Building Domain-Specific Languages	2007	9780978739256	384
The Passionate Programmer: Creating a Remarkable Career in Software Development	2009	9781934356340	200
ThoughtWorks Anthology	2008	9781934356142	240
Ubuntu Kung Fu: Tips, Tricks, Hints, and Hacks	2008	9781934356227	400
Web Design for Developers: A Programmer's Guide to Design Tools and Techniques	2009	9781934356135	300
iPhone SDK Development	2009	9781934356258	576

The Home of Ruby and Rails

The RSpec Book

RSpec, Ruby's leading Behaviour Driven
Development tool, helps you do TDD right by
embracing the design and documentation aspects
of TDD. It encourages readable, maintainable
suites of code examples that not only test your
code, they document it as well. *The RSpec Book* will
teach you how to use RSpec, Cucumber, and other
Ruby tools to develop truly agile software that gets
you to market quickly and maintains its value as
evolving market trends drive new requirements.

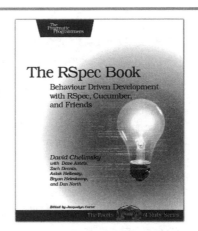

**The RSpec Book: Behaviour Driven
Development with RSpec, Cucumber, and
Friends**
David Chelimsky, Dave Astels, Zach Dennis, Aslak
Hellesøy, Bryan Helmkamp, Dan North
(350 pages) ISBN: 978-1-9343563-7-1. $42.95
http://pragprog.com/titles/achbd

Security on Rails

Security on Rails provides you with the tools and
techniques to defend your Rails applications
against attackers. With this book, you can conquer
the bad guys who are trying to exploit your
application. You'll see the very techniques that
hackers use, and then journey through this
full-fledged guide for writing secure Rails
applications.

Security on Rails
Ben Poweski and David Raphael
(350 pages) ISBN: 978-19343564-8-7. $34.95
http://pragprog.com/titles/fr_secure

The Pragmatic Bookshelf

The Pragmatic Bookshelf features books written by developers for developers. The titles continue the well-known Pragmatic Programmer style and continue to garner awards and rave reviews. As development gets more and more difficult, the Pragmatic Programmers will be there with more titles and products to help you stay on top of your game.

Visit Us Online

Metaprogramming Ruby's Home Page
http://pragprog.com/titles/ppmetr
Source code from this book, errata, and other resources. Come give us feedback, too!

Register for Updates
http://pragprog.com/updates
Be notified when updates and new books become available.

Join the Community
http://pragprog.com/community
Read our weblogs, join our online discussions, participate in our mailing list, interact with our wiki, and benefit from the experience of other Pragmatic Programmers.

New and Noteworthy
http://pragprog.com/news
Check out the latest pragmatic developments, new titles and other offerings.

Save on the eBook

Save on the eBook versions of this title. Owning the paper version of this book entitles you to purchase the electronic versions at a terrific discount.

PDFs are great for carrying around on your laptop—they are hyperlinked, have color, and are fully searchable. Most titles are also available for the iPhone and iPod touch, Amazon Kindle, and other popular e-book readers.

Buy now at pragprog.com/coupon.

Contact Us

Online Orders:	www.pragprog.com/catalog
Customer Service:	support@pragprog.com
Non-English Versions:	translations@pragprog.com
Pragmatic Teaching:	academic@pragprog.com
Author Proposals:	proposals@pragprog.com
Contact us:	1-800-699-PROG (+1 919 847 3884)